T0339285

INTRODUCING THEOLOGICAL METHOD

A Survey of Contemporary Theologians and Approaches

MARY M. VEENEMAN

Baker Academic

a division of Baker Publishing Group
Grand Rapids, Michigan

© 2017 by Mary M. Veeneman

Published by Baker Academic
a division of Baker Publishing Group
P.O. Box 6287, Grand Rapids, MI 49516-6287
www.bakeracademic.com

Printed in the United States of America

All rights reserved. No part of this publication may be reproduced, stored in a retrieval system, or transmitted in any form or by any means—for example, electronic, photocopy, recording—without the prior written permission of the publisher. The only exception is brief quotations in printed reviews.

Library of Congress Cataloging-in-Publication Data
Names: Veeneman, Mary M., 1981– author.
Title: Introducing theological method : a survey of contemporary theologians and approaches / Mary M. Veeneman.
Description: Grand Rapids : Baker Academic, 2017. | Includes bibliographical references and index.
Identifiers: LCCN 2017032147 | ISBN 9780801049491 (pbk. : alk. paper)
Subjects: LCSH: Theology—Methodology.
Classification: LCC BR118 .V44 2017 | DDC 230.01—dc23
LC record available at https://lccn.loc.gov/2017032147

Unless otherwise indicated, Scripture quotations are from the New Revised Standard Version of the Bible, copyright © 1989, by the Division of Christian Education of the National Council of the Churches of Christ in the United States of America. Used by permission. All rights reserved.

Scripture quotations labeled KJV are from the King James Version of the Bible.

In keeping with biblical principles of creation stewardship, Baker Publishing Group advocates the responsible use of our natural resources. As a member of the Green Press Initiative, our company uses recycled paper when possible. The text paper of this book is composed in part of post-consumer waste.

To my North Park mentors:
Stephen Spencer, Charles Peterson,
and Liza Ann Acosta

CONTENTS

Introduction: *The Context of Modern Theology*   1

1. The Work of Theology   7

2. Ressourcement and Neo-orthodox Theologies   15

3. Theologies of Correlation   35

4. Postliberal Theologies   61

5. Evangelical Theologies   81

6. Political Theologies   111

7. Feminist Theologies   141

8. Theologies of Religious Pluralism and Comparative Theology   169

Conclusion: *Where Do We Go from Here?*   187

Suggested Reading List for Students   191

Bibliography   192

Index   198

CONTENTS

INTRODUCTION

The Context of Modern Theology

In the summer of 1914 Europe ignited in war, ending what had generally been a century of peace on the continent. Many have argued that the war was inevitable because of the role of imperialism on the international scene.[1] Regardless of who started the war and who prevailed, World War 1 marked a turning point in Protestant theology and serves as an illustration of the importance of theological method.

Karl Barth was schooled in Protestant liberalism, the dominant theological school in Germany in the nineteenth century. Among several notable teachers was Adolf von Harnack, who famously argued that the essence of Christianity is the fatherhood of God and the brotherhood of all people.[2] Although during the early stages of his work Barth called himself a disciple of Harnack, World War 1 was the occasion for a major break between Barth and his teachers.

Albrecht Ritschl, Harnack's teacher, had closely tied Christianity to the culture of the time. Ritschl saw Christianity as primarily emphasizing the work of God in redeeming humanity and the work of human beings to bring about the kingdom of God. As a result, Ritschl (and subsequently Harnack's theology) was very optimistic about what the human being could do. Ritschl assumed that language in Jesus's teachings about the kingdom of God meant the gradual improvement of society over time. Additionally, Ernst Troeltsch, another prominent theologian of the period, argued that Christianity had become part and parcel

---

1. Allen Weinstein and David Rubel, *The Story of America* (London: DK, 2002), 422.

2. Adolf von Harnack, *What Is Christianity?*, trans. Thomas Bailey Saunders (New York: Harper, 1957), 51.

of European culture. Ultimately, they saw Christianity as simply the religious manifestation of European culture.[3]

If Christianity is simply the religious manifestation of European culture, then Christianity is not in a position to critique culture. The results of this line of thinking were made clear at the advent of World War I. Karl Barth's theology would experience a significant shift as a result of this.

At the outbreak of the war, Barth's theological teachers were among a number of German intellectuals who signed their support to the Kaiser's war effort.[4] Barth was profoundly dismayed by this move and saw it as evidence of a fundamentally bankrupt theology that was unable to do anything but endorse the actions of the culture. He broke with Protestant liberalism and sought a new theology that did not make a quick link between the idea of the kingdom of God and social action. His new theology would seek to begin with the Word of God and to read it fresh, apart from historical criticism and apart from any captivity to the culture of the day.[5]

Why tell this story? In a book that covers numerous twentieth-century theologians, why is Barth treated in the introduction? Barth's story is important for a discussion of theological method because it clearly shows what is at stake in these kinds of conversations. Theological method is a work of prolegomena.[6] Its work is crucial because it sets the ground rules for how theology is tied to the world around it, what texts are read, and what questions are asked. Protestant liberal thinkers came to the conclusions they did about World War I because of earlier methodological moves and assumptions. When one sees religion as part and parcel of culture, there isn't a clear warrant for religion standing apart from culture. Similarly, the theological moves Barth made came about from his own methodological assumptions. His critique of Protestant liberalism was grounded in a fundamental assumption about the relationships between God, the Word of God, and human beings.

Although the story of Karl Barth and his teachers during World War I is a particularly good illustration of the potential problems with theological method,

3. William C. Placher, *A History of Christian Theology: An Introduction* (Louisville: Westminster John Knox, 1983), 286.

4. This document, commonly referred to as the "Manifesto of the Ninety-Three German Intellectuals," can be found at Brigham Young University's World War I document archive, http://wwi .lib.byu.edu/index.php/Manifesto_of_the_Ninety-Three_German_Intellectuals.

5. Daniel W. Hardy, "Karl Barth," in *The Modern Theologians: An Introduction to Christian Theology since 1918*, ed. David F. Ford with Rachel Muers (Malden, MA: Blackwell, 2005), 22. Barth's theology, born out of a methodological critique, will be subject to the methodological critiques of other thinkers. This will be discussed further in chap. 2.

6. Prolegomena covers preliminary issues or could be expressed as the things that must be said before arriving at the topic at hand (in our case, that topic is theology itself).

the contemporary setting can also provide examples of where method can lead to poor theology. One example of this is the kind of theology that arises out of a flat biblical hermeneutic. Hermeneutics deals with questions about how texts are to be read and interpreted.[7] The way one reads the biblical text is part of any discussion of theological method, as is the way one chooses to prioritize the biblical text in theological work. A flat hermeneutic is one that reads the text for what the words literally say. Typically, this is an approach that does not pay sufficient attention to genre or to historical setting.

An example of this has been highlighted and critiqued by the recent emphasis on the new perspective on Paul, a school of thought that argues that the apostle Paul, particularly in Protestant circles, has been too readily associated with Martin Luther and thus pulled out of his original context. This earlier view results from a flat reading of Paul that associates his statements about the works of the law with Luther's statements about legalism in late medieval Catholicism. The problem with reading Paul through the thought of Martin Luther, this school of thought argues, is that first-century Judaism is read to be quite similar to late medieval Catholicism. A historical study of first century Judaism shows that the comparison between it and late medieval Catholicism breaks down and is thus not particularly helpful for interpreting Paul.

Like the story of Barth and Protestant liberalism, the new perspective on Paul illustrates that the way theological method is approached is of crucial importance. The way in which one thinks about the roles of various theological sources, including the biblical text and the Christian tradition, as well as the types of questions to bring to the table, will have an impact on one's theology.

Theological method matters because it drives how theological questions are asked and the ways in which texts are read. How those things are carried out will have a direct impact on one's theological conclusions. A theology that starts with the idea of God and the Word of God is going to say quite different things from a theology that starts with human cultural experience.

Readers should be particularly attentive to the following methodological concerns:

1. What are the *primary sources* for theological reflection? Some theologians will argue that the biblical text alone should inform theological work. Others will argue that creation itself or philosophy and the natural and social sciences are important sources for theological work. Some theologians will argue that the Christian tradition should inform theological work, while

---

7. Stanley J. Grenz, David Guretzki, and Cherith Fee Nordling, *The Pocket Dictionary of Theological Terms* (Downers Grove, IL: InterVarsity, 1999), 59.

others will advocate a theology that explicitly avoids a consideration of the tradition.

2. What *questions* should a theologian answer? Some theologians argue for a standard set of questions, while others argue that the questions should arise from the contemporary context.

3. What is the *starting point* of theological work? For example, some of the theologians studied in this text will be very concerned with the contemporary situation in specific contexts, while others will look to universal human experience. Other theologians will argue that God or the biblical text, apart from human context, must be the starting point for theological reflection.

As readers work through these differing theologies and theological methods, they should regularly ask themselves *how* the theological claims are tied back to the theological method employed and compare the various methods studied. One way students can approach this is to ask themselves what kinds of conversations would arise if all the theologians studied could be gathered into a room and asked these critical questions.

To be clear, a good theological method is not a guarantee of good theological results. One may employ a good method but come to conclusions that are problematic for one reason or another. At the same time, a good theological method is a necessary starting point for good theological work. Theologians who have not thought about methodology do not have solid ground on which to build their theological work.

This book will introduce the reader to some of the most important theologians of the twentieth century, including Karl Rahner, Karl Barth, Paul Tillich, Avery Dulles, and George Lindbeck. It will also give careful attention to liberation and feminist theologies, evangelical theologies, and comparative theology. Each section will consider the thinker's background, underlying assumptions, use and interpretation of sources, and driving questions. This book will not advocate for a particular theological method. Rather, it will advocate having a conversation about method and becoming more aware of one's own background, underlying assumptions, use and interpretation of sources, and driving questions. Of course, an exhaustive treatment of Christian theological method would be many volumes long and require a lifetime's worth of study. This volume chooses twentieth- and twenty-first-century theologians to study because they are close to the present in terms of historical location and thus may introduce ideas that students find to be more immediately applicable. At the same time, it is important to stress that (as Bernard of Chartres put it) we stand on the shoulders of giants, and that is true for any Christian theologian. Each of the individuals discussed in this book was influenced by many Christian thinkers who came before. A thorough study of theology requires a significant amount of time spent in the tradition of the church. By studying the methodologies of theologians who came before those covered in this book, a fuller understanding of Christian history as a cohesive and coherent narrative will emerge.[8]

Stanley Grenz and Roger Olson open their book *Who Needs Theology?* by stating that everyone is a theologian.[9] The statement that usually follows this kind of assertion is that the only remaining question is whether one is a good theologian. Similarly, everyone has a theological method, even if that method is not explicitly known. The only question is whether one employs a good method. This book is intended to help the reader become a better theologian by developing a good theological method.

---

8. While a full treatment of other theological methods is beyond the scope of this book, students who want to broaden their understandings of theological method across the history of the church should see Paul L. Allen, *Theological Method: A Guide for the Perplexed* (New York: T&T Clark, 2012). A number of works focus on the method of a particular historical figure or period. These include Timothy Smith, *Thomas Aquinas' Trinitarian Theology: A Study in Theological Method* (Washington, DC: Catholic University of America Press, 2003); Paul Avis, *In Search of Authority: Anglican Theological Method from the Reformation to the Enlightenment* (New York: Bloomsbury T&T Clark, 2014); and Mark A. Noll, ed., *The Princeton Theology 1812–1921: Scripture, Science, and Theological Method from Archibald Alexander to Benjamin Warfield* (Grand Rapids: Baker Academic, 2001). Considerations of theological method in specific confessional contexts include John G. Stackhouse Jr., ed., *Evangelical Futures: A Conversation on Theological Method* (Grand Rapids: Baker Books, 2000), and Christopher A. Stephenson, *Types of Pentecostal Theology: Method, System, Spirit* (New York: Oxford University Press, 2013). Finally, consideration of theological method through a doctrinal lens can be found in Howard W. Stone and James O. Duke, *How to Think Theologically* (Minneapolis: Fortress, 2013).

9. Stanley J. Grenz and Roger E. Olson, *Who Needs Theology? An Invitation to the Study of God* (Downers Grove, IL: InterVarsity, 1996).

1

The Work of Theology

Looking at the history of Christianity, as well as the variety of modern church practices, makes one important point clear: Christians do not always agree about how the Christian life is to be led. Disagreement about Christian belief and practice is ultimately disagreement about theology. Ongoing questions about Christian faith and practice require that Christians continue to do the work of theology. This book seeks to take a step back from that work and instead consider how one goes about doing the work of theology.

What Is Theology?

The Greek roots of the term *theology* are *theos*, "God," and *logos*, "word" or "words." Alister McGrath refers to theology as "talking about God" and to Christian theology as "talking about God in a Christian way."[1] "To study theology," McGrath writes, "is to think systematically about the fundamental ideas of Christianity. It is intellectual reflection on the act, content, and implications of the Christian faith."[2] Daniel Migliore writes this about theology: "I propose to describe the work of theology as a continuing search for the fullness of the truth of God made known in Jesus Christ. Defining the theological task in this way emphasizes that theology is not mere repetition of traditional doctrines, but a persistent search for the truth to which they point and which they

1. Alister E. McGrath, *Theology: The Basics*, 2nd ed. (Malden, MA: Blackwell, 2004), vii.
2. Ibid.

7

only partially and brokenly express."[3] Shortly after that statement, Migliore refers to Augustine's description of "faith seeking understanding."[4] Thomas Oden describes theology this way: "The study of God is an attempt at orderly, consistent, and reasoned discussion of the Source and End of all things. . . . The term theology is itself a rudimentary definition indicating discourse about God."[5]

There are a number of reasons for taking up theological work. Some undertake theological work to help explain reality. Others do so to organize Christian teaching. Still others do so to critique the contemporary life and thought of the church. Of course, these reasons for doing theology are not mutually exclusive. Many people will take up the theological task with all three of these aims in mind. Knowing the goals and the purposes for undertaking theological work is important—these things can help give us a focus and direction for our work. At the same time, knowing the reason for doing theological work is only the first step—it is important to also spend some time thinking about *how* theological work should be done, or what *theological method* should be. We must ask some key questions about method: Where should we begin? What sources should we use? What specific questions should we ask?

The Work of Theology

McGrath suggests a few ways we might go about answering the question of how to "do" theology. One way would be to study some prominent theologians and examine how they carry out this task.[6] Here are some examples of two theologians from earlier in the history of Christianity and two theologians from the twentieth century.

- Thomas Aquinas: He wrote during the medieval period and is well known for taking the philosophy of Aristotle and trying to synthesize it with Christian theology. He also drew heavily on the work of Augustine and on the Bible.
- John Calvin: He was one of the second generation of leaders during the Protestant Reformation. He is well known for emphasizing the providence of God in his theological system, though the role of providence in his

3. Daniel L. Migliore, *Faith Seeking Understanding: An Introduction to Christian Theology*, 2nd ed. (Grand Rapids: Eerdmans, 2004), 1.
4. Ibid., 2.
5. Thomas C. Oden, *Classic Christianity: A Systematic Theology* (San Francisco: HarperOne, 2009), 5.
6. McGrath, *Theology*, xii.

thought has often been misunderstood. He saw the Bible as the primary source of Christian theology.

- Karl Barth: Probably the best-known Protestant theologian of the twentieth century, he reacted strongly to the Protestant theology of the nineteenth and early twentieth centuries and called for a theology that starts with God and focuses on the Word of God.
- Karl Rahner: The best-known Catholic theologian of the twentieth century, he reacted to the common Catholic theology of the early twentieth century and believed that theology must be made comprehensible to contemporary people. He argued that theology should start with religious experience that all people have.[7]

There are a couple of problems with trying to make determinations about methodology by studying one particular theology. Each of these theologians has written thousands of pages. There are scholars who devote their entire careers to studying one of them and still never get through all of the writings! That makes this approach to studying theological method very difficult. Additionally, each of these theologians has a very different approach.[8] If you were able to put them in a room and talk with them about method, you would probably have a very interesting and lively discussion, but you would quickly see that each of them has a different starting point for undertaking theological work:

- Thomas Aquinas would draw on the philosophy of Aristotle, the theology of Augustine and the Bible, giving significant weight to each of those.
- John Calvin would insist on giving a place of primary importance to the Bible.
- Karl Barth would say that theology must start with God and the Word of God, but he would explain that somewhat differently than Calvin would.
- Karl Rahner would want to start with a particular kind of human experience—this would be a universal religious experience that he claims each person has whether or not he or she is aware of it.

Because of this, how would you know which approach is the best one to take? You might go with the one that is closest to you in historical location, but Barth and Rahner worked in roughly the same time period and clearly have very different approaches. We are going to have that discussion across the pages of this book. We are going to talk about method, and we will do that by looking

7. Ibid., xiii.
8. Ibid.

at various theologians. In order to get to the place where we can have that conversation, though, we need to first talk about the various sources of theology and look at method in general before we will be in a position to compare the methodological proposals of various theologians.

There are two important things to keep in mind as we move forward. First, while there is not complete agreement on how we should go about doing theology either historically across the tradition or today, there is some broad agreement on what sources we should generally consider. McGrath reminds us that "throughout its long history, Christian theology has made an appeal to three fundamental resources: the Bible, tradition, and reason."[9] Christians generally agree on the importance of the Bible for theological work (as well as living the Christian life), even though there are disagreements over how to interpret it and what its relationship to other theological sources might be.

In addition to this, theological work has been shaped by the historical location of those who do theology, whether or not the theologian is aware of it. Certainly, Thomas Aquinas's work was significantly shaped by the rediscovery of Aristotle's philosophy during the medieval period. Calvin's outlook in his major work, *The Institutes of the Christian Religion*, is clearly shaped by his context—his writings reflect many of the debates that were taking place during the Protestant Reformation. Barth's theological work reacted strongly to nineteenth- and early twentieth-century Protestant theology. Rahner's work reflects both the influence of twentieth-century philosophy and a reaction to late nineteenth- and early twentieth-century Catholic theology. Further, that theological work is historically influenced also makes sense in that Christianity is fundamentally a faith that is rooted in history. Christian theology is focused on the person of Christ, and the story of Christ tells us about God breaking into history in a particular time and place. Because we also live in a particular time and place, we must take that into consideration. Taking the time and place or *location* of the theologian into account will result in some theological questions being the same, while others will be different; this will be apparent in subsequent chapters as theologians are introduced.

Sources for Theology

Theology must be done with consideration to such things as revelation, sources, orienting questions, and starting point. We need to address these topics before talking about specific theological methodologies.

9. Ibid., xv.

Above all else, if theology is talk about God, it is crucial to gain knowledge about this God. Christians believe that God has chosen to reveal Godself to humanity. This act is referred to as "divine revelation." Divine revelation generally comes in two forms: general revelation and special revelation.[10] General revelation comes from an understanding of the entire world as created by God. If God created all that is, then all that is can be seen as a communication from God. As a result, investigations of creation can reveal true things about God. Often, general revelation is explored through the natural sciences (which investigate the created order) and philosophy (which investigates reality via the use of human reason). Special revelation is revelation from God to a particular group of people. This is revelation that goes beyond what is revealed in God's act of creating. In Christian theology, the chief act of special revelation is in the Christ event. God's word as revealed in the biblical text is also understood by most theologians to constitute special revelation.

Some have argued that the best way to describe the difference between special revelation and general revelation is to hold that general revelation is revelation for all people, while special revelation is revelation for a select group of people (i.e., Christians). The problem with this view is that, outside of certain circles that heavily emphasize predestination, most Christians have held that Christ died for all people. If this is the case, the group "Christian" is potentially universal, even if it is not universal in actuality. Perhaps it is better to argue that general revelation is that revelation from which all people can know some truths, regardless of religious persuasion. Special revelation is potentially for all people, but in order for one to receive it as revelation, a prior religious decision is required. Avery Dulles's *Models of Revelation* offers a helpful extended treatment of this particular issue.[11]

Thinking about revelation leads to a consideration of a larger issue in Christian theology. What sources should be used? The answer to this question largely depends on who is asked. All Christian theologians will argue that the Bible is important, but they will differ on exactly what role the Bible should have.

Martin Luther, along with other Reformers, argued for a principle of *sola scriptura*. Although it was not Luther's intention, some have interpreted the *sola scriptura* principle to insist that the biblical text must be the only source of theology and that no other sources have any bearing on that work.

There are two problems with this view. The first problem is one of history: Luther did not intend the *sola scriptura* principle to suggest that scripture should

---

10. Not all theologians hold that knowledge of God can be gained via general revelation. Karl Barth is one prominent example of a theologian who holds such a view.

11. See Avery Dulles, *Models of Revelation* (Maryknoll, NY: Orbis Books, 1992).

be the only source of theology. His understanding of *sola scriptura* was that scripture is to be the chief source of theology. In other words, scripture holds the trump card or has veto power over any other potential sources. An added problem comes when considering the question of what it might mean to have scripture as the only source of theology. One need only look at the history of Christianity and the breadth of contemporary Christianity to know that not all Christians read the Bible in the same way. Despite claims about the Bible being self-interpreting, it seems that there often isn't an immediately apparent plain reading of the text. Further, the biblical text is not made up of one genre. Two particularly significant types of genres for the purposes of this discussion are poetry and parables. These are genres that are explicitly not intended to be taken literally. As a result, no "plain" or "flat" meaning of the text can be gleaned apart from the work of interpretation.

If interpretation is required (and in actuality it is required for the whole of the biblical text), it is hard to argue that the biblical text can be one's sole source of theology. If the text does not convey clear meaning apart from interpretation, then one's interpretation must also play a role in understanding. If that is the case, something is added to the biblical text in order to gain meaning from it. The question that arises from the necessity of interpretation is what informs one's interpretation.

As noted earlier, theologians have often argued that all Christians are theologians; the important question is whether one is a good theologian. All Christians are theologians in that they all hold particular beliefs about God that they get from scripture and other sources of theology. As a result, they make particular theological judgments. In a similar way, all readers of the biblical text are interpreters. They make particular judgments about what the text means. What must be asked is what informs those judgments.

This gets us into a conversation about the kinds of sources needed for theology. As we have seen, *sola scriptura* did not historically mean that the Bible is the only source of theology. Many people today would ask if it is actually possible to have a theology that is based on the Bible alone. If it isn't, then what other sources can help theologians better understand revelation?

Historically, theologians have discussed tradition, reason, and experience, in addition to scripture, as potential sources for theological work. Tradition can refer to the tradition of one particular branch of Christianity or the history of the church as a whole. The extent of tradition is typically defined by the community claiming that tradition. One thing to be mindful of when thinking about traditions is that most definitions of Christian tradition are focused on one branch or smaller subset of Christianity. This influences how various Christians come to understand the term *tradition*.

The value of tradition is that it seems to offer an aid to reading scripture. If scripture is better interpreted in community rather than alone, the tradition broadens out the reading community of the one who approaches scripture. With the tradition, reading sacred texts in a community does not just involve reading with people in one's own context, or even with people outside one's context but living at the same time, but it involves reading with others who have lived in different places and in different times. This kind of reading community can help a reader begin to identify blinders that are culturally conditioned and start to see other options for interpreting the text. While tradition is defined differently in different Christian communities, all Christian communities have traditions. This means that claiming not to have a tradition is problematic. Further, those that argue that they do theology free from tradition are likely not being honest about the ways in which their own contexts influence how they read and interpret the Bible.

In addition to tradition, many theologians consider human reason to be a source for theology. This ties back to the earlier discussion of general revelation. If God created all that exists, as Christian theology claims, then God created the human intellect and endowed human beings with the ability to investigate the world around them. It follows, then, that the use of reason in theology should be permissible. Different thinkers will make different claims about how reason is employed. Some will argue that reason is part of methodology and has to do with how theological arguments are constructed. Others will argue that reason is a genuine source and so will consult the work of philosophers in constructing theological arguments.

Experience is a final potential source for theology. The "Wesleyan Quadrilateral" includes scripture, tradition, reason, and experience. In this context, experience is seen as one of four sources of authority for theology.[12] In other contexts, experience might be the thing that brings critical questions in need of addressing.

Two final considerations, those of orienting questions and starting point, must be made concerning theological methodology. Orienting questions are the questions that drive a particular thinker's theological approach. These questions might be about the needs of the contemporary context, the philosophical basis for theological assertions, the claims of the tradition, or the claims of the biblical text. Let's return to Karl Rahner for a moment to consider the importance of an orienting question. Rahner was interested in the joining of

12. For more information about the Wesleyan Quadrilateral, see Don Thorsen, *The Wesleyan Quadrilateral: Scripture, Tradition, Reason, and Experience as a Model of Evangelical Theology* (Lexington: Emeth, 2005).

Thomistic theology with the transcendental method. One key question for the transcendental method involved the necessary conditions for a given thing to happen. This drove Rahner to begin his work by asking whether the necessary conditions for human beings to receive revelation from God were present, should God choose to reveal Godself to humanity.

Orienting questions are connected to starting points in one critical way, as can be seen with the example from Rahner. If Rahner begins by asking the question about the human being receiving revelation from God, his starting point will be in search of the answer to that question. Rahner begins his work in *Hearer of the Word* by considering the human being and showing how human beings might receive revelation from God, should God choose to give it.

Other thinkers have very different starting points. While Rahner essentially begins his work with the human being, Karl Barth protested vigorously against approaches that begin with the human being. Barth was concerned about what he saw as anthropocentrism (human-centeredness) in nineteenth-century Protestant liberalism. Because of this, he wanted to find a theology that was fundamentally not anthropocentric. As a result, he insisted that theology must start with God and the Word of God, and not the human being. In addition to considerations of God and humanity, many thinkers start their theological work with questions that arise from the contemporary context. We will see this clearly in the work of Tillich, Dulles, and others. Thus various thinkers have significant orienting questions for their theological work, and many of these arise from their distinctive starting points.

Conclusion

This book will introduce you to the approaches of several theologians across a number of Christian theological traditions. It will raise questions of sources, starting points and orienting questions, and theological assumptions. While this book will not offer one definitive conclusion about theological methodology, it will hopefully create space in your own mind and spark conversations about what is at stake in doing the work of theology.

2

Ressourcement and Neo-orthodox Theologies

The theologies covered in this chapter are theologies that react against late nineteenth- and early twentieth-century theology in Catholicism and Protestantism, but in ways that are different from the methodologies described in chapter 3. Both movements seek to recover older doctrines or beliefs that had been central at earlier stages of the church's history and were perceived to have been forgotten in the modern era. Additionally, both movements seek to use their various retrievals to create a theology that speaks more clearly to the contemporary person. Both neo-orthodoxy (within Protestantism) and ressourcement theology have been critiqued by their respective traditions.[1]

AVERY DULLES

Dulles's Faith

Avery Dulles was born in 1918 in New York. He was educated in boarding schools in both New England and Switzerland and eventually attended Harvard College, graduating in 1940. If his name sounds familiar, it is likely because his father was John Foster Dulles, the US secretary of state under President

1. On ressourcement theology see Karl Rahner and Herbert Vorgrimler, "Nouvelle Theologie" in *Theological Dictionary* (New York: Herder and Herder, 1965), 318. On neo-orthodoxy see Stanley Grenz and Roger Olson, *20th-Century Theology: God and the World in a Transitional Age* (Downers Grove, IL: InterVarsity, 1992), 63–65.

Eisenhower. His uncle was Allen Dulles, the first civilian director of the Central Intelligence Agency.

Dulles's grandfather was a Presbyterian minister, and Dulles was raised in that faith. By the time he went to college, however, he did not hold any significant religious convictions. After his graduation from Harvard College, he entered Harvard Law School for a year and a half before serving in the US Navy. When he had completed his time in the navy in 1946, Dulles entered the Jesuit order.[2]

Although he entered college with significant doubts about God, and although his university studies did not draw him any closer to belief in a God, Dulles recounted a story in which, while on a walk in Cambridge, he saw a tree beginning to bud. He was struck at that moment with the thought that there must be a greater order to the world around him.[3] From this point, Dulles began to move toward the Christian faith. In his final public address he explained:

> Happiness, I gradually came to see, is the reward given for holding fast to what is truly good and important. To some extent the philosophers of antiquity identified these goals. But Christian revelation brought a tremendous increase of light. God alone, I learned from the New Testament, was good and true in an unqualified sense. And the same God in all his beauty and majesty became one of our human family in Jesus Christ, the truth, the way and the life. The most important thing about my career, and many of yours, I feel sure, is the discovery of the pearl of great price, the treasure hidden in the field, the Lord Jesus himself.[4]

Dulles's Theological Orientation

As a theologian, Dulles sought to be a moderate who worked to bring disparate perspectives together. His many books and articles address both classic questions of Christian theology and current debates in the church. Dulles's approach to questions of classic Christian theology is one that often seeks to give the reader the state of the question before offering a personal perspective. This approach can be seen most clearly in his *Models of Revelation* and *Models of the Church*, in which he lays out various ways of understanding the topic at hand

2. Biographical information on Cardinal Dulles can be found at Fordham University, http://legacy.fordham.edu/dulles. For his obituary with some additional information about his conversion, see Robert D. McFadden, "Cardinal Avery Dulles, Theologian, Is Dead at 90," *New York Times*, December 12, 2008, http://www.nytimes.com/2008/12/13/us/13dulles.html. Dulles also discusses his conversion story in *A Testimonial to Grace and Reflections on a Theological Journey* (New York: Sheed & Ward, 1996). He often seemed reluctant to speak of his conversion and seemed uninterested in emphasizing it as a conversion from Protestantism to Catholicism.

3. McFadden, "Cardinal Avery Dulles."

4. Avery Dulles, "A Life in Theology: 39th McGinley Lecture," *America*, April 21, 2008, http://americamagazine.org/node/148690. This is the written version of Dulles's final public address.

and then offers his own proposal, which seeks to build on the strengths of the various models described while also arguing that they are somewhat inadequate.

Dulles and Neo-scholasticism

While Dulles's approach to theology is clear across the entirety of his writing, it is particularly clear in his *Craft of Theology* and in his final public lecture. As a Catholic theologian, both sacred scripture and the tradition of the church are important sources for Dulles. As a Catholic theologian who worked in the twentieth century, Dulles was educated in a particular type of theology that was common in Catholic circles in the first part of the twentieth century: neo-scholasticism.[5] Dulles describes this approach well:

> Characteristic of that system was the division of theology into tracts or treatises, each of which was broken down into a series of theses. These theses, generally formulated in language echoing the official teaching of popes and councils, were set forth in a standard pattern. After the enunciation of the thesis came the definitions of the key terms, followed by a listing of adversaries, and a theological note indicating the degree of certitude and emphasis attaching to the thesis. Next came a series of proofs from authoritative church teaching, from the Bible, from tradition, and from theological reasoning. Finally the arguments of the adversaries were summarized and answered. The entire thesis was sometimes followed by corollaries and scholia dealing with connected questions.[6]

This was often referred to as the "theology of the manuals," as the results of this type of work would be published in books that sought to offer this kind of information on any given doctrine.

Some twentieth-century Catholic theologians were quite critical of this approach to theology. Dulles takes a moderate position toward this type of work. Among its strengths he counts its respect for previous generations of theological thinkers, an interest in reconciling disparate views, a respect for official church teaching, and a sense of working for the church. This approach also has an interest for method and systematic theology, clarity about the state of the question (which is always important for Dulles), an interest in responding to theological objections, and awareness that not all answers or theological convictions hold

5. Scholasticism refers to the theological method dominant in Western Christianity during the High Middle Ages. Examples of this theological school of thought include Thomas Aquinas and Anselm of Canterbury. The Protestant Reformers often took issue with medieval Scholasticism, though they were more familiar with late medieval Scholasticism than they were with Anselm and Thomas Aquinas.

6. Avery Dulles, *The Craft of Theology: From Symbol to System*, expanded ed. (New York: Crossroad, 1995), 41–42.

equal weight. While other thinkers express regret or frustration over the theology of the manuals, Dulles argues that it is precisely this method that exposed him to the history of theology and theological controversy and that showed him how to mount a theological argument.[7]

Despite the positive things he identifies in its approach, Dulles does not claim that neo-scholasticism is the way that theology should move forward. He argues that although the method taught him much, "it could not be described as adequate."[8] Because Dulles was studying at a time (the 1950s) in which Catholic thinkers were seeking to find new approaches to theology, he had the benefit of considering their work, as well as the work of Protestant biblical theologians, alongside neo-scholasticism.[9] That Dulles had access to types of theology beyond neo-scholasticism likely made neo-scholasticism more palatable. For him, it was the dominant form of theology but not the only form to which he was exposed.

Despite some of the benefits of neo-scholastic theology Dulles enumerates, he ultimately sees it as inadequate for a fairly significant reason. Neo-scholasticism, in its early twentieth-century form, involves taking the statements of theologians and councils out of context. Inevitably, a compilation of theological opinions from the tradition will pull those statements from their original contexts. This leads to a failure on the part of the theologian to truly grasp the position of the person or council in question. Dulles writes, "The theologian, therefore, could not adequately deal with thinkers of another school by looking at their answers to isolated questions. Since each theologian's answers had to be considered within his or her own intellectual framework, it was necessary for system to confront system."[10] In addition to this problem, Dulles argues that neo-scholasticism could at times represent an entrenchment of its participants; it left thinkers content to dwell in their own schools of thought, considering opposing viewpoints only long enough to refute them.[11]

Dulles's Theological Approach

In understanding Dulles's own position, it is important to consider both the role of the biblical text and the role of tradition. Dulles is clear that sacred scripture is the locus of divine revelation and, therefore, is a central source for theological work. At the same time, he is clear that approaching scripture is not

7. Ibid., 42–43.
8. Ibid., 44.
9. Ibid.
10. Ibid., 45.
11. Ibid., 46.

without some complications. While the biblical text is necessary for the church to remain faithful to the teachings of Christ, the Bible is not a text with a clear and unambiguous interpretation at all points. Because of this, the Bible, rightly used, must be understood by the theologian to be "a book of the Church."[12]

Dei Verbum, the document from Vatican II on revelation, identifies two types of interpretation of scripture. The first is the literal sense, which is essentially an effort to get back into the mind of the author to understand the original, intended meaning. The second is what Dulles refers to as "the further understanding," that comes both from considering scripture as a whole and looking at it through the lens of the tradition of the church.[13]

In Dulles's usual fashion, in considering how scripture is used in theology, *The Craft of Theology* outlines ten hermeneutical approaches. These include (1) the classical doctrinal approach, which understands the Bible as a collection of doctrinal statements; (2) biblical theology, which attempts to draw together the teachings of the whole of scripture on one particular theological topic; (3) spiritual exegesis, which is seen most clearly in the writings of the Eastern church fathers; (4) Word theology, which Dulles associates with the approach of Karl Barth; (5) existential hermeneutics, which Dulles associates with the approach of Rudolf Bultmann; (6) the experiential-expressive approach, which can be seen in the approach of Karl Rahner (discussed in chap. 3); (7) seeking authorial intention; (8) historical reconstruction (as is seen in various approaches to biblical criticism); (9) the cultural-linguistic approach (discussed in chap. 5); and (10) the approach of liberation theology (discussed in chap. 6).[14]

While he notes that he has not exhausted all the possible hermeneutical approaches, Dulles has come close with this list. In offering the list, Dulles is ultimately making a case for diversity. Each of these positions can be found in the work of some notable contemporary theologians, and, as a result, none should be dismissed out of hand. Further, it is not possible to take all of these approaches and synthesize them into a single approach.[15]

What does one do with so many approaches? Dulles says that one's approach might depend on the types of questions being asked. A theologian may select an approach as a primary lens through which to read the biblical text for a particular question he or she is exploring. At the same time, Dulles does not seem to suggest that these methods are all of equal value.

Out of these ten approaches, Dulles writes that his own method is one that makes use of historical critical scholarship under the guidance of tradition and

---

12. Ibid., 69.
13. Ibid., 70–71. He notes that this view affirms the "harmony that exists among revealed truths."
14. Ibid., 71–85.
15. Ibid., 85.

magisterial teaching.[16] To be appropriately theological, this data must also be considered in light of the best of biblical theology and spiritual exegesis. For Dulles, this is "a comprehensive approach, combining scientific and spiritual exegesis," which remains faithful to the Catholic tradition and also addresses the needs of systematic theology.[17]

Concerning tradition, Dulles is careful to show how Catholic theology has developed over time. He writes that prior to the Council of Trent, there were a few different approaches to the role of tradition in theology. The first approach saw tradition as a prerequisite for a right interpretation of scripture. This was a view held by several of the church fathers and by Thomas Aquinas. An additional approach posited that revelation itself was given to the church partially in the form of the scriptures and partially in the oral tradition that originates with the apostles. A final view noted by Dulles was one that saw the Holy Spirit continually working within the Catholic Church to provide ongoing "inspiration or illumination."[18]

The Council of Trent, which was held in the mid-sixteenth century in the wake of the Protestant Reformation, spoke definitively on this subject. Trent stated that scripture alone was insufficient for right doctrine. In order to correctly interpret scripture, one must rely on the tradition of the church, both in the writings of earlier theologians and in the councils of the church. Each of the three pre-Trent positions outlined above supports this view. In addition to this, Trent essentially affirmed a two-source theory of revelation, which held that revelation is contained partially in scripture and partially in the church's unwritten traditions, though the final wording of the text could be taken to suggest that revelation is contained wholly in scripture or wholly in tradition. Ultimately, Trent seems to suggest that tradition is not in any way subjugated to scripture. This was usually interpreted to mean that tradition was something orally handed down from the time of the apostles and that it was static, rather than something that developed over time.[19]

Vatican II (1962–65) took a slightly different approach to the relationship between scripture and tradition. *Humani Generis*, keeping with the logic of the Council of Trent, had stated in 1950 that scripture and tradition were two sources of revelation and that there were truths contained in the tradition that were not contained in scripture. Further, the magisterium (the teaching office of the Catholic Church) was the official interpreter of both streams of revelation.[20]

---

16. Ibid., 85. Magisterial teaching refers to the official teachings of the Catholic Church coming out of the Vatican.

17. Ibid., 85.

18. Ibid., 87–88.

19. Ibid., 89.

20. Ibid., 93.

While this type of reasoning was found in the preparatory documents for Vatican II, the 1960s were a very different time than the 1660s, and an affirmation of two sources of revelation was viewed as problematic for Catholic-Protestant relations.[21]

While Vatican II did not change the church's understanding of tradition and its relationship to scripture, it did shift its emphasis. Tradition, in the Vatican II document *Dei Verbum*, is the custodian of the Word of God. While scripture alone is insufficient for the articulation of doctrine, tradition allows for the right understanding of the Word of God.[22] In other words, it is the task of tradition to help the faithful interpret the biblical text.

Dulles makes several important affirmations coming out of this history. Ultimately, he argues that tradition involves a shared "sense of the faith" that is in the church via the work of the Holy Spirit. Additionally, the tradition is found within the context and community of faith. Dulles does argue that tradition

> to some degree found normative expression in the writings of the fathers, in liturgical texts, and in other ecclesially certified "monuments of tradition." . . . Tradition, as a sense of the faith nourished in the Church by normative texts or "monuments" provides an element of continuity in the development of Christian doctrine. Tradition is "divine" insofar as it is aroused and sustained by God; it is "apostolic" insofar as it originates with the apostles; it is "living" insofar as it remains contemporary with every generation.[23]

Dulles wants to be clear that in some sense tradition is prior to scripture. He argues that it holds equal weight to scripture but that it was instrumental to the church in determining what texts should be canonical. At the same time, he says that tradition is less than scripture in that it itself is not in the canonical texts. Ultimately, Dulles claims, the magisterium is the interpreter of both scripture and tradition. He writes, "The ecclesiastical magisterium, making use of Scripture and tradition, is the authoritative judge of the conformity of particular doctrines and practices, including human traditions, with the word of God."[24]

---

21. Ibid.
22. Dulles writes,
   Scripture is formally insufficient. In other words, tradition is needed for a sufficient grasp of the word of God, even though it be assumed that all revelation is somehow contained in Scripture. It is not from Scripture alone that the Church draws its certainty about everything that has been revealed. Tradition is the means by which the full canon of the sacred books becomes known, and by which the meaning of the biblical text is more profoundly understood and more deeply penetrated. (Ibid., 97)
23. Ibid., 103.
24. Ibid., 104.

If for Dulles the magisterium is the ultimate judge of right doctrine, it is important to briefly examine how he understands the work of the magisterium to fit into the larger project of theological reflection. Dulles cites *Dei Verbum*, the Vatican II document on sacred scripture, which holds that tradition and scripture are one "sacred deposit of the word of God," and that this deposit has been given to the church.[25]

One of the things for which Dulles's work is known is his consideration of the place of theological dissent in the Catholic Church. This is a pressing question in Catholic theology, because the locus of authority is somewhat different from Protestant theology. To be clear, Catholics and Protestants alike argue for the primacy of the Word of God, which reveals the person of Christ in the biblical text. The difference is that the Catholic Church has official church teaching that comes out of the magisterium in a way that is quite different from Protestantism. Official church teaching holds that the magisterium is authorized by God to interpret both scripture and tradition. The question that particularly interests Dulles is whether Catholic theologians can ever dissent or disagree with the magisterium.[26]

The Congregation for the Doctrine of the Faith (CDF), the Vatican group charged with making judgments about right doctrine, issued a document in 1990 on the relationship between Catholic theologians and the magisterium. In it, the CDF acknowledges that theologians go about their work in different ways to different ends than does the magisterium. Because the magisterium is charged with the work of conveying official church teaching to the church as a whole, it does not need to use the same methods of argumentation as theologians do. Similarly, as theologians are engaged in the work of theological argumentation, they are not going to simply appeal to the authority of popes and councils but will rather seek to construct clearly reasoned doctrinal positions.[27] Despite these distinct roles, the magisterium and theology have also been mutually dependent. Certainly, theology across the history of the church has relied on official statements of the church. It would be impossible to talk about the nature of the Trinity without referring to the Council of Nicaea or the nature of Christ without talking about the Council of Chalcedon. At the same time, the magisterium has made use of the work of theology throughout its history. Dulles points out that every council has made use of the work of theologians, and that almost every papal encyclical was written with the help of theologians.[28]

25. Ibid., 105.
26. Ibid.
27. Ibid., 106–7. Here Dulles is citing the CDF document *Instruction on the Ecclesial Vocation of the Theologian*.
28. Dulles, *Craft of Theology*, 107.

What is often misunderstood about Catholic theology is that magisterial statements do not all carry the same weight. While most outsiders assume that anything stated by the Vatican must be held by all believers, the reality is that some statements carry less weight than others. Dulles delineates four categories. One category is made up of definitive things that all Catholics are to accept as divinely revealed. A related but different category is made up of things that Dulles refers to as "definitive declarations of nonrevealed truths" that stem from the revealed truths in the first category. Following the first two categories in weight, a third category is made up of "nondefinitive but obligatory" teaching that helps one understand revelation. The final category is made up of teachings that are important for a particular time or place.[29]

Of these categories, Dulles argues that the first is accepted by all Catholics and is explicitly mentioned in both Vatican I and Vatican II. The second category is not explicitly found in either Vatican I or Vatican II but, according to Dulles, is implied by both. Dulles locates the third category in the teachings of popes and councils and in Vatican II, and the fourth category has been articulated by Joseph Ratzinger (while he was the head of the CDF).[30]

While Dulles does not address dissent to the first two categories mentioned above (noting that things in the first two categories enjoy a wide consensus in the church and denying them would render one not Catholic), he points out that some theologians do express dissent with matters of the third and fourth categories. Because things in the third and fourth categories (which he calls "reformable") do not have definitive (infallible) claims attached to them, it is legitimate for Catholic theologians to acknowledge that they could be wrong. Dulles writes, "It stands to reason that the theologian, like any other Catholic, must be antecedently disposed to accept the reformable teaching of the magisterium, which has the divinely given office of determining the doctrine of the Church. But it may happen that an individual theologian, as already mentioned, could be unsuccessful in attempting to achieve personal conviction."[31] In other words, there is an explicit place in Catholic theology for disagreements concerning certain matters of faith. The possibility of this lies in the reality that there are many places one might turn to for knowledge. Dulles writes,

> Other sources to be used by theologians in forming their judgment include the teaching of Scripture, the testimony of ancient Christian tradition, the prayer and worship of the Church, the opinions of other theologians, the sense of the faithful and the evidence of history, experience, or reason. If a reformable teaching

29. Ibid., 108–9.
30. Ibid., 109–11.
31. Ibid., 112.

appears to be at odds with one or more of these other sources, a theologian who has personally looked into the matter may be inclined to disagree.[32]

Dissent can be a problem in the church. Prominent theologians who dissent can cause significant disagreement within the church. Vatican II inherently addressed the legitimacy of some dissent in the church through the prominent place given to a number of well-known scholars who had been disciplined or called into question by the Vatican prior to the council. Dissent continued to be a pressing issue for the church after Vatican II, but from the opposite end of the theological and ideological spectrum. While the theologians who were called into question prior to Vatican II and who participated in the council tended to be on the left, a number of right-wing Catholics questioned Vatican II and some of the other social teachings of the church, while questions from the left remained.[33]

Dulles notes that the US bishops have affirmed the legitimacy of disagreement with some "nondefinitive" church teachings. In a group statement, they wrote, "The expression of theological dissent from the magisterium is in order only if the reasons are serious and well-founded, if the manner of the dissent does not question or impugn the teaching authority of the Church and is such as not to give scandal."[34] Of course, these criteria can raise more questions than they answer. Dulles writes, "Who was to say whether the reasons were well-founded? How could one establish that the authority of the magisterium was not being impugned when its teaching was being denied? How could scandal be avoided when theologians were openly saying that the pope's teaching was wrong?"[35]

Despite the complexities dissent entails, Dulles acknowledges the importance of having a place in the church for some dissent, though he certainly does not extend this possibility to cover dissent on definitive church teachings. At the same time, it is important to be aware that space for dissent exists in the church and is upheld to a small degree by the teachings of the CDF. An awareness of this reality combats both the idea that Catholic theologians all exist in lockstep with the Vatican and the idea that creative thinking is impossible within the church. As someone who saw himself as a moderate, Dulles worked to build bridges between positions that might initially be seen as at odds with one another,

32. Ibid.

33. Dulles writes, "After the council, the problem of dissent became still more acute. Many right-wing Catholics dissented from the social teaching of the Church, and a few, including Archbishop Marcel Lefebvre, frankly dismissed Vatican II as a heretical council. On the left, many progressive theologians differed from papal teachings such as, most particularly, the doctrine of Paul VI on birth control (*Humanae Vitae*, 1968)" (ibid., 113).

34. Ibid. He quotes the United States Conference of Catholic Bishops, *Human Life in Our Day* (Washington, DC: United States Catholic Conference, 1968), 18.

35. Dulles, *Craft of Theology*, 113.

and he consistently came across as generous to a variety of positions and not merely those in line with his own. While he was viewed as a more conservative Catholic theologian later in his career, Dulles's work sought to create space for conversation about theological dissent, showing that Catholic theology was about far more than simply restating past positions. Also, his work was always done in such a way that earned respect, even from those who vigorously disagreed with him. As a result, Dulles's theological work will continue to have great value for anyone interested in questions of methodology, particularly Catholic methodology.

KARL BARTH

Protestant Liberalism

The introduction to this book discusses nineteenth-century Protestant liberalism. To examine the work of Karl Barth requires returning to this movement to consider the context in which he was educated.

Nineteenth-century Protestant liberalism, like all theology, came in a specific context. It was situated in a period in which science and industry had grown, and new knowledge coming out of those areas led some to question various tenets of the Christian faith. One example of this is Charles Darwin's theory of natural selection. By the late nineteenth century, this theory had gained acceptance in the broader culture. Darwin's theory posed some problem to Christian theology in that it appeared to contradict Christian claims that the earth is young and was created in six days.[36]

One response to such ideas is to distrust any knowledge that appears to contradict the biblical text. This is the fundamentalist approach. Another approach is to reject Christianity altogether. This stance holds that if the findings of the natural sciences contradict the biblical text or religious beliefs, the natural sciences must be correct.

Protestant liberalism tries to take a course in between these two extremes. It holds that there is something important about the Christian faith that would be lost with total abandonment, but it also holds that Christianity as it has been traditionally expressed is not compatible with new scientific knowledge. In considering major Christian doctrines, Protestant liberalism tends to take one of two approaches. First, it rejects some Christian claims as not original to the teachings of Christ. This is the major task of the history of dogma movement—to look at

36. Regarding this point, it is important to understand that the view of a young earth and six days of creation was not universally held across the history of the church. Augustine famously wrote that the creation story in Genesis is clearly not a story intended to be taken literally.

Christian beliefs and determine their actual origins. One significant claim of this movement is that while Jesus is the originator of true Christianity, Paul was the great Hellenizer who brought Greek thought forms into Christian theology. Because these ideas did not actually originate with Jesus, they are not authentically Christian views. Second, if it does not outright reject beliefs that it finds problematic, it reconstrues them. In other words, liberal Protestants may refer to Jesus as the Son of God, but they aren't necessarily affirming Nicene and Chalcedonian orthodoxy. When they affirm the sonship of Jesus, what they mean by it is that Jesus is particularly connected to God or that Jesus points other human beings to God. What they don't mean by it is that Jesus is fully God and fully human.

Adolf von Harnack is one of the most important Protestant liberal theologians, and he is particularly relevant for this discussion because he was one of Barth's teachers. Harnack held that the message of Jesus has been made complex throughout the history of Christian dogma but in its original form is quite simple. For Harnack, the message of Jesus is about the fatherhood of God, the infinite value of the human soul, and the brotherhood of all people.[37] Initially, when students encounter Harnack's argument, they do not see its potential problems. Certainly those who hold to Nicene and Chalcedonian orthodoxy could also agree that Jesus taught about the fatherhood of God, the infinite value of the human soul, and the brotherhood of all people. That seems nonobjectionable enough. The potential problem raised by some critics is that this is the totality of what Harnack claims. In other words, critics are concerned not so much with what Harnack does say but with what he doesn't say.

The other significant feature of Protestant liberalism for the purposes of this discussion is its understanding of human progress. The nineteenth century saw significant scientific and industrial progress and was also a period of relative peace. Protestant liberalism tended to understand society as progressing, and it also considered religion and culture to be connected to each other.

Barth's Disillusionment

In 1914 war broke out in Europe. Barth, who had been trained as a Reformed minister under Harnack and Wilhelm Hermann, was dismayed when his theological teachers signed a document giving formal endorsement to the German war effort. For Barth, this led to disillusionment with the Protestant liberalism in which he was trained. It was clear to him that in endorsing the war plans of the German government, Christianity had failed to be prophetic. This would eventually lead to a new approach to Christian doctrine for Barth.

37. Harnack, *What Is Christianity?*, 51.

In 1919 Barth released the first edition of his *Epistle to the Romans*. Although it was not immediately widely distributed, it was soon circulated broadly by a new publisher. Barth received quite a bit of attention for this book and was soon given an honorary professorship of theology.[38]

Barth's newfound theology was developed in *The Epistle to the Romans* and in a lecture he gave in 1920, with Harnack in attendance, titled "Biblical Questions, Insights, and Vistas." In this lecture Barth developed an understanding of the otherness of God. In the lecture and in other places, Barth argued that the problem with Protestant liberal theology is that it is far too anthropocentric. Theology, according to Barth, must start with and be grounded on the Word of God. He writes, "Theology stands and falls with the Word of God, for the Word of God precedes all theological words by creating, arousing, and challenging them. Should theology wish to be more or less or anything other than action in response to that Word, its thinking and speaking would be empty, meaningless and futile."[39]

The Word of God

For Barth, theology must start with God and with the Word of God. Further, it must be utterly grounded in the Word of God. He writes, "Theology's whole illumination can be only its human reflection or mirroring (in the precise sense of 'speculation'!); and its whole production can only be a human reproduction. In short, theology is not a creative act but only a praise of the Creator and of his act of creation."[40]

The Word of God comes first, according to Barth, because human beings cannot think or reflect on the Word until they are themselves created, and this is an act that only God can do. Without the Word first, true theology is impossible. Further, it is not the task of the theologian to interpret or explain the Word of God, but rather the theologian is to announce and confirm the Word.[41] He writes, "Not only does this Word regulate theology and precede all theological interpretation; it also and above all constitutes and calls theology forth out of nothingness into being, out of death into life. This Word is the *Word of God*. The place of theology is in direct confrontation with this Word, a situation in which theology finds itself placed, and must again and again place itself."[42] Barth refers

38. Hardy, "Karl Barth," 23.
39. Karl Barth, *Evangelical Theology, an Introduction*, trans. Grover Foley (New York: Holt, Rinehart and Winston, 1963), 17.
40. Ibid.
41. Ibid., 17–18.
42. Ibid., 18.

to the Word as that which God has spoken and will speak to human beings. It is through the Word of God that God enters into relationship with humanity and reveals Godself to humanity.

It is important to understand Barth's definition of the Word of God, because it will differ somewhat from what is commonly associated with the term. For Barth, the Word of God is found chiefly in the person of Jesus Christ. The Word of God is also found in the biblical text and Christian preaching, both of which bear witness to the Word. Barth writes, "Theology responds to the Word which God *has spoken, still speaks,* and *will speak again* in the history of *Jesus Christ* which fulfills the history of Israel. To reverse the statement, theology responds to that Word spoken in the history of *Israel* which reaches its culmination in the history of Jesus Christ."[43] Christ is the Word of God and the ultimate act of revelation from God. Theology must always start with this Word of God.

Speaking about God

Barth affirms with the Christian tradition that God created all that exists. He parts company with some in the tradition, though, regarding how to understand the creation. Barth's work in the early 1920s, particularly in "Biblical Questions, Insights, and Vistas," emphasizes God as creator who is wholly other from the creation.[44] Because God is wholly other from creation, human beings cannot come to know true things about God from that creation. Barth rejects what theologians usually refer to as the *analogia entis* or "analogy of being."[45] This idea can be found in the work of several theologians, but it is chiefly found in the work of Thomas Aquinas. The analogy of being holds that if God created all that is, the creation itself must tell human beings something about God. Thomas Aquinas couches this in terms of how human beings speak about God. He argues that God has points of contact with creation, but that it is important to be clear about how we are using language about God.

When human beings use human language (the only thing at their disposal) to speak about God, it must be clear that they are not using terms univocally. In other words, to say that God is "one" means something beyond any human understanding of oneness. Individual human beings are in and of themselves one, but that oneness cannot be said to be exactly the same as God's oneness.

43. Ibid. (emphasis in original).
44. Karl Barth, "Biblical Questions, Insights, and Vistas," in *The Word of God and the Word of Man*, trans. Douglas Horton (New York: Harper Torchbooks, 1956), 52–54.
45. Barth famously refers to the *analogia entis* as "the invention of the anti-Christ" in the preface to *Church Dogmatics* I/1, ed. G. W. Bromiley and T. F. Torrance (Edinburgh: T&T Clark, 1956). See also Keith L. Johnson, *Karl Barth and the Analogia Entis* (New York: Continuum, 2010), 123.

Because of that, the term cannot be used univocally to speak about God and human beings.

At the same time, Thomas says, we cannot say that language about God is equivocal. To use a term equivocally would be to refer to a particular kind of bird and a particular piece of building equipment as "cranes." Both things carry the name "crane," but they are two completely different things. At first glance, it may look like Thomas has left his readers no way in which to speak about God. In reality, though, he forges a middle way.

Thomas argues that we can speak about God analogically. Human beings can use their limited language to say that God is like particular things found in creation. In other words, God's goodness is something like human goodness, even though it is a far greater and incomprehensible good. Similarly, God's beauty is something like the beauty of creation, even though God's beauty is far greater.[46]

Barth essentially rejects this claim. He argues that God is wholly other[47] from creation, and therefore anything that might be seen in creation is inadequate to reveal to human beings anything about God. Theologians often call this claim in Barth "God's 'No'" to creation. There is a clear distinction between God and creation, and human beings can know nothing about God from the creation.

It is important to recognize that Barth's theology is by no means wholly negative. To say that God is other from creation and that therein is found God's "No" is not to give a full summation of Barth's understanding of the relationship between God and creation. Barth also spends time, particularly later in his life, talking about God's "Yes" to humanity in Jesus Christ. He writes,

> The dawn of the new time, of the sovereignty of him which is and which was and which is to come—this is the meaning of Easter. Resurrection means the *new world*, the world of a new quality and kind. Our discovery of the significance of the world we live in, that its life comes from death, our knowledge that its origin is in God because our own is in God, is not a continuation of anything that has been or is, either in the spiritual or in the natural realm, but comes to our mind spontaneously as a new creation. Reality as we have known it, even if it be understood in the optimistic way of the reformers as a process of growth, is neither verified nor explained by this new truth; but in the light of this truth, it is seen to be clothed upon with new reality.[48]

This is the heart of Barth's theology. God is wholly other from God's creation, and yet God becomes radically connected to the creation in covenant via Jesus

---

46. This is addressed in Thomas Aquinas, *Summa Theologiae* 1a.13.5.

47. Karl Barth, "The Righteousness of God," in *The Word of God and the Word of Man*, trans. Douglas Horton (New York: Harper Torchbooks, 1956), 24.

48. Barth, "Biblical Questions," 90–91 (emphasis in original).

Christ. It is for this reason that Barth's theology, which might initially be read as pessimistic, is actually a theology of hope and reconciliation.

WOLFHART PANNENBERG

Barth was a theological giant of the twentieth century, and many have argued that he is the most important Protestant theologian of that era. Despite this, not everyone adopted his method. The next chapter will discuss Paul Tillich, whose approach to theology could almost be characterized as diametrically opposed to Barth's. In the middle, though, is another theologian, Wolfhart Pannenberg, who has both some of the convictions of Barth and yet values some of the same sources as Tillich. As a result, he serves as an effective bridge between the two.

Pannenberg and His Light Experience

Wolfhart Pannenberg was born in 1928 in Stettin, Germany (which is today located in Poland). His family was not particularly religious, though Pannenberg would have an experience as a teenager that led him toward a quest for God. He writes,

> The single most important experience occurred in early January 1945, when I was 16 years old. On a lonely two-hour walk home from my piano lesson, seeing an otherwise ordinary sunset, I was suddenly flooded by light and absorbed in a sea of light which, although it did not extinguish the humble awareness of my finite existence, overflowed the barriers that normally separate us from the surrounding world. . . . I did not know at the time that January 6 was the day of Epiphany, nor did I realize in that moment Jesus Christ had claimed my life as a witness to the transfiguration of this world in the illuminating power and judgment of his glory. But there began a period of craving to understand the meaning of life, and since philosophy did not seem to offer the ultimate answers to such a quest, I finally decided to probe the Christian tradition more seriously than I had considered worthwhile before.[49]

This early experience led the young Pannenberg to pursue philosophical and theological study. In 1950 he went to study under Karl Barth. Reflecting on Barth's thought, he wrote, "I was impressed by the Barthians' emphasis on the sovereignty of God in his revelation, and it seemed self-evident to me that God was to be conceived of as utterly sublime and majestic if there was any God at

49. Wolfhart Pannenberg, "God's Presence in History," *Christian Century*, March 11 (1981), 261.

all, and when I came to Basel in 1950 to study under Karl Barth himself, I was almost convinced of the appropriateness of his approach."[50]

While Pannenberg was drawn to Barth's thought, he had some reservations. He was concerned about what he saw as dualism in Barth's thought. He sensed that philosophy and theology should not be separated, but rather that every single reality should remain "incomprehensible" apart from God, if God truly was the creator of all that is. Further, Pannenberg understood Barth's understanding of the relationship between God and the world to be such that the world was a strange place to God, rather than home. Barth's sharp distinction between the creator and the creation makes it impossible to understand God as being somehow at home, or native, to God's creation.[51]

As he continued his studies, Pannenberg strengthened the ties in his own mind between philosophy and theology. This came about in large part, he writes, through his reading of the church fathers. At this point he began to realize the importance of history for God's revelation. He understood that it was in history that God's work in creation is revealed.[52]

Revelation

The locus of God's revelation is found in different places for different people. Some thinkers, like Barth, place it first in Christ and then through the work of the Holy Spirit via the Word of God (scripture). Other thinkers, like Millard Erickson (who will be discussed in chap. 5), place it squarely in the biblical text. Karl Rahner (who will be discussed in chap. 3) locates it first in human experience of God. For Pannenberg, God's revelation is chiefly found in history. He writes,

> Now historical experience, tradition and critical exegesis, together with philosophical and theological reflection on their content and implications, became the privileged medium to discuss the reality of God. That meant that there is no direct conceptual approach to God, nor from God to human reality, by analogical reasoning, but God's presence is hidden in the particulars of history. . . . We finally arrived at the conclusion that even God's revelation takes place in history and that precisely the biblical writings suggest this solution of the key problem of fundamental theology.[53]

Directly responding to Barth's understanding of revelation, Pannenberg writes, "In the end it became discernible that it is in history itself that divine revelation

50. Ibid.
51. Ibid.
52. Ibid.
53. Ibid.

takes place, and not in some strange Word arriving from some alien place and cutting across the fabric of history."[54]

In other words, God is known precisely through the ways in which God acts in history. When encountering this idea, some students will ask how one knows in what places God acts in history and in what places the normal course of human events is occurring. They will also sometimes cite the problem of interpretation: How does one evaluate a historical event to know God's intentionality? These are both significant questions that do not go unanswered in Pannenberg's work. Pannenberg is clear that the most significant acts of God in history are God's work through the people of Israel and the revelation of God in Jesus Christ.[55] This means that the Bible serves as the record of the most significant revelation.

While there are many important acts of God in history, according to Pannenberg, the most important act of God in history is the resurrection. Pannenberg understands himself as an eschatological realist. To unpack this term, *eschatology* literally means "speech about the end." It is typically understood as the study or discussion of the end times. This can mean different things in different contexts. In evangelical popular culture, one prominent example of this is the *Left Behind* series, which suggests that Christians will be removed from the earth before a period of tribulation that must precede the return of Christ to earth and the inauguration of the millennium, a thousand-year period of rule of Christ on earth. *Realism* refers to the view that there is an objective reality that stands alone from any individual's perception. For Pannenberg, it is only by bringing these two words together that one can adequately describe the type of knowledge about God and reality that is available to human beings.

Eschatological realism, for Pannenberg, means that while there is an objective truth or reality, human beings cannot know it in its fullness until the end of time. He writes,

54. Ibid.
55. Pannenberg affirms the importance of history here: "The Christian faith depends wholly upon the historical events of nearly two thousand years ago and on the meaning inherent within their context. It has no truth independent of this. The God of Israel himself demonstrated through these events before all the world that he alone is the true God. Therefore, our belief in God depends directly upon the events which constitute the fate of Jesus of Nazareth" ("Jesus' History and Our History," trans. Ted Peters, *Perspectives in Religious Studies* 1, no. 2 [1974]: 140). At times, there is a question about the relationship between history and scripture. He writes, "I am not saying that it is biblically inappropriate to speak of God revealing himself in his Word. My point is that this thesis needs more nuanced biblical justification than can be given simply by adducing John 1:1 and Hebrews 1:1–2. Since the Bible offers other ideas of revelation as well as that of the Word of God, it is essential to inquire into the relation of those other ideas to that of the Word" (*Systematic Theology*, trans. Geoffrey W. Bromiley [Grand Rapids: Eerdmans, 1991], 1:237).

There is knowledge of God only in retrospect of his past action in history, just as Moses sees God's glory only when it has gone by. Since the basic knowledge of God in Israel does not rest on a single divine action, but on a series of divine communications from the promises to the fathers by way of the exodus to occupation of the land of promise, the knowledge of God that is thereby imparted can stand only at the end of a sequence of revelatory events.[56]

In other words, no one will know the complete truth until that truth is understood from the perspective of the end of time. This is so, for Pannenberg, because all events are part of a larger whole, one cohesive story.[57] This isn't the end of the story concerning what can be known in the here and now. Pannenberg argues that human beings can anticipate what will ultimately be revealed through the person of God. After all, for Pannenberg, the end of time involves the full inauguration of God's kingdom. The kingdom of God has preliminarily come in the person of Christ. As a result, via the resurrection, human beings can have proleptic (i.e., anticipatory) knowledge of what will be known in the end.[58] For Pannenberg, the reality of the kingdom of God, which will come in fullness at the end of all things, is at the core of the Christian understanding of revelation.[59]

The payoff of Pannenberg's understanding of revelation in history is clear. Because revelatory events are found in historical events, rather than primarily in the biblical text, this revelation is accessible to all.[60] History is not the only publicly accessible source of knowledge, according to Pannenberg. He also argues that theology and the natural sciences need to be in dialogue with each other: "If the God of the Bible is the creator of the universe, then it is not possible to understand fully or even appropriately the processes of nature without any reference to God. If on the contrary, nature can be appropriately understood without reference to the God of the Bible, then that God cannot be the creator of the universe, and consequently he cannot be truly God and be trusted as a source of moral teaching either."[61]

Theology, the Natural Sciences, and Religious Experience

For Pannenberg, theology and the natural sciences need to be in dialogue with each other. Scientific questions do not often get at questions asked in the course

56. Pannenberg, *Systematic Theology*, 1:244–45.
57. Stanley J. Grenz, *Reason for Hope: The Systematic Theology of Wolfhart Pannenberg*, 2nd ed. (Grand Rapids: Eerdmans, 2005), 45. Grenz notes here that this claim has not been universally accepted.
58. Pannenberg, *Systematic Theology*, 1:246–47.
59. Ibid., 1:247. See also Grenz's explanation of Pannenberg's position in *Reason for Hope*, 45.
60. Pannenberg, *Systematic Theology*, 1:250.
61. Wolfhart Pannenberg, "Theological Questions to Scientists," *Zygon* 16, no. 1 (March 1981): 66.

of theological work. At the same time, the natural sciences, in Pannenberg's mind, provide universally accessible knowledge about the surrounding world.

Along with considering revelation as history, the nature of known truth, and the role of science in human knowledge, Pannenberg says that religious experience is basic to human beings. He argues that religion is a fundamental part of what it means to be human. While he acknowledges that modernity has tried to stifle the religious impulses in human beings, it has never been able to fully do that. Religious tendencies among human beings reveal something fundamental about them. Pannenberg writes, "The universal presence of religious themes corresponds to the feature of human behavior that is described as openness to the world, ec-centricity, or self-transcendence."[62] In this sense, Pannenberg has some important agreement with Karl Rahner, who will be discussed further in the next chapter. While Pannenberg claims that religious inclinations in human beings do not prove the existence of God, within a framework that believes in the existence of God, this offers evidence that all human beings have an orientation toward the God who created them. Pannenberg writes, "If the one God is to be the Creator of the human race, then as self-conscious beings we must have some awareness, however inadequate, of this origin of ours. Our human existence necessarily bears the mark of creaturehood, and this cannot be totally hidden from our awareness of ourselves."[63]

In the end, Pannenberg's approach to theology is unique among those examined in this book because of his focus on revelation as history. With this focus Pannenberg has moved beyond some of the claims of Barth while still emphasizing God and the Word of God. As will be seen in the next chapter, Paul Tillich's theology takes a different approach to the locus of revelation and the understanding of God. It is between his views and the views of Karl Barth that Pannenberg stands.

---

62. Pannenberg, *Systematic Theology*, 1:155–56.
63. Ibid., 1:157.

3

Theologies of Correlation

Theologies of correlation are fundamentally interested in dialogue. This dialogue is often found between the church and the broader world and between theology and other disciplines, be they philosophy, literature, the social sciences, or the natural sciences. While two of the figures in this chapter are Roman Catholic, the first figure treated here, Paul Tillich, is Protestant. As a result, it is clear that just as neo-orthodox theology is not limited to Protestantism, so theologies of correlation are not limited to Roman Catholicism.

PAUL TILLICH

Tillich's Stand against the Nazis

Paul Tillich was born in 1886 to a Lutheran pastor and his wife. He studied at a number of German universities and eventually received a PhD in 1911. In addition to his philosophical training, he received divinity training and was ordained as a pastor before serving in a congregation for a few years. In 1914, when World War I broke out, Tillich found himself in the German army, serving as a chaplain. During that period, Tillich saw firsthand the devastation of the war, and it represented a significant turning point in his life.[1]

1. David H. Kelsey, "Paul Tillich," in *The Modern Theologians: An Introduction to Christian Theology Since 1918*, ed. David F. Ford with Rachel Muers (Malden, MA: Blackwell, 2005), 62.

After the end of the war, Tillich taught as part of the religious studies faculties at many German universities.[2] He published a book in 1933 (during the same month the Nazis came to power) titled *The Socialist Decision*, which explicitly attacked Nazi ideology. As a result, he was dismissed from his position at the University of Frankfurt. Because his safety was ultimately in jeopardy, Tillich and his family left Germany for the United States. There Tillich took a faculty position at Union Theological Seminary in New York City. This means that at the age of forty-seven, Tillich essentially started his career over in a language that was not his own.[3] What is perhaps most impressive about this is that some of Tillich's most well-known work, particularly his *Systematic Theology*, was published after this point in his life.

Tillich's Method of Correlation

Tillich's theological methodology comes in part from his experience as an immigrant. He noted that the experience of coming to America opened up for him a new mode of being, living in two worlds at once. Immigrants live in the tension of seeking to adapt to the new milieu while preserving their connection to the old one.[4] This experience led to some key questions for Tillich.

For Tillich, theology is a function of the church, and its work is to serve the church. He writes, "Theology, as a function of the Christian church, must serve the needs of the church. A theological system is supposed to satisfy two basic needs: the statement of the truth of the Christian message and the interpretation of this truth for every new generation. Theology moves back and forth between two poles, the eternal truth of its foundation and the temporal situation in which the eternal truth must be received."[5] Tillich here argues that the work of theology is to address the questions that come out of the contemporary situation with the Christian message or resources from Christian theology. This is not an easy task. Tillich writes, "Not many theological systems are able to balance these two demands perfectly. Most of them either sacrifice elements of the truth or are not able to speak to the situation."[6]

One common misconception about Tillich's claim is that theology or the Christian message itself somehow changes to accommodate itself to the contemporary situation. What he makes clear in his statement about the difficulty

---

2. The one exception to this was the University of Marburg, where Tillich was appointed to the theological faculty from 1924 to 1925.

3. Kelsey, "Paul Tillich," 62.

4. Charles W. Kegley and Robert W. Bretall, eds., *The Theology of Paul Tillich* (New York: Macmillan, 1964), 19.

5. Paul Tillich, *Systematic Theology*, 3 vols. (Chicago: University of Chicago Press, 1951–63), 1:3.

6. Ibid.

of the task at hand is that he is not suggesting that the Christian message or Christian theology changes, but rather that it must be articulated anew for each new situation. This also does not mean that theology can be the work of simply restating what was said before. Tillich writes, "Some of them [theologians] combine both shortcomings. Afraid of missing the eternal truth, they identify it with some previous theological work, with traditional concepts and solutions, and try to impose these on a new, different situation. They confuse eternal truth with a temporal expression of this truth."[7] Tillich identifies this approach with fundamentalism in the United States.[8] What is perhaps most interesting about this point is that Tillich concedes that fundamentalist theologies can be very popular, but that that has no bearing on the truth of them. What makes good theology, for Tillich, is what successfully accomplishes the two tasks he laid out. To say that theology must address the current "situation" does not mean that it is supposed to address the situation of one specific person or group. "Theology is not preaching or counseling," he writes, and so its usefulness for those two tasks is not relevant to questions about the truth of theology.[9]

It is important to be aware of how Tillich understands the term *situation* and how he uses it to describe the theological task. He writes, "The 'situation' to which theology must respond is the totality of man's creative self-interpretation in a special period."[10] What he means by this is that when theology considers the situation, it is chiefly focusing on the way in which human beings reflect on a particular event or reality, rather than the event or reality itself. "Thus theology is not concerned with the political split between East and West, but it *is* concerned with the political interpretation of this split. Theology is not concerned with the spread of mental diseases or with our increasing awareness of them, but it *is* concerned with the psychiatric interpretation of these trends."[11]

It is notable that Tillich is particularly concerned with responses or interpretations to contemporary events or situations, because his understanding of the human situation as a whole mirrors that. Tillich wants to be clear that "situation" is only one part of the theological picture. It is also crucial for theology to be grounded in the truth of the Christian message. Tillich identifies this kind

7. Ibid.

8. Religious fundamentalism is typically associated with a literalistic interpretation of religious texts and with a rejection of the findings of secular disciplines when they appear to contradict religious texts. In the United States, fundamentalism is often associated with the conservative Protestant movement that took issue with Darwin's theory of natural selection and advocated a more literal reading of the biblical text.

9. Tillich, *Systematic Theology*, 1:3–4.

10. Ibid., 1:4.

11. Ibid.

of theology as "kerygmatic" theology (from the Greek *kerygma*, to preach or proclaim). It is different from fundamentalism in that it subjects every theology to "the criterion of the Christian message." This raises the question of what comprises the Christian message itself. Tillich writes, "This message is contained in the Bible, but it is not identical with the Bible. It is expressed in the classical tradition of Christian theology, but it is not identical with any special form of that tradition."[12] He identifies Martin Luther, who was under attack by orthodox thinkers of his time, and Karl Barth, who was under attack by fundamentalists, as theologians whose work serves as examples of kerygmatic theology. Both Luther and Barth, according to Tillich, "made a serious attempt to rediscover the eternal message *within* the Bible and tradition, over against a distorted tradition and a mechanically misused Bible."[13] Barth and Luther, as a result, stand as theologians who are faithful to the Christian message itself, rather than distortions of that message.

In focusing on the truth of the message over against distortions of that truth that arise from misunderstandings, theology must not miss the "situation" as well. While theology must remain faithful to a good reading of that message, it cannot neglect the situation. Here Tillich assesses Luther slightly differently. He writes, "Yet the 'situation' cannot be excluded from theological work. Luther was unprejudiced enough to use his own nominalist learning and Melanchthon's humanist education for the formulation of theological doctrines. But he was not conscious enough of the problem of the 'situation' to avoid sliding into orthodox attitudes, thus preparing the way for the period of Protestant orthodoxy."[14] Tillich's assessment of Barth is also significant. He argues that Barth's strength is that he is continually correcting himself and seeking to "not become his own follower," but in doing that, Tillich says, he ceases to be "a merely kerygmatic theologian." Tillich argues that he becomes "neo-orthodox," and his use of that term suggests that he sees Barth as potentially falling prey to some of the problems of the earlier Protestant orthodoxy.[15]

12. Ibid.

13. Ibid., 1:4–5.

14. Ibid., 1:5. The period of Protestant orthodoxy to which Tillich refers is a historical period that follows the Reformation but is characterized by a different kind of theology. While the Reformers started from the assumption that the biblical text is the Word of God and thus the foundation of theology, Protestant orthodox thinkers believed that theology had to be built on a foundation of first principles that are a priori truths. Once these truths are established, the work of theology can begin. Protestant orthodoxy is generally remembered as a spiritually stagnant period in the history of Protestantism, and it gave rise to the composition of lengthy systematic theologies that were built on the philosophical foundations so prized by their writers. This was the catalyst for the rise of Pietism, which focused on one's daily spiritual life and connection to God rather than philosophical and theological claims.

15. Ibid. Chap. 2 above discusses Barth's neo-orthodox theology in detail.

For Tillich, the theologian must be attentive to situation. Just as it is deeply problematic to step away from the truth of the Christian message, it is also deeply problematic to neglect situation, which he again defines as "modern man's interpretation of existence."[16] A failure to be attentive to a situation can result in things like the nationalism of the German Christians during World War Il.

In light of these problems, Tillich articulates his method of correlation. He gives this summation of his position:

> The following system is an attempt to use the "method of correlation" as a way of uniting message and situation. It tries to correlate the questions implied in the situation with the answers implied in the message. It does not derive the answers from the questions as a self-defying apologetic theology does. Nor does it elaborate answers without relating them to the questions as a self-defying kerygmatic theology does. It correlates questions and answers, situation and message, human existence and divine manifestation.[17]

Tillich and Symbol

To understand Tillich's methodology, it is important to consider his approach to symbol. Tillich argues that religious truths must be expressed symbolically, because symbol is the only adequate way to describe that which is beyond human language. To understand what Tillich means by symbols, it is helpful to consider his comparison with signs. Symbols, he writes, are like signs in that they point to something else. Examples of how this works with signs can be seen in our everyday experiences. If you are reading this book for a particular class, you may attend that class in a particular classroom. Your walking into that classroom may have nothing directly to do with your taking a theology course, but you walk into a classroom because your schedule told you that the course was being held in a particular location, and the classroom's sign (indicating the room number) told you that you were in the right place.[18] In other words, you interpreted something concrete (a room number) to indicate something else (that you were in the right place for your class).

Signs are helpful, but sometimes they are confused with symbols, and at that point they become problematic. Signs and symbols are different things, and when

16. Ibid., 1:5.
17. Ibid., 1:8.
18. Tillich gives the example of a red light and the stopping of a car. He writes, "The red sign at the street corner points to the order to stop the movements of cars at certain intervals. A red light and the stopping of cars have essentially no relation to each other, and conventionally they are united as long as the convention lasts. The same is true of letters and numbers and partly even words. They point beyond themselves to sounds and meanings" (*Dynamics of Faith* [New York: Harper & Row, 1957], 41).

one is mistaken for another, confusion occurs. Tillich argues that the difference between signs and symbols is that "signs do not participate in the reality of that to which they point, while symbols do."[19] This means that there is an essential difference between signs and symbols. Symbols are connected in their being to the thing to which they point. Because signs are not, signs can be replaced at any point necessary.[20] If your school decided to change the numbering of the classrooms, that wouldn't change anything about the function of the classrooms themselves or what goes on inside any given classroom.

Symbols are different. The symbol participates in what it signifies. Tillich uses the example of a flag, arguing that the flag is a symbol rather than a sign, because it is a part of what a particular nation communicates about itself. As a result, flags of nations do not change unless there is some event that ultimately leads to the nation fundamentally changing its identity. Tillich rightly points out that people often react strongly to an attack on a flag.[21] Symbols also have the role of showing us things that we otherwise would not grasp. Art, for example, helps human observers grasp things that were previously unconsidered. In addition to doing this, a symbol also makes us aware of parts of ourselves that were previously not grasped. Tillich writes, "A great play gives us not only a new vision of the human scene, but it opens up hidden depths of our own being. Thus we are able to receive what the play reveals to us in reality. There are within us dimensions of which we cannot become aware except through symbols, as melodies and rhythms in music."[22]

This is a tall order for a symbol. The symbol points to something else in which it participates, and it makes us aware of new things about the world and about ourselves. How does one create such a symbol? This question suggests Tillich's final two characteristics of the symbol. The symbol cannot be "intentionally produced" or "invented."[23] In other words, anyone hoping to create something that would have the effects described above will likely be disappointed. A powerful symbol can emerge out of culture at any time, but it is something that arises organically rather than something that is intentionally built. Symbols come out of a number of arenas of human life, including politics, arts, religion, and history.[24] It is unsurprising that Tillich, as a theologian, is particularly interested in religious symbols. To fully understand the way in which religious symbols function in Tillich's thought, it is important to first consider his view of ultimate concern.

19. Ibid., 42.
20. Ibid.
21. Ibid.
22. Ibid., 42–43.
23. Ibid., 43.
24. Ibid.

The Object of Theology for Tillich

For Tillich, theological method and the system that comes out of it belong together and must be considered together.[25] Because of that, it is important to consider his understanding of both the object of theology and of Christ.

Tillich writes that no one can fully call oneself a theologian. This is because of the reality of both faith and doubt, which is present for all who would call themselves Christian. He writes,

> No one can call himself a theologian, even if he is called to be a teacher of theology. Every theologian is committed *and* alienated; he is always in faith *and* in doubt; he is inside *and* outside the theological circle. Sometimes the one side prevails, sometimes the other; and he is never certain which side really prevails. Therefore, one criterion alone can be applied: a person can be a theologian as long as he acknowledges the content of the theological circle as his ultimate concern.[26]

The idea of ultimate concern is at the heart of Tillich's theological system. He writes, "In view of this age-old struggle, it must be restated that the theologian belongs inside the theological circle but that the criterion whether or not he is in it is the acceptance of the Christian message as his ultimate concern."[27]

What is ultimate concern? For Tillich, it is that with which the theologian must be primarily occupied. This could at first glance be open to the charge of relativism. Is the object of theology thus defined as simply that which is of utmost importance to a given individual? Some have criticized Tillich for using the language of ultimate concern for exactly that reason. Yet those who critique him for this don't seem to fully understand what he is saying here. Tillich writes,

> Ultimate concern is the abstract translation of the great commandment: "The Lord, our God, the Lord is one; and you shall love the Lord your God with all your heart, and with all your soul and with all your mind, and with all your strength." The religious concern is ultimate; it excludes all other concerns from ultimate significance; it makes them preliminary. The ultimate concern is unconditional, independent of any conditions of character, desire, or circumstance. The unconditional concern is total: no part of ourselves or of our world is excluded from it; there is no "place" to flee from it. The total concern is infinite: no moment of relaxation and rest is possible in the face of a religious concern which is ultimate, unconditional, total, and infinite.[28]

25. Tillich, *Systematic Theology*, 1:8.
26. Ibid., 1:10 (emphasis in original).
27. Ibid., 1:11.
28. Ibid., 1:11–12. Tillich cites Mark 12:29 and Ps. 139.

In other words, ultimate concern is not the thing that one particular individual or group of individuals values most. Rather, it is that which is preliminary to all other concerns. In the Christian context, for Tillich, that is the being that most call "God."

It is at this juncture that Tillich's general treatment of symbols becomes relevant for his theological work. He argues that ultimate concern can be expressed only symbolically.[29] Human beings are finite and will never have adequate language to describe that which is infinite. As a result, human beings are able to speak only symbolically about God. Tillich writes, "Religiously speaking, God transcends his own name. This is why the use of his name easily becomes an abuse or blasphemy. Whatever we say about that which concerns us ultimately, whether or not we call it God, has a symbolic meaning. It points beyond itself while participating in that to which it points."[30] Tillich argues that there is no other language than symbol that works for the task of speaking about faith.[31]

God in Tillich's Thought

In Tillich's theological system, "God" is the symbol of human ultimate concern. Tillich argues that that symbol can be found "in any act of faith, even if the act of faith includes the denial of God."[32] This initially seems to be an odd claim, but he explains as follows:

> Where there is ultimate concern, God can be denied only in the name of God. One God can deny the other one. Ultimate concern cannot deny its own character as ultimate. Therefore, it affirms what is meant by the word "God." Atheism, consequently, can only mean the attempt to remove any ultimate concern—to

29. Tillich's discussion in *Dynamics of Faith* gives good insight:
   One may ask: Why can it not be expressed directly and properly? If money, success or the nation is someone's ultimate concern, can this not be said in a direct way and without symbolic language? Is it not only in those cases in which the content of the ultimate concern is called "God" that we are in the realm of symbols? The answer is that everything which is a matter of unconditional concern is made into a god. If the nation is someone's ultimate concern, the name of the nation becomes a sacred name and the nation receives divine qualities which far surpass the reality of the being and functioning of the nation. The nation then stands for and symbolizes the true ultimate, but in an idolatrous way. Success as ultimate concern is not the natural desire of actualizing potentialities, but is readiness to sacrifice all other values in life for the sake of a position of power and social predominance. The anxiety about not being a success is an idolatrous form of the anxiety about divine condemnation. Success is grace; lack of success, ultimate judgment. In this way concepts designating ordinary realities become idolatrous symbols of ultimate concern. (50–51)
30. Ibid., 45.
31. Ibid.
32. Ibid.

remain unconcerned about the meaning of one's existence. Indifference toward the ultimate question is the only imaginable form of atheism. . . . In any case, he who denies God as a matter of ultimate concern affirms God, because he affirms ultimacy in his concern.[33]

In other words, to deny God is to affirm that there is something that concerns humanity ultimately, and for Tillich, that is in the end an affirmation of God.

Further, to ask about the existence of God is to ask the wrong question, because asking about existence is to ask about something that exists "within the whole of reality," and then the answer to the question of existence is no. This might seem a little confusing at first. Is Tillich, who works in the area of Christian theology, denying the existence of God? He is actually denying only an erroneous claim about God. Tillich writes, "God does not exist. He is being-itself beyond essence and existence. Therefore, to argue that God exists is to deny him."[34] Tillich argues that there is a fundamental flaw in cosmological arguments for the existence of God. Such arguments look at the surrounding world and then find characteristics of the world that point to God. The problem is that such claims imply that God is "derived from the world," even if that does not imply some kind of dependence of God on the world. But if God is derived from the world, God cannot transcend the world. This, Tillich claims, also denies the reality of God as that which is wholly beyond the world.[35]

That God is wholly beyond the world explains why symbolic language must be used to speak of God. Nothing in this world adequately accounts for the nature of God. The problem is that human beings are in this world and have natural limitations to their abilities. Only symbolic language can even begin to get at the nature of a reality that is beyond the present world. This is why Tillich says that the word *God* itself is a symbol of faith.

33. Ibid., 45–46. He further writes,
   It is obvious that such an understanding of the meaning of God makes the discussions about the existence or nonexistence of God meaningless. It is meaningless to question the ultimacy of ultimate concern. This element in the idea of God is in itself certain. The symbolic expression of this element varies endlessly in the whole history of mankind. Here again, it would be meaningless to ask whether one or another of the figures in which an ultimate concern is symbolized does "exist." If "existence" refers to something which can be found within the whole of reality, no divine being exists. The question is not this, but which of the innumerable symbols of faith is most adequate to the meaning of faith? In other words, which symbol of ultimacy expresses the ultimate without idolatrous elements? This is the problem, and not the so-called "existence of God"—which is in itself an impossible combination of words. God as the ultimate in man's ultimate concern is more certain than any other certainty, even that of oneself. God as symbolized in a divine figure is a matter of daring faith, of courage and risk. (46)
34. Tillich, *Systematic Theology*, 1:205.
35. Ibid.

The Human Condition in Tillich's Thought

Tillich's approach to Christian theology is born out of his own unique context. He sees the human experience as one that is fundamentally characterized by the awareness of death. This leads human beings to ask some critical questions. He writes, "Perhaps it is not too bold to assume that the words for life first arose through the experience of death. In any case, the polarity of life and death has always colored the word 'life.'"[36] The very nature of living also implies death: "'Living Beings' are also 'dying beings,' and they exhibit characteristics under the predominance of the organic dimension. This *generic* concept of life is the pattern after which the ontological concept of life has been formed."[37]

The fundamental human problem for Tillich is the experience of despair. He argues that human beings see the human condition "in terms of disruption, conflict, self-destruction, meaninglessness, and despair in all realms of life."[38] At this juncture he makes clear that the questions facing humanity at the time of his writing are different questions than ones faced earlier in the church. While the Reformation involved the question of finding a merciful God and becoming reconciled to that being, according to Tillich, the question facing human beings in the mid-twentieth century is something different. Tillich writes, "It is the question of a reality in which the self-estrangement of our existence is overcome, a reality of reconciliation and reunion, of creativity, meaning, and hope."[39] If human beings are seeking to overcome their own self-estrangement, exactly what is this self-estrangement to begin with? Tillich argues that Genesis 1–3 gives the clearest picture of what this looks like. For Tillich, while the human being has freedom, which distinguishes it from all other creatures, that freedom comes in the context of finitude. Further, the human being is aware of finitude both individually and in the larger world.[40] Prior to the fall, humanity can be described as "dreaming innocence."[41] This innocence stands in for an unaware human state. Tillich suggests that when the human being becomes aware of his or her own existential estrangement, the state of "dreaming innocence" will end.[42]

In speaking of the fall, Tillich wants to be clear about one common misunderstanding concerning the man and the woman in the garden. He writes that many theologians have indicated that prior to the fall, the man was perfect.

36. Ibid., 2:11.
37. Ibid. (emphasis in original).
38. Ibid., 1:49.
39. Ibid.
40. Ibid., 2:31.
41. Ibid., 2:33.
42. Ibid.

Whether they intend to or not, Tillich says that to make these claims suggests that the man is being placed in a position close to Christ. "Dreaming innocence" is not like perfection, though. It implies potentialities that may become actualized, but it does not imply perfection.[43]

Where does the human being end up after the fall? According to Tillich, after the fall the human being exists in a situation in which he or she is aware of human finitude. While all creatures are finite, the distinction with human beings is that they are aware of this finitude and perceive it as threatening. This awareness is described as "anxiety." As a result, although the human being is free and is aware of that freedom, it can best be described as a freedom that is "united with anxiety" or "anxious freedom."[44]

The fall is the point at which human beings transition from dreaming innocence to anxious freedom.[45] This is the point at which things begin to go wrong for the human being. Tillich writes, "At the moment when man becomes conscious of his freedom, the awareness of his dangerous situation gets ahold of him. He experiences a double threat, which is rooted in his finite freedom and expressed in anxiety. Man experiences the anxiety of losing himself by not actualizing himself and his potentialities and the anxiety of losing himself by actualizing himself and his potentialities."[46] This is the human condition, for Tillich. Human beings exist in a state of estrangement from "the ground of being" (God), from others, and from themselves. For Tillich, the move away from dreaming innocence to the awareness of estrangement results in "personal guilt and universal tragedy."[47] Tillich wants to be clear that this is not a departure from the biblical understanding of the human problem but is rather fundamentally in keeping with it. He argues that even though the term *estrangement* is not to be found in the Bible, the idea of estrangement is present in most of the Bible's descriptions of the human problem. He writes, "It is implied in the symbols of the expulsion from paradise, in the hostility between man and nature, in the deadly hostility of brother against brother, in the estrangement of nation from nation through the confusion of language,

---

43. Ibid., 2:34. Tillich writes,

> Orthodox theologians have heaped perfection upon perfection upon Adam before the Fall, making him equal with the picture of Christ. This procedure is not only absurd; it makes the Fall completely unintelligible. Mere potentiality or dreaming innocence is not perfection. Only the conscious union of existence and essence is perfection, as God is perfect because he transcends essence and existence. The symbol "Adam before the Fall" must be understood as the dreaming innocence of undecided potentialities. (Ibid., 2:34)

44. Ibid., 2:35.
45. Ibid.
46. Ibid.
47. Ibid., 2:44–45.

and in the continuous complaints of the prophets against their kings and people who turn to alien gods."[48]

Tillich also sees estrangement present in Paul's descriptions of the human condition. Despite this, Tillich also argues that estrangement cannot be understood as sin per se. Much of this has to do with problems with the way sin is described. Tillich points out that Paul makes use of the term in a particular way. When Paul uses the term in the singular and without an article, he sees it as that which has hold over the world. This is a very different use of the word from its common meaning today—individual moral failings. The way the term is currently used does not have much to do with estrangement in Tillich's mind, but the way in which Paul uses the term gets at exactly what Tillich means by estrangement. Tillich doesn't intend to dismiss the term *sin* altogether, though, arguing that it does express something not covered by estrangement—the personal act of rejecting the ground of one's being.[49]

Christ in Tillich's Thought

The solution to the problem of estrangement is found in "the New Being in Jesus as the Christ," according to Tillich: "Therefore, if the Christ is expected as mediator and savior, he is not expected as a third reality between God and man, but as him who represents God to man. He does not represent man to God, but shows what God wants man to be. He represents to those who live under the conditions of existence what man essentially is and therefore ought to be under these conditions."[50] In other words, it is Christ who shows who human beings can be in the face of estrangement. Ultimately, Christ is the one who has lived in the reality of estrangement, but "without being conquered by [it]."[51] This is a critical insight into Tillich's thought. If the human predicament is the experience of estrangement, the solution to this predicament is new being in Christ, because Christ is the one who has shown humanity how to live in its reality without being ruled by it.

At the same time, it is important to understand what Tillich does not affirm about Christ. He writes, "It is inadequate and a source of a false Christology[52] to say that the mediator is an ontological reality beside God and man. This could only be a half-god who at the same time is half-man. Such a third being could neither represent God to men nor man to men."[53] In other words, Tillich does

---

48. Ibid., 2:45.
49. Ibid., 2:45–46.
50. Ibid., 2:93.
51. Ibid., 2:94.
52. Christology is the study of the person of Christ.
53. Tillich, *Systematic Theology*, 2:93–94.

not affirm the doctrine of the incarnation as it has been historically articulated. If the historic understanding of the incarnation is that in Jesus one finds true humanity and true divinity, as articulated in the Nicene Creed and the Chalcedonian Definition, Tillich parts company with the doctrine.

He does address the doctrine head-on, though, writing that the doctrine of the incarnation is in need of a revision. He notes that it is not a biblical term, though he also concedes that that is not an argument against using the term theologically. Ultimately, Tillich argues that "God become man" is a "nonsensical statement." The problem in Tillich's mind is that "God" points to "ultimate reality," and what that means is that whatever God can do, God cannot in any way "cease to be God." If God were to become human, God would then have stopped being God. As a result, the concept of incarnation is not one that should be at home in Christianity. Tillich writes, "[Incarnation] is, on the contrary, a characteristic of paganism so far as, within it, no god has overcome the finite basis on which he stands. Because of this, the mythological imagination within polytheism has had no difficulty in transforming divine beings into both natural objects and human beings. The unqualified use of the term 'Incarnation' in Christianity creates pagan, or at least superstitious, connotations."[54]

Tillich does not claim that the term must be abandoned altogether, though. He notes that one way to perhaps shift the Christian understanding of incarnation is to use John's statement about the Word having become flesh. Tillich says that "Logos" stands for the way in which God shows Godself to creation and throughout history. "Flesh" refers to historical existence rather than some kind of concrete thing (e.g., a body). The term *became* refers to God participating in something which is not God.[55] Incarnation, then, for Tillich, means God's revelation sharing in human history. If this is the meaning of incarnation, then Tillich is happy to retain the term, though he expresses some concern that it might in practicality be quite difficult to keep it from being misunderstood by many as God actually becoming human.[56]

What is one to take away from considering Tillich? He clearly has a view that Christ *creates* a way past the human predicament. If the human predicament is the experience of estrangement, or the awareness of one's own mortality, the Christ, for Tillich, is someone who lives with this reality and is yet not conquered by it. This is a powerful claim, and in some sense Tillich is saying, along with classical Christianity, that Christ is the ultimate solution to the human problem. At the same time, Tillich denies the claim central to classical Christianity that

54. Ibid., 2:94–95.
55. Ibid., 2:95.
56. Ibid.

Christ is God become human, and in doing that, he clearly denies the historical understanding of Christianity that Christ is truly human and truly divine.

KARL RAHNER

Karl Rahner was born to a religious German family in 1904. After completing
secondary school in 1922, he entered the Society of Jesus. It would be the spirituality of Ignatius of Loyola, the founder of the Society of Jesus, that would have
a significant impact on Rahner throughout his career. For that reason, it is important to discuss briefly the Ignatian spirituality that characterizes the Society.

Rahner was asked in an interview why he decided at the age of eighteen to
become a Jesuit. His answer is instructive.

> Well, I must say that I actually can't give you any special information about that.
> Sometime ask an average man, married some fifty or sixty years, what really
> prompted him to marry this particular Maria Meier. If he doesn't fib or hasn't
> lived a life of intense self-reflection, he's likely to say, "I completely admit the fact
> that I did that. I was faithful to my decision and was happy throughout the fifty
> or sixty years of my marriage. I also accept the fact that normal human motiva-
> tions prompted my decision. But I cannot give you any more exact psychological
> information."[57]

Rahner said that his own description of his Jesuit vocation would sound much
the same. While he could suggest reasons why one might wish to undertake
a religious vocation and describe blessings that come out of priestly ministry,
those things do not specifically comment on his own case. Rahner did note that
his older brother, Hugo (who once famously promised to translate the writings
of Karl Rahner into German—understandable German, that is), had entered the
Society of Jesus three years earlier and that that may have had some influence
on his decision to join.[58]

The Society of Jesus was formed by Ignatius and his followers in 1534, and
the group decided to go on pilgrimage to Jerusalem and to offer themselves in
service to the pope. Right away, there was a different emphasis in Ignatius's movement than what had been seen in a number of other monastic movements. In
the earlier part of the medieval period, the dominant form of monasticism was
cenobitic monasticism, which was focused on praying the hours and common
work. The mendicant orders, most notably the Dominicans and the Franciscans,

---

57. Karl Rahner, *I Remember: An Autobiographical Interview*, trans. Harvey D. Egan (New York:
Crossroad, 1984), 35.

58. Ibid., 36.

offered a different vision of the monastic vocation that did not involve life se-
cluded from the world in a monastery.

The Jesuit order drew on the best of both cenobitic and mendicant monasticism. Unlike cenobitic orders, the Jesuits did not spend a significant part of
each day praying the hours. Ignatius emphasized the idea that the carrying out
of one's vocation was in itself prayer. While the Jesuits were criticized by some
of the other orders for being lazy and like the world for not keeping the hours,
Ignatius was adamant about not separating one's daily tasks from prayer itself.[59]
If one's vocation were to teach (and that has been the case for many Jesuits), for
example, Ignatius would argue that in teaching, one was also engaging in prayer.

This spirituality had a significant impact on Rahner and would come to
influence much of his theological work. That Rahner was a priest was also
a significant factor in his theological work. His concern was always that his
theology be applicable to the contemporary person.

Rahner's Theology

Rahner first says that in speaking of theology, he always has in mind an orthodox Catholic theology, because a theology that is not obedient to revelation
as it is proclaimed in the church would not be Catholic theology at all. At the
same time, Rahner says that he envisions a Catholic theology that is courageous
and does not shy away from potential conflicts with church officials. This kind
of theology would be conversant with the larger contemporary context and be
able to live within it.[60]

Further, this theology must be that of a worldwide church. Rahner says that
theology cannot only consider its medieval (and European) history, but must also
consider approaches from Latin America, Africa, and Asia. Echoing ideas found
in *Foundations of Christian Faith*, Rahner envisions a theology that would allow
human beings to truly understand the message of freedom and redemption. It
would stem not necessarily from what is Christian, Rahner says, but rather from
the historical situation (both in its intellectual and social elements).[61] Such a
theology would move beyond the kind of theology done in the late nineteenth
and early twentieth centuries and make possible new pronouncements of the
church. This kind of theology would see itself as an interpretation of the reality
that grace makes present in every human being, and it would be through this
theology that this reality would find itself. Rather than considering itself to be

59. Placher, *History of Christian Theology*, 176.
60. Karl Rahner, foreword to *Theology and Discovery: Essays in Honor of Karl Rahner, SJ*, ed. William J. Kelley (Milwaukee: Marquette University Press, 1980), n.p.
61. Ibid.

an example of clarity in theology, this kind of theology would look continually to the incomprehensibility of God.[62]

Rahner says that though he could say much more on this subject, he is not seeking to deride the older theology, "whose grateful children we are and remain." Rather, he seeks to issue a prophetic call to theologians that the theological task is far from finished.[63]

With the eye toward practicality that his priestly vocation would require, Rahner has stressed that the contemporary situation dictates that theology must be approached differently than how it has been approached in the past. Christianity as a truth claim is no longer taken for granted, and the larger culture is not in any way the Christendom of medieval Europe. As a result, Rahner argues in many places that theology must take its historical situation/location into account so that it can be intelligible to the contemporary person.

Making the human person the starting point of theology begins to answer this concern. Because the idea of contact with God is no longer taken for granted in society, it is critical to first establish that the human being has the capacity to receive revelation from God. By doing the work to make that claim, Rahner lays the groundwork necessary for subsequent assertions about revelation, the content of that revelation, and God's intention for humanity.

Rahner applies the idea of contemporary contextualization in dogmatic theology to the question of theological anthropology.[64] In an essay in *Theological Investigations* on theology and anthropology, Rahner writes that dogmatic theology today must be theological anthropology. Because of this, an anthropocentric view is necessary and helpful for the theological task. The question of the human being's ability to hear a word from God and to respond if one is uttered is not one particular topic in theology but rather the whole of dogmatic theology itself.[65]

This position does not contradict theocentrism in theology, Rahner argues, citing Thomas Aquinas's assertion that God is the formal object of all revealed theology. Once the human being is understood as the being that is absolutely transcendent with respect to God (one who can receive revelation from God), anthropocentrism and theocentrism are no longer opposites but rather the same thing seen from two sides. Further, an anthropological focus in theology does

62. Ibid.
63. Ibid.
64. Anthropology, generally defined, is the study of human beings and cultures. Theological anthropology is the theological study of human nature. Theological anthropology seeks to give a theological account of the human being.
65. Karl Rahner, "Theology and Anthropology," *Theological Investigations*, trans. Graham Harrison (London: Darton, Longman & Todd, 1972), 9:28.

not compete with a christological focus. Rahner writes that anthropology and Christology mutually determine each other within Christian theology if they are both understood correctly. Christian anthropology, according to Rahner, is able to fulfill its purpose only if it takes the union between God and humanity in Christ into account.[66]

The Human Subject and the Supernatural Existential

For Rahner, the terms of the conversation are clear. Theology must have an eye toward the human subject and must address the concerns of the contemporary person. In order to understand how he approaches the theological task, it is important to know some of Rahner's underlying assumptions. The first and most important assumption is that human existence is a graced existence. Rahner holds that God's grace is present throughout creation. Further, human beings are endowed with what he calls the "supernatural existential." The supernatural existential is the component of the human being that makes it possible for the human being to be a recipient of God's grace. It is that which makes human beings able to respond to God's offer of grace. Because of this, Rahner argues that all human beings have a prethematic (subconscious) awareness of and orientation to God, if not an explicit awareness of and orientation toward God. Even the person who denies the existence of God has this orientation, at a minimum, on the subconscious level.[67]

This reality must be true of all people at all times. Rahner argues that human beings must be able to receive the love of God, if that love is ever going to be a human reality. As a result, it must be possible for human beings to receive and embrace divine love. For Rahner, this reality is at the center and root of what it means to be human. Further, it must be possible for human beings to receive this love as a free gift. The supernatural existential, that which makes it possible for human beings to receive God's grace and love, must be something that is added to human nature. Were it a necessary component of human nature, it would become necessary that God grant it to human beings. Were that the case, God's grace would no longer be a gratuitous gift, and there would be a constraint on God. God would have to give this necessary thing to humanity. This is not the case, according to Rahner. Rather, the supernatural existential (humanity's ability to receive the grace of God) comes as something apart from fundamental human nature, and yet it is a reality for all human beings. Thus

66. Ibid., 28–29.
67. Karl Rahner, "Relationship between Nature and Grace: The Supernatural Existential," in *A Rahner Reader*, ed. Gerald McCool (New York: Crossroad, 1975), 185–87. This material was originally published in Karl Rahner, *Theological Investigations*, 1:300–302, 310–15.

it is something true of all humans, yet it is also something that is added on, so to speak, to human nature.

This already indicates one of Karl Rahner's theological priorities. Remember that Barth held that theology must begin with God and the Word of God. For Barth, liberal Protestant theology had become far too anthropocentric. He believed that this was the reason for the failure of so many theologians to speak out against the German government's war efforts. For Rahner, theology has to start with a discussion of whether the human being can know anything about God. Rahner believes in an analogical approach to the relationship between God and creation. He views the world as infused with grace, and he believes that one can look at creation and know true things about God from it.[68]

Rahner starts his theological work from the human being for another reason. He argues that all human beings are oriented toward "holy mystery," or God, even if this is only experienced by the human being on the subconscious level. Rahner writes,

> This unthematic and ever-present experience, this knowledge of God which we always have even when we are thinking of and concerned with anything but God, is the permanent ground from out of which that thematic knowledge of God emerges which we have in explicitly religious activity and in philosophical reflection. It is not in these latter that we discover God, just as we discover a particular object of our experience within the world. Rather, both in this explicitly religious activity directed to God in prayer and in metaphysical reflection we are only making explicit for ourselves what we already know implicitly about ourselves in the depths of our personal self-realization. Hence we know our subjective freedom, our transcendence and the infinite openness of the spirit, even where and when we do not make them thematic at all.[69]

What Rahner means by this is that all people have some kind of awareness of or orientation toward God, even if that is only on the implicit or subconscious level. Even when human beings are explicitly aware of God and undertake religious activity that is directed to God, they are only experiencing something at an explicit level that has always been known on an implicit level. All human beings are turned toward God.

This view leads to some important implications for Rahner. One of the most important is his understanding of the anonymous Christian. Rahner acknowledges that proclaiming the Christian faith as the absolute religion and true

68. Karl Rahner, *Foundations of Christian Faith*, trans. William V. Dych (New York: Crossroad, 1989), 71, 53.
69. Ibid., 53.

conduit of salvation has always been troubling for those who are not Christian.[70] To consider the question, Rahner starts with two key assumptions. The first assumption is the universal salvific will of God. He writes, *"First of all*, we shall presuppose a universal and supernatural salvific will of God which is really operative in the world. This implies the possibility of supernatural revelation and faith everywhere, and hence throughout the whole length and breadth of the history of the human race."[71] In other words, God wills that all people be saved, and this must mean that God works everywhere, at all points in human history.[72] Rahner's second assumption is that non-Christians can attain salvation though "faith, hope and love," and as a result, non-Christian religions cannot be understood as playing no role or only a negative one in salvation.[73]

This, of course, raises an additional theological question, which Rahner identifies as the actual theological question at hand. Rahner writes, "How can Jesus Christ be understood to be present and operative in non-Christian religions from the perspective of Christian dogmatic theology? . . . How is Jesus Christ present and operative in the faith of the individual non-Christian?"[74] Rahner argues that Christ's presence in non-Christians is mediated via the Holy Spirit.

With this argument as its foundation, Rahner coins the term *anonymous Christian* to indicate the kind of salvific faith that might be possible among non-Christians. He writes,

> We prefer the terminology according to which that man is called an "anonymous Christian" who on the one hand has *de facto* accepted of his freedom this gracious self-offering on God's part through faith, hope, and love, while on the other he is absolutely *not yet a Christian* at the social level (through baptism and membership of the Church) or in the sense of having consciously objectified his Christianity to himself in his own mind (by explicit Christian faith resulting from having hearkened to the explicit Christian message). We might therefore put it as follows: the "anonymous Christian" in our sense of the term is the pagan after the beginning of the Christian mission, who *lives in the state of Christ's grace* through faith, hope and love, *yet who has no explicit knowledge* of the fact that his life is orientated in grace-given salvation to Jesus Christ.[75]

70. Ibid., 312.
71. Ibid., 313 (emphasis in original).
72. Ibid., 314.
73. Ibid.
74. Ibid., 315.
75. Karl Rahner, "Observations on the Problem of the Anonymous Christians," in *Theological Investigations*, trans. David Bourke (London: Darton, Longman & Todd, 1976), 14:283 (emphasis in original).

Rahner argues that the concept of anonymous Christianity is crucial because it solves an otherwise impossible problem. In giving this account of the possibility of salvation for non-Christians, Rahner offers a system that makes clear that salvific faith must somehow reference Christ, even if it is on the level of the implicit. At the same time, it avoids consigning all non-Christians to hell by denying them the possibility of salvation.[76]

It is important to note that while this idea was taken up by the Catholic Church at the Second Vatican Council, it was cast in slightly narrower terms than those used by Rahner. *Lumen Gentium* states, "Those also can attain to salvation who through no fault of their own do not know the Gospel of Christ or His Church, yet sincerely seek God and moved by grace strive by their deeds to do His will as it is known to them through the dictates of conscience."[77]

Rahner's Influence on the Second Vatican Council

Although his work had been questioned by the Vatican prior to the Second Vatican Council, Rahner was appointed by John XXIII as an expert adviser. He was involved in the writing of *Lumen Gentium* and is believed to have been involved in writing an early draft of *Gaudium et Spes*. One of the most important achievements of Vatican II was a recasting of relationships between Catholic and Protestant Christians, as well as between Catholics and non-Christians. The Catholic Church has always held that there is no salvation outside the Catholic Church. Prior to Vatican II, this meant that the salvation of Protestant Christians was in question in the minds of Catholics (and, to be fair, Protestants also questioned the salvation of Catholics). Vatican II explicitly referred to Protestant Christians as "separated brethren," who were brothers and sisters in Christ with Catholics. Although not part of one institutional church, and still not able to share in the communion table together, Protestants and Catholics were ultimately seen as being part of one church and one salvation.

As was mentioned above, Rahner's idea of the anonymous Christian was picked up in *Lumen Gentium*. It was here that the Catholic Church affirmed that it is possible to actually be a part of the church and be saved even if one does not explicitly know the name of Christ. Because of this, the council also affirmed that non-Christian religions "often reflect a ray of truth that enlightens all men." The council even goes so far as to say that any goodness found among

---

76. Karl Rahner, *Theological Investigations*, trans. David Morland (London: Darton, Longman & Todd, 1979), 16:218.

77. *Lumen Gentium* 16. Document available at http://www.vatican.va/archive/hist_councils /ii_vatican_council/documents/vat-ii_const_19641121_lumen-gentium_en.html.

atheists (and the assumption is that there is goodness to be found) is looked on by the church as a preparation for the gospel.

At the council, a number of theologians whose work had previously been questioned and at times suppressed were actively involved. The church's approach to their theological positions seemed to be somewhat different after the council.

BERNARD LONERGAN

Bernard Lonergan is less well known than Karl Rahner or Avery Dulles (discussed in chap. 2), but like them is also significant for his contribution to Catholic theological method. He is placed in this chapter because of his correlationist approach to theology. In many ways, he shares much in common with Rahner; however, his published works focus much more on method and epistemology, while Rahner's published works cover the breadth of Catholic theology.

Lonergan was a Canadian Jesuit who, like Rahner, lived from 1904 to 1984. He was raised in a religious family in Quebec and attended a Jesuit secondary school. After his completion of secondary school, Lonergan entered the Society of Jesus in 1922. From a relatively early age, while in secondary school, Lonergan experienced dissatisfaction with the education he was receiving and the state of Catholic education generally. This would direct him to his life's work, which was calling for a renewal of Catholic education and Catholic studies.[78]

Insight, Lonergan's most well-known text, was initially written as a prolegomenous work to a treatment of theological method.[79] Although the work on theological method did appear, *Insight* became a seminal book in its own right. In *Insight*, Lonergan is interested in showing what happens when human beings go through the process of knowing. His goal is to spur his reader toward greater awareness of the process of knowing and of knowledge itself.[80] *Method in Theology* seeks to bring the ideas found in *Insight* into the specific task of theological work.

"A theology," according to Lonergan, "mediates between a cultural matrix and the significance and role of a religion in that matrix."[81] This claim is ultimately what makes Longeran's theology a theology of correlation. Even though he is putting it somewhat differently, it is clear from this statement that theology is intended to connect a particular religious tradition to a particular context.

78. Bernard Lonergan, "Insight Revisited," in *A Second Collection*, ed. William F. J. Ryan and Bernard J. Tyrrell (Philadelphia: Westminster, 1974), 263–64.

79. Lonergan, *Second Collection*, 268.

80. Bernard Lonergan, *Insight: A Study of Human Understanding* (Toronto: University of Toronto Press, 1992), introduction.

81. Bernard Lonergan, *Method in Theology*, 2nd ed. (New York: Herder & Herder, 1972), xi.

Lonergan's first statement about method in this text also gives some indication of what theology is not. He writes, "Method is not a set of rules to be followed meticulously by a dolt. It is a framework for collaborative creativity. It would outline the various clusters of operations to be performed by theologians when they go about their various tasks."[82] In other words, as many of the other thinkers in this book clearly hold, theological method is not a set of precise steps that, when undertaken correctly, will yield a predictable and reliable answer. While this might make the work of theology easier, it would perhaps also make it far less interesting.

Lonergan outlines eight key tasks for contemporary theology: "research, interpretation, history, dialectic, foundations, doctrines, systematics, and communications."[83] He then claims that to offer a model does not suggest that his model should be repeated step by step. Rather, he argues that the model he puts forward is something that might be helpful for theologians to have at hand as they do theological work. In writing about method, Lonergan wants to be clear that he is more interested in how theologians go about their work than what they actually say.[84]

Method in theology is often understood in one of three ways. It can be understood as an art rather than a science; this view sees theology as something that doesn't have a set procedure. Another approach, though, is to treat theology as a science. Those who hold this view will often look to the sciences and take up some of their procedures. Finally, there are those who "often have to be content if their subject is included in a list not of sciences but of academic disciplines."[85] What this statement shows is that the question of the nature of theology is unsettled and debated.

This leads to the question of what counts as a method for Lonergan. He writes this about method in the natural sciences:

> A method is a normative pattern of recurrent and related operations yielding cumulative and progressive results. There is a method, then, when there are distinct operations, where each operation is related to the others, where the set of relations forms a pattern, where the pattern is described as the right way of doing the job, where the operations in accord with the pattern may be repeated indefinitely, and where the fruits of such repetition are, not repetitious, but cumulative and progressive.[86]

82. Ibid.
83. Ibid.
84. Ibid., xii.
85. Ibid., 3.
86. Ibid., 4.

Lonergan writes that, in the sciences, method brings about the work of asking questions, and this is something that is done throughout the process. Ultimately, as the scientist investigates further and repeats various processes with different variables, the results come together to advance the scientist's knowledge. Results of inquiry also confirm that the work is going either in the correct direction or in a problematic direction. Scientific work builds on itself to the benefit of all who undertake it.[87]

To this point, Lonergan has focused on the natural sciences, but he argues that this kind of observation can tell theologians something about method. While the specifics of methodology do not easily transfer to other disciplines, this kind of observation does offer a sense of what method as a whole is supposed to do. He writes, "It illustrates a preliminary notion of method as *a normative pattern of recurrent and related operations yielding cumulative and progressive results.*"[88]

One of Lonergan's principal concerns in doing any sort of intellectual work is understanding the processes by which human beings come to know things. He suggests that a failure to understand and be attentive to these processes can lead one's own knowledge astray. He distinguishes levels of consciousness and intentionality experienced by human beings while they are awake.[89] Lonergan first notes the empirical level, stating that it is on this level that we have sensate experiences. The next level, the intellectual level, is that on which human beings engage with the structures of thinking. The rational level is that level on which human beings make decisions or judgments about what has been considered. A final level described by Lonergan is the responsible level on which human beings consider how the things engaged on the first three levels come to bear on their own lives.[90]

Lonergan argues that all the operations on these four levels are "intentional and conscious."[91] At the same time, human self-awareness and intention toward particular ends will vary from level to level. Lonergan argues that human beings

87. Ibid., 5.

88. Ibid. (emphasis in original).

89. He writes, "In our dream states consciousness and intentionality commonly are fragmentary and incoherent. When we awake, they take on a different hue to expand on four successive, related, but qualitatively different levels" (ibid., 9).

90. Lonergan writes,

There is the *empirical* level on which we sense, perceive, imagine, feel, speak, move. There is an *intellectual* level on which we inquire, come to understand, express what we have understood, work out the presuppositions and implications of our expression. There is the *rational* level on which we reflect, marshal the evidence, pass judgment on the truth or falsity, certainty, or probability, of a statement. There is the *responsible* level on which we are concerned with ourselves, our own operations, our goals, and so deliberate about the possible courses of action, evaluate them, decide, and carry out our decisions. (Ibid., 3, emphasis in original)

91. Ibid., 9.

experience self-awareness at each of these levels, but starting with the empirical level and moving up to the responsible level, human beings have greater self-awareness.[92] In addition to this, the information gained at one of these epistemological levels leads to gained knowledge on higher levels. Ultimately, each of these levels takes us to a subsequent level. Lonergan writes, "So intelligence takes us beyond experiencing to ask what and why and how and what for. Reasonableness takes us beyond the answers of intelligence to ask whether the answers are true and whether what they mean is really so. Responsibility goes beyond fact and desire and possibility to discern between what is truly good and what only apparently is good."[93] Lonergan has a beautiful way of putting this:

> The many levels of consciousness are just successive stages in the unfolding of a single thrust. . . . To know the good, [the good] must know the real; to know the real, [the real] must know the true; to know the true, [the true] must know the intelligible; to know the intelligible, [the intelligible] must attend to the data. So from slumber, we awake to attend. Observing lets intelligence be puzzled, and we inquire. Inquiry leads to the delight of insight, but insights are a dime a dozen, so critical reasonableness doubts, checks, makes sure. Alternative courses of action present themselves and we wonder whether the more attractive is truly good. Indeed, so intimate is the relation between the successive transcendental notions, that it is only by a specialized differentiation of consciousness that we withdraw from more ordinary ways of living to devote ourselves to a moral pursuit of goodness, a philosophic pursuit of truth, a scientific pursuit of understanding, and artistic pursuit of beauty.[94]

Further, Lonergan argues that all people make use of the transcendental method insofar as they go through the four stages of knowledge delineated above. Despite this, it is hard to make use of this method fully, because it is something that does not come about through study but rather comes about through heightening one's consciousness, and that happens only through one's individual agency.[95]

92. Ibid.
93. Ibid., 11.
94. Ibid., 13.
95. Ibid., 14. Lonergan writes this in a footnote:
   I conceive method concretely. I conceive it, not in terms of principles and rules, but as a normative pattern of operations with cumulative and progressive results. I distinguish the methods appropriate to particular fields and, on the other hand, their common core and ground, which I name transcendental method. Here, the word transcendental is employed in a sense analogous to Scholastic usage, for it is opposed to the categorical or predicamental. My actual procedure also is transcendental in the Kantian sense, inasmuch as it brings to light the conditions of the possibility of knowing an object in so far as that knowledge is *a priori*. (Ibid., 14n2)

When defining doctrine, Lonergan makes a number of important points. He says that there are two types of doctrine: doctrine of the original message and doctrines about that doctrine. The original message is scripture, and doctrines about doctrine comes through the church's interpretation of the original message.[96]

Lonergan divides doctrine about doctrine into a few different categories, including *church doctrines*, which trace back to the New Testament, though they are more than simply restatements of scripture or tradition. He wants to be clear that doctrine cannot stop on this level. While some will argue that doctrine need be no more than that which is derived from the New Testament, one can merely look at the history of Christian theology to see that doctrine has developed in ways that meet the needs of the particular context from which they come. In other words, it is erroneous to claim that theology needs only the New Testament to make its affirmations.[97]

Theological doctrines are those that reflect on the revelation found in and through Christ. This type of work was primarily done in the early church to respond to particular questions or controversies, but by the late patristic period there was some movement toward a more comprehensive approach to theology. In the medieval period, theology was worked on for its own sake rather than just in response to a crisis or controversy. Medieval theologians compiled earlier statements of theology, as in Peter Lombard's *Sentences*, and wrote extensive commentaries on scripture. There was also a move to systematize theology by writing comprehensive accounts of Christian theology by drawing on both scripture and resources from the tradition.[98]

Lonergan is clear that systematizing theology is not enough. While it is important to be aware of this particular thought process, theological method does not end there. He writes, "One must also ask what one is doing when one is doing theology, and one's answer must envisage not only the Christian encounter with God but also the historicity of Christian witness, the diversity of human cultures, the differentiations of human consciousness."[99]

Theological doctrines have particular functions. Lonergan states that these doctrines offer instruction and directives to the believing community, and they show the origins of the community and give the community direction for the future. In addition, doctrine makes the community what it is. Lonergan writes, "It is constitutive of the community, for the community exists inasmuch as there is a commonly accepted set of meanings and values shared by people in

96. Ibid., 295.
97. Ibid., 296.
98. Ibid., 296–97.
99. Ibid., 297.

contact with one another."[100] In addition, theological doctrines communicate what Christ gave to the apostles and what the apostles gave to their successors.[101]

In addition to this, Lonergan argues that there is a *methodological doctrine*. Theology reflects on revelation and church doctrine, and methodology reflects on theology. Methodology does not intend to tell theologians what they should say; rather, it intends to address how theologians should go about doing their work. Theological doctrines come out of that work.[102]

Doctrines can also be of value to the unconverted. Lonergan notes that conversion can happen on the intellectual, moral, or religious level. A lack of conversion can lead to a loss of faith, but a lack of conversion may also exist in a person who doesn't actually understand what conversion entails. These individuals may claim the name Christian, but their lives don't reflect Christian conversion. Doctrine may help this group see that there is something larger to be grasped. Lonergan writes, "Accordingly, while the unconverted may have no real apprehension of what it is to be converted, at least they have in doctrines the evidence both that there is something lacking in themselves and that they need to pray for illumination and to seek instruction."[103]

Conclusion

While theologies of correlation work in conversation with other disciplines, they are sometimes critiqued by another set of theologies: political theologies. While Rahner and others are interested in human experience, they have been accused of defining it too broadly and implying that all human experience is the same. Political theologies are interested in defining human experience specifically and looking at individuals in their sociohistorical context. These theologies will be discussed in detail in chapters 6 and 7, but before that, an examination of postliberal theology, born out of the theologies of correlation is in order.

---

100. Ibid.
101. Ibid.
102. Ibid., 298.
103. Ibid., 299.

4

Postliberal Theologies

The previous chapter raised the question of the back-and-forth between the historic Christian faith and the contemporary context. The thinkers covered in that chapter responded with a type of correlation method of theology. Postliberalism, a theological school from the last part of the twentieth century that seeks to avoid the pitfalls of propositionalism and the reliance on experience that characterizes liberalism, also asks questions about religion and culture, but it does so in a very different way. For the postliberal thinkers, doctrine is learned in the same way that a language or a culture is learned. This has significant implications for the ways in which these thinkers go about the theological task. Postliberal theologians include George Lindbeck and Hans Frei, though the central postliberal thinker is Lindbeck. Lindbeck's work sets out the key methodological features that mark the approach, but Hans Frei's incorporation of narrative into the postliberal conversation is a significant addition. These two thinkers shape the discussion in this chapter.

GEORGE LINDBECK

George Lindbeck was born in 1923 to Lutheran missionaries in China. He arrived in the United States at the age of seventeen to begin his education at Gustavus Adolphus College. After graduating, he attended Yale University, where he received a bachelor of divinity degree and a PhD in divinity. Before completing his PhD, Lindbeck started teaching at Yale Divinity School. Lindbeck quickly became involved in ecumenical work and served as an observer representing the Lutheran World Federation at the Second Vatican Council. He was involved in Lutheran-Catholic dialogue throughout his career.[1]

The Nature of Doctrine: Religion and Theology in a Postliberal Age is Lindbeck's most well-known book. It was originally intended to be a precursor to a longer book on doctrinal agreements and disagreements among the various major Christian traditions.[2] To date, that book has not appeared. Lindbeck clearly thinks that *The Nature of Doctrine* is important in its own right, writing that the book is by itself a contribution to conversations about doctrine.[3] The book has been taken this way by many thinkers.

The Nature of Doctrine

In *The Nature of Doctrine*, Lindbeck considers the question of doctrine in terms of how it arises, how it functions, and how it changes. He lays out fairly narrow parameters from the outset, noting that his considerations will be strictly theoretical. What he means by this is that he is not interested, for the purposes of the book, in making judgments about the truth claims of any particular religion. The book is about, in Lindbeck's words, "how to think [rather than] what to assert about matters of fact."[4] Stemming from this, Lindbeck argues that the claims in the book are intended to be acceptable to all traditions.[5] One interesting point made by Lindbeck at the outset, though, is that although he is working within a framework of doctrinal neutrality, he is not working within a framework of theological neutrality. He sees theology as a reflection on "the data of religion," which includes doctrinal data.[6] He argues that theology as methodology, in the sense in which he speaks of it, is potentially open to critique because it depends on ideas coming out of a theory of religion.[7]

Lindbeck's Critique of Other Theologies

In order to understand Lindbeck's proposal, it is first important to under-stand the critiques he makes of three other prominent approaches to theology.

1. Biographical information taken from Lindbeck's faculty profile on the Yale Divinity School website: "George A. Lindbeck, 1946 B.D., 1955 Ph.D.," http://divinity.yale.edu/alumni/alumni-awards/award-recipients/george-lindbeck-1946-bd-1955-phd.

2. George A. Lindbeck, *The Nature of Doctrine: Religion and Theology in a Postliberal Age* (Louisville: Westminster John Knox, 1984), 8.

3. Ibid.

4. Ibid., 9.

5. Lindbeck also writes, "Nor does the suggested outlook prejudge the issue of whether Christianity or any other religion is right or wrong, and it might therefore be helpful to Christians in discussions with adherents of other religions or no religion at all" (ibid.).

6. Ibid., 10.

7. Ibid.

The first is what he refers to as the "cognitive-propositionalist" approach. This approach understands doctrines as "informative propositions or truth claims about objective realities."[8] In this view, religious claims are similar to claims in philosophy or science as they were traditionally understood. Lindbeck argues that this is the approach that was taken by a number of different expressions of traditional orthodoxy.[9] In Roman Catholicism, cognitive propositionalism is seen in the neo-scholastic approach to theology described in chapter 2. This is the theology of the manuals that seeks to compile theological statements made by past councils and church fathers. In American evangelicalism, this approach seeks to take individual statements from the biblical text and group them according to doctrine. For example, if writing about the church, a proponent of this approach would seek to draw out every statement in the biblical text that could be understood as being about the church in order to arrive at an understanding of doctrinal truth. (This is the approach against which Stanley Grenz reacts, as will be described in chap. 5.)

The second approach Lindbeck discusses is the "experiential-expressive" approach. This position sees doctrines as nondiscursive expressions of religious experience, attitudes, and "existential orientations."[10] It draws connections between religion and aesthetics, and as a result, it is friendly toward F. D. E. Schleiermacher and his successors.[11] This approach can be seen to some degree in the theology of Paul Tillich, and it can also be seen in some elements of nineteenth-century Protestant liberalism.

A final approach laid out by Lindbeck is a middle position particularly favored by Catholics who are "ecumenically inclined." It seeks to combine elements of the cognitive-propositional approach with elements of the experiential-expressive approach. Lindbeck writes of this approach, "Both the cognitively propositional and the expressively symbolic dimensions and functions of religion and doctrine are viewed, at least in the case of Christianity, as religiously significant and valid." Lindbeck argues that this position is held, among others, by Bernard Lonergan and Karl Rahner.[12]

The problem with all these positions, according to Lindbeck, is that there is no way to find "doctrinal reconciliation without capitulation."[13] What he means by this is that there is no way to bring disparate doctrinal positions into conversation with one another without one position or the other making

8. Ibid., 16.
9. Ibid.
10. Ibid.
11. Ibid.
12. Ibid.
13. Ibid.

significant concessions. Lindbeck notes that for the cognitive propositionalist, "if a doctrine is once true, it is always true, and if it is once false, it is always false."[14] The experiential-expressivist position has the opposite problem, according to Lindbeck. For those who adopt this position, doctrines can remain the same even when the understood meanings behind them change, and doctrines can change even when the underlying meaning does not.[15] The problem with this, in Lindbeck's words, is that "there is thus at least the logical possibility that a Buddhist and a Christian might have basically the same faith, though expressed very differently."[16]

The third position, which is the middle position between cognitive-propositionalism and experiential-expressivism, has as a strength a greater readiness to account for both differences and similarities in religious belief systems, but it does not seem to have much success with combining disparate positions. Lindbeck writes of proponents of this approach, "Even at their best, as in Rahner and Lonergan, they resort to complicated intellectual gymnastics and to that extent are unpersuasive. They are also weak in criteria for determining when a given doctrinal development is consistent with sources of faith, and they are therefore unable to avoid a rather greater reliance on the magisterium." This kind of view is the most helpful of the three for ecumenical work, but its account of how "doctrinal reconciliation without capitulation" comes about is too complicated to be taken seriously, according to Lindbeck.[17]

Lindbeck's Rule Theory

Lindbeck's aim is to articulate a position that moves the conversation beyond these three options. He wants to find a way toward "doctrinal reconciliation

---

14. Lindbeck goes on to say, "This implies, for example, that the historic affirmations and denials of transubstantiation can never be harmonized. Agreement can be reached only if one or both sides abandon their earlier positions. Thus, on this view, doctrinal reconciliation without capitulation is impossible because there is no significant sense in which the meaning of a doctrine can change while remaining the same" (ibid.).

15. Lindbeck writes,

> Both transubstantiationist and nontransubstantiationist conceptualities—to continue with the previous example—can express or evoke similar or dissimilar experiences of divine reality, or no experience at all. The general principle is that insofar as doctrines function as nondiscursive symbols, they are polyvalent in import and therefore subject to changes of meaning or even to a total loss of meaningfulness, to what Tillich calls their death. They are not crucial for religious agreement or disagreement, because they are constituted by harmony or conflict in underlying feelings, attitudes, existential orientations, or practices, rather than by what happens on the level of symbolic (including doctrinal) objectifications. (Ibid., 17; citing Tillich, *Systematic Theology*, 1:240)

16. Lindbeck, *Nature of Doctrine*, 17.

17. Ibid.

without capitulation," and to do so he will need to find a position that avoids the major pitfalls mentioned above.

The solution to the impasse outlined by Lindbeck is what he refers to as a "rule theory." This theory makes some key assumptions about doctrines and their role in faith communities. Lindbeck argues, "Church doctrines are communally authoritative teachings regarding beliefs and practices that are considered essential to the identity or welfare of the group in question. They may be formally staged or informally operative, but in any case, they indicate what constitutes faithful adherence to a community."[18] Lindbeck elaborates by arguing that it is just these types of teachings or beliefs that determine whether one is inside or outside a particular community. If such a teaching or belief did not have the power to determine whether a person is inside or outside, it would no longer be formative for that particular community. In other words, doctrines are necessary for identity, even if the community in question denies their importance.[19]

One key element of this argument is that doctrine cannot be avoided. While some Christian traditions, for example, claim a "creedless Christianity," Lindbeck states that this is actually not possible, arguing that claims of a creedless Christianity become a creed unto themselves.[20] Lindbeck clarifies here that most biblicist Protestants would affirm the contents of the Nicene Creed but would argue that Nicaea's views are clearly found in scripture.

In order to make sense out of this, it is important to grasp a key distinction at work in Lindbeck's understanding of doctrine. For him, there are two types of doctrine: operational doctrines and official doctrines. If one considers a given religious community, it probably wouldn't be all that hard to find doctrines that are officially proclaimed but yet do not play a determinative role regarding who is inside and who is outside the community. Without some kind of distinction between official and operational doctrines, Lindbeck's major claims would seem to ignore both the reality that some written doctrines aren't held with utmost conviction by a given community and the reality that communities often have "doctrines" that fit the definition given by Lindbeck but that are not actually written anywhere. This is where the operational/official distinction comes in. Lindbeck argues that some doctrines may cease to be official, even though they remain operational. To return to his example of biblicist Protestants and the Nicene Creed, Lindbeck argues that, for these Protestants, the creed is still operational, because its tenets are held, even though it is not official, in that

18. Ibid., 74.
19. Lindbeck writes, "In any case, operative doctrines, even if not official ones, are necessary to communal identity. A religious body cannot exist as a recognizably distinctive collectivity unless it has some beliefs and/or practices by which it can be identified" (ibid.).
20. Ibid.

the basis of its acceptance is in scripture rather than in its inherent authority. Similarly, doctrines can remain official long after they have ceased to be operational within the community.[21]

If this is the case, the next question is how and why "rules," or doctrines, change and what those changes reflect in a given community. According to Lindbeck, communities make doctrinal decisions as a result of disputes, either about beliefs or practices.[22] This seems to fit well with the history of Christianity, particularly when one looks at early Christianity. During the apostolic period, for example, there wasn't a debate about gentile Christians and how they should be incorporated into the church until that was a pressing pastoral issue. Similarly, the early church did not formally address the divinity of Christ until theological controversies about the nature of Christ arose.

Lindbeck himself argues that the Marian dogmas of 1854 and 1950 (the dogmas concerning the immaculate conception of Mary and the bodily assumption of Mary into heaven) are really the only two significant exceptions to this in the history of Christianity.[23] Lindbeck finds two key points coming out of this assertion. Doctrines must be understood in context, which means that the opposing positions must be understood alongside them. Further, the official doctrines of a given community may not give an accurate picture of all that the community believes or does.[24]

To illustrate that final point, Lindbeck quotes Cardinal Newman, who argued that doctrinal debates can rage over what appear to be frivolous matters, but which actually are quite significant because of the implicit doctrines that come out of them. Lindbeck offers two examples. First, he reminds readers about debates about vestments and images during the Protestant Reformation. The actual issue may appear to be one of minutiae. At the same time, that question serves as a proxy for broader questions about the nature of Christian worship that many Christians would find extremely important. Similarly, today there are debates about the use of gendered language for God. It may at first glance seem like a more minor issue, but a consideration of the question leads one to

21. Ibid.
22. Ibid., 75.
23. Ibid.
24. Lindbeck writes,

> In any case, insofar as doctrines are the products of conflict, there are two important consequences: first, they must be understood in terms of what they oppose (it is usually much easier to specify what they deny than what they affirm); and, second, the official doctrines of a community may poorly reflect its most important and abiding orientations or beliefs, either because some of the latter may never have been seriously challenged (and therefore never officially denied) or because points that are under most circumstances trivial may on occasion become matters of life and death. (Ibid., 74)

ask questions about the nature of God, human beings as created in the image of God, and salvation itself.[25]

Doctrine versus Theology

This point gets at a final distinction that must be made in Lindbeck's thought— the difference between doctrine and theology itself. Lindbeck argues that they are clearly different, because there are various ways that one can articulate the Christian faith within a particular community and its set of doctrines. Lindbeck points out that those who agree on doctrines may disagree about how to understand or explain them, while there can be consensus on theology across confessional lines.[26] While theology and doctrine are usually connected to each other, such that confessional divides also indicate some theological divide, there are ways in which, for example, some Protestant groups might find themselves sharing a theological outlook with the Catholic Church, even though those two groups remain divided on issues of church polity and sacraments.[27] At this juncture, it is important to point out that Lindbeck is using the term *doctrine* in a much more narrow way than it is typically used. Books with the terms *doctrine* or *dogmatics* in their titles are often actually works of theology. The difference, according to Lindbeck, is that works of theology often deal with a fairly comprehensive set of beliefs, while he defines doctrine as beliefs that are essential to the community.[28]

The potential problem with Lindbeck's model (in his mind) is that doctrines (using his definition) are frequently not taken seriously enough. This is because "communal norms" are often incompatible with the contemporary mind-set, which tends to be individualistic.[29] This comes from a couple of different trends in the contemporary context. Pluralism has led to a loss of confidence in any one community or position. Individualism has prized the autonomy of the self and sees the very idea of communal norms as problematic.[30] Lindbeck writes,

> The suggestion that communities have the right to insist on standards of belief and practice as conditions of membership is experienced as an intolerable infringement of the liberty of the self. This reaction is intensified by the growing contradiction between traditional standards and the prevailing values of the wider society as communicated by education, the mass media, and personal contacts.

25. Ibid., 76.
26. Ibid.
27. Ibid.
28. Ibid.
29. Ibid., 77.
30. Ibid.

The very words "doctrine" and "dogma" have the smell of the ghetto about them, and to take them seriously is, it seems, to cut oneself off from the larger world.[31]

How exactly does doctrine function for Lindbeck? He argues that religion is an intellectual framework within which one has particular kinds of experiences and makes particular kinds of claims.[32] He goes on to say that doctrine sets up rules that guide the community and through which the community understands and interprets its experience.[33]

This is an interesting position to take, because Lindbeck is essentially arguing for some middle position between cognitive-propositionalism and experiential-expressivism. Cognitive-propositionalism holds that doctrines are statements of propositional truth that stand for all time. The receiving community has nothing to do with the shape these propositional truths take. On the other end of the spectrum, experiential-expressivism takes individual religious experiences and sees them as a source of doctrine. At the same time, Lindbeck sees himself as doing theological work in a way quite different from what is done by Rahner and Lonergan, since he sees their approaches as inadequate.

Lindbeck's postliberalism walks the middle line by holding that doctrine is a rule that is normative for the community, but that it is through this lens that the experiences of community members are viewed, rather than the other way around. In addition to that, doctrines are fluid insofar as faithfulness to them doesn't involve simply parroting what has been said before. Lindbeck writes, "Faithfulness to such doctrines does not necessarily mean repeating them; rather, it requires, in the making of any new formulations, adherence to the same directives that were involved in the first formulation. It is thus . . . that faithfulness to an ancient creed such as the Nicene should be construed."[34] This position also walks the line between the belief that doctrine is an unchanging collection of propositional truths and that doctrine is always changing according to the shifting experiences of members of the community.

Lindbeck wants to be clear that church doctrine is flawed (as are the human beings who make up respective religious communities).[35] Despite this, he also argues that doctrine, just as grammar, has an ongoing value, particularly for those who are just becoming acquainted with the community, those who are not well grounded in the community, and those who may be coming close to distorting it or evacuating it of meaning.[36]

31. Ibid.
32. Ibid.
33. Ibid., 81.
34. Ibid.
35. Ibid.
36. Ibid., 82.

Christian Community in Doctrine

Because this book is about the practice of Christian theology, it is important to discuss how doctrine, as defined by Lindbeck, is arrived at in the Christian community, and we need to consider the relationship between doctrine and theology in the Christian community. Lindbeck argues that there are different types of doctrine. One such type is the "unconditionally necessary" doctrine. These doctrines are elements of the faith that cannot change without the fundamental character of the community changing as well. In the Christian tradition, Lindbeck offers the example of the "law of love." This is an unconditionally necessary doctrine for Christianity because there aren't any times or places where Christians are not supposed to practice love of God and neighbor.[37]

Other doctrines are not quite as central. Lindbeck refers to these as "conditionally essential." To illustrate this point, he offers the example of Christians participating in war. In the early church, this was a fairly universal rule; early Christians generally did not participate in the Roman military prior to the conversion of Constantine.[38] Today, pacifism is not seen as required across the entire Christian tradition, though some subsets of Christians may hold it as essential. Lindbeck also notes that this type of doctrine may one day become mandatory because of the development of weapons of mass destruction. As a result, this doctrine, which is mandatory at some times and not at others, is conditionally essential. Lindbeck writes that pacifism "is not, so most churches hold, an unconditionally necessary consequence of the Christian rule of love, though it may be conditionally necessary."[39]

Whereas unconditionally necessary doctrines are permanent—the Christian rule of love will always be a central feature of what it means to be a Christian, for example—Lindbeck says that conditional doctrines can be either permanent or temporary. A permanent conditional doctrine is one that applies at all times, because the circumstances that must be present for it to be operative are assumed to be always present. Lindbeck suggests that calls to feed the poor fall into this category because, presumably, there will always be people who are poor. Regarding temporary doctrines, Lindbeck offers the example of debates in churches about sexual ethics. These debates, in his mind, consider whether the conditions under which the biblical text's moral tenets were developed still exist today, or whether developments over the past several centuries are significant enough to render these doctrines temporary.[40]

37. Ibid., 85.
38. As a side note, there is debate about whether this was because many early Christians were pacifists or because participation in the Roman military also often involved pagan religious practices.
39. Lindbeck, *Nature of Doctrine*, 85.
40. Ibid.

Temporary doctrines can be further divided into reversible and irreversible doctrines. Lindbeck's earlier example of war serves as an example of a reversible doctrine in that its status as a Christian teaching can shift back and forth depending on the particular context. Other teachings come out of irreversible historical events, according to Lindbeck. These are things that cannot be so easily changed. Lindbeck offers the condemnation of slavery as one example of this. While Christians at one point saw slavery as an unavoidable reality (even if they did see it as unnatural or a result of the fall), they eventually saw, as a result of historical developments, examples of societies without the institution of chattel slavery. That such societies were possible led Christians to rethink their biblical commitments. While there is no scriptural text that explicitly condemns slavery, Christians started to realize that the biblical narrative as a whole shows concern for the marginalized and implies that slavery is unacceptable. Now, Lindbeck says, "the Christian obligation to oppose slavery is irreversible even though conditional."[41] What Lindbeck seems to be saying here is that doctrine can develop and shift in response to broader societal developments. While the biblical text nowhere explicitly condemns slavery, Christians came to see the institution of slavery as something that was fundamentally unchristian, even though they did not have explicit statements from scripture to support that claim.

A final type of doctrine discussed by Lindbeck is the "accidentally necessary" doctrine. These doctrines typically involve longstanding practices in the church that could have been different at the outset but now cannot be changed. To illustrate this, Lindbeck gives the nontheological example of driving on the right side of the road in the United States. Certainly, a decision could have been made at the outset to have everyone drive on the left side of the street, but it would be nearly impossible, not to mention hazardous, to try to change which side of the street Americans drive on today. To give a theological example, many of the post–New Testament liturgical developments (such as the ways in which Christmas or Easter is observed) could have been different from the outset, but now many elements of those observances are functionally unchangeable.[42]

To be clear, Lindbeck argues that the historic creeds of the early church (and here he is referring to the Apostles' Creed, the Nicene Creed, and the Chalcedonian Definition) have been treated as "unconditionally and permanently essential."[43] In contrast, a doctrine like the immortality of the soul could be seen

41. Ibid., 85–86.
42. Ibid., 86.
43. Ibid.

as "conditional, temporary, and reversible."[44] At first blush this seems odd. Does not the Christian tradition teach the immortality of the soul just as strongly as it teaches the Nicene and Chalcedonian positions concerning Christ? Lindbeck makes a critical argument at this juncture: "A doctrine such as the immortality of the soul, in contrast, could perhaps be classified as . . . temporary. It could be argued that this belief is necessary to the integrity of the Christian faith only when believers think in terms of a classical mind-body dualism, but not when their anthropology is Hebraic or modern."[45] In other words, immortality of the soul depends on a particular understanding of the makeup of the human being, and for Lindbeck, it is a live question what things would look like, theologically, if one's understanding of the human being is different.

One question that must be asked about any approach to theology is whether it works. It is interesting that Lindbeck is deeply committed to ecumenical work, particularly dialogue between Lutherans and Catholics. Since Lindbeck is articulating this approach to doctrine while grounded in the Lutheran perspective, it stands to reason that one should ask whether this "works" from the Catholic perspective. Lindbeck anticipates that question and answers in the affirmative. He argues that temporary and reversible doctrines could actually become permanent and conditional. As a result, the possibility of temporary, reversible doctrines does not contradict Catholic claims about the permanency of doctrine.[46] Here he refers to his affirmation that the immortality of the soul may be necessary only when one holds to a traditional mind-body dualism. If one holds to a different understanding of the human being, then the necessity of this doctrine may not follow. He writes, "Whatever one may think of this particular example, it illustrates the logical possibility of conditionally permanent doctrines. Whenever such and such a condition prevails, such and such doctrine applies. It is thus the condition, not the doctrine, which is temporary or 'reformable.'"[47] Here Lindbeck emphasizes that it is not doctrine per se that changes, but rather the circumstances under which doctrine arises. When those circumstances are different, different doctrine may apply. In the course of this discussion, Lindbeck does not shy away from noting that while Nicaea and Chalcedon have traditionally been understood as unconditional and permanent, in the contemporary context questions have been raised about whether these statements about the nature of the Trinity and the nature of Christ are instead "conditional and perhaps reversible."[48]

44. Ibid.
45. Ibid.
46. Ibid., 87.
47. Ibid.
48. Ibid.

Intratextuality

It has already been noted that Lindbeck makes a distinction between doctrine and theology. As this work is about methods of theology, it is important to connect what he says about doctrine (which is central to his entire mode of thought) to the work of theology. "The task of descriptive (dogmatic or systematic) theology is to give a normative explication of the meaning a religion has for its adherents," Lindbeck writes.[49] He makes a distinction between intratextual approaches, which he sees as compatible with his rule theory, and extratextual approaches, which he argues fit better with propositional or experiential-expressivist approaches to religion.[50] The key difference is that extratextual approaches find religious meaning outside the textual or linguistic system to which it refers, while intratextual approaches find meaning in the way a particular language is used. Lindbeck writes, "Thus the proper way to determine what 'God' signifies, for example, is by examining how the word operates within a religion and thereby shapes reality and experience rather than by first establishing its propositional or experiential meaning and reinterpreting or reformulating its uses accordingly."[51] Theological work is thus fundamentally intratextual. Lindbeck notes that intratextuality is not exclusive to religion but can be observed in all rule-governed human behaviors. Lindbeck argues that the experiences we have in the world make sense insofar as they fit into particular systems of meaning.[52] To give an example of this, Lindbeck points out that one does not identify a particular scheduled train route from the suburbs into the city by studying the history of trains, or even by observing the specific trains that are used in a given system. A different train might travel this route from one day to the next, but the thing that identifies the train is that it goes from one place to another at the same time every day. In other words, the overall system identifies what it is.[53]

Lindbeck argues that intratextuality is greatest in natural languages, cultures, and religions, which is consistent with his account of the similarities between these three things. Religion can describe things from within itself, but it can also describe everything as inside the system and interpreted by and acted on from within the religious system.[54] The task of the theologian is one of "thick description,"[55] according to Lindbeck. Thick description looks to the system as a

---

49. Ibid., 113.
50. Ibid., 114.
51. Ibid.
52. Ibid., 114.
53. Ibid., 114.
54. Ibid., 114–15.
55. Ibid., 115. Lindbeck takes this term from Clifford Geertz, who borrows it from Gilbert Ryle.

whole, rather than considering individual parts in isolation from one another.[56] Ultimately, this has to map onto the important texts of a given faith. Lindbeck argues that, in religious systems, intratextuality is a real thing rather than just a metaphorical concept. He argues that this is true precisely because the major world religions all have authoritative writings, and, as a result, faithfulness to them can be gauged by considering how descriptions fit with the world found within those authoritative texts.[57]

Texts are, in Lindbeck's mind, an important element to a religious tradition because they offer some kind of "transpersonal authority" that can resolve matters of conflict. Lindbeck also argues that nontextual religions oftentimes cannot survive major change in the surrounding context. Scripture itself, according to Lindbeck, can offer a framework through which religious adherents interpret their experiences in this world. Lindbeck puts this aptly, writing, "A scriptural world is thus able to absorb the universe."[58] Additionally, he argues that this is a practice well established in the Christian tradition, noting that Augustine did this with his own experiences, Aquinas did this with Aristotelianism, and Friedrich Schleiermacher did this with German romantic idealism to the extent that when they addressed things not explicitly covered in scripture, they were much more deeply influenced by scripture than their formal methodologies might suggest.[59]

While this trend is significant, Lindbeck also acknowledges examples of this approach gone awry. This happens when what is being interpreted becomes the interpretative framework itself. In other words, if the biblical text is the interpretative framework, problems would arise if the surrounding culture became the interpretative framework for the text itself.[60] It seems that this move would bring one close to experiential-expressivism. Lindbeck also suggests that this is exactly what happened with gnosticism during the first and second centuries. In that system, Hellenism became the interpreter of the biblical text rather than the thing being interpreted by the biblical text.[61] He also argues that it is important to understand the genre of texts and to look at the function of a text in the community from which it comes.[62] In the end, Lindbeck's system rests on

56. Ibid.
57. Ibid., 115–16.
58. Ibid., 117.
59. Ibid., 118
60. Ibid.
61. Ibid.
62. He writes,
    The meaning must not be esoteric: not something behind, beneath, or in front of the text; not something that the text reveals, discloses, implies, or suggests to those with extraneous metaphysical, historical, or experiential interests. It must rather be what the text says

a fundamental resistance to foundationalism. (Foundationalism will be covered in greater detail in chap. 5.)

HANS FREI

Hans Frei (1922–88), a colleague of Lindbeck at Yale, is particularly well remembered for his work on narrative theology. As an additional representative of postliberalism, his understanding of theology will share much in common with Lindbeck's. Frei argues that modern Christian theology has been preoccupied with apologetics and has focused on anthropology. Modern Christology has been focused on the historical Jesus and the work of Christ in the New Testament rather than with metaphysical definitions of Christ's being, as was seen in the fourth and fifth centuries.[63] Frei argues that the focus of theology for the past three centuries has been on seeing the revelation of Christ reflected in human experience.[64] What this means is that it has been the role of Christian theology to "validate the *possibility* and, hence, the meaning of Christian claims concerning the shape of human existence and the divine revelation to it, even though the *actual occurrence*—and thus the *verification* of the claim—is a matter of divine, self-authenticating action and revelation."[65] In other words, theology has been put in the position of proving its claims with evidence taken from human experience and rationality. Further, Frei argues that this can be and sometimes is done in a patchwork way that pieces together different manners of conceiving human experience that might not actually go together.[66]

Frei calls for a different approach to Christian theology. He argues that Christian theology should not seek to prove Christian truth. Christian theologians have as their work the description of Christian belief (and here Frei explicitly states that this work is description rather than explanation or argument). Further,

---

in terms of the communal language of which the text is an instantiation. A legal document should not be treated in quasi-kabbalistic fashion as first of all a piece of expressive symbolism (though it may secondarily be that also); nor should the Genesis account of creation be turned fundamentalistically into science; nor should one turn a realistic narrative (which a novel can also be) into history. (Ibid., 120)

63. Hans Frei, "Remarks in Connection with a Theological Proposal," in *Theology and Narrative: Selected Essays*, ed. George Hunsinger and William C. Placher (New York: Oxford University Press, 1993), 27–28. Note: Frei addresses the question of the narrative structure of the biblical text after modern scholarship in his seminal work, *The Eclipse of the Biblical Narrative: A Study in Eighteenth and Nineteenth Century Hermeneutics* (New Haven: Yale University Press, 1974). This book should be on the reading list of any students interested in the history of interpretation. See p. 307 for Frei's description of how the sense of narrative changed in the eighteenth and nineteenth centuries.

64. Frei, "Remarks," 29.

65. Ibid., 30 (emphasis in original).

66. Ibid.

this work does not seek to describe what moves human beings to a state of belief.[67] Frei puts it this way:

> My plea here is—the more formal, the less loaded one can make the notion of understanding, the better. And that, in turn, involves a search, in deliberate opposition to most of what I find in contemporary theology, for categories of understanding detached from the perspectives we bring to our understanding, including our commitments of faith. Whether such a thing can be successful remains to be seen. In any case, it involves a search for a notion of understanding that is as little as possible moved by considerations of man's understanding as moved by his being—existential, historical, or ontological.[68]

It is far from clear that this is possible. Frei argues that the next move in theology should be to ask Adolf von Harnack's famous question about the essence of Christianity. He calls for this question to be answered in what he refers to as a "nonperspectivist way," though he also seems to concede that doing this might not be possible. He further concedes that there is not even agreement among theologians about what sources to consider. He notes that some might call for examining all of Christian history to find some central tradition, while others might call for a focus strictly on the Bible. Even with a strict focus on the Bible, the problem of which sections to privilege comes to the forefront once it becomes clear that it may not be so easy to find biblical unity on all subjects.[69]

Frei isn't interested in raising this question without offering an answer. He argues that this work should begin with the Synoptic Gospels. This is the best place to start because they are narratives. Frei argues that narratives offer the possibility of some hermeneutical moves that are not possible with other genres in the New Testament. Once one has looked at the Gospels, one can then branch out into other parts of the New Testament to see if they fit with the hermeneutical moves already made in the Gospels.[70]

Frei is interested in narrative because he believes that it has been largely lost in recent biblical interpretation.[71] Prior to the Enlightenment, Frei argues, Christians read the Bible as one large story from Genesis to Revelation and saw that story as having a normative world of its own. The Bible served to provide the church with a way of living the Christian life.[72] The Bible was a frame of

67. Ibid.
68. Ibid., 31.
69. Ibid.
70. Ibid., 32.
71. See also Frei, *Eclipse of the Biblical Narrative*, 3–4.
72. Frei, *Eclipse of the Biblical Narrative*, 3–4. See also James Fodor, "Postliberal Theology," in *The Modern Theologians: An Introduction to Christian Theology since 1918*, ed. David Ford with Rachel Muers (Malden, MA: Blackwell, 2005), 234.

reference for the believing community[73] that offered a particular vision of the Christian life. Frei argues that the Bible is best read as a narrative. In other words, the story is the meaning of the text. It is important to understand that, for Frei, this is a meaning contained in the text itself. The historical context contributes to the meaning, but the meaning cannot be reduced to the historical context. Perhaps most important, the story and its meaning cannot be moved into other interpretative schemes without complication. Frei argues that work in biblical studies since the Enlightenment has at times tried to fit scripture into a predetermined set of categories. In doing this, one has moved out of the world of the text and into another world. Frei calls this a "great reversal," in which the biblical story has been fit into another story. He argues that a theology that is faithful to the biblical narrative will see it as a whole, complete in its own context. The one thing that sets the biblical text apart from others, though, is that the narrative is one in which all Christians live.[74]

Frei argues that some biblical texts can have "normative" interpretations. He writes,

> My proposal, which I can really test only in application and not in abstraction . . . is that in regard to aesthetic or quasi-aesthetic texts, particularly narratives—and the Gospels are such in part—"normative" interpretations may be possible. That is to say, the meaning of the text remains the same no matter what the perspectives of succeeding generations of interpreters may be. In other words, the constancy of the meaning of the text is the text and not the similarity of its *effect* on the life-perspectives of succeeding generations. No reference to the situation of the interpreter is necessary in understanding the text.[75]

In other words, Frei argues that existential and hermeneutical approaches to understanding a text are often restrictive, while his aesthetic approach sees the meaning of a text in the story world that it creates. He also says that the aesthetic approach allows for several methods to be used for interpretation and prioritizes the text itself over the methods used to interpret it.[76]

For Frei, meaning must be "firmly grounded in the text and nowhere else."[77] Starting at this point—a text-centered approach to truth and meaning—is critical for Frei. He acknowledges that his approach is limited by the reality that only one narrative can be considered at any one time. Even each of the Synoptic Gospels, he claims, demands its own consideration.[78]

---

73. Fodor, "Postliberal Theology," 234.
74. Ibid., 235.
75. Frei, "Remarks," 32 (emphasis in original).
76. Ibid., 42.
77. Ibid.
78. Ibid.

Frei's approach takes the integrity of the text seriously by looking at it as a coherent whole. Rather than asking questions about sources or earlier forms, Frei calls on those who would take up his approach to consider the text as a whole and to find meaning in the story the text tells. This approach may appeal to a broad range of views on the biblical text that range from those that reject the historical-critical method because of its assumption that it is possible to reconstruct history, to those that reject the historical-critical method because of the way it breaks apart the original text. Postliberal theology emphasizes coherence—the coherence of particular communities and their doctrines and the coherence of the story found in the biblical text. Because of this, its approach will be of interest to a broad range of theological perspectives.

One of the most interesting things about postliberalism is its theological orientation. Postliberalism focuses on doctrine that arises out of believing communities. Lindbeck's work has emphasized the ways in which one learns doctrine. Frei's work is clearly connected to that when he holds that the work of Christian theology is to describe (not argue for or evaluate) Christian beliefs. To do this, Frei points to the narrative of the biblical text as that which informs Christian belief and thus Christian practice.

Postliberalism and Evangelicalism

There is a lively debate to be had about the exact status of the work of Lindbeck, who initiated this new movement of postliberal thinkers. Postliberals have found themselves in conversation with Protestant evangelicals, perhaps most notably at the 1994 Wheaton Theology Conference, the proceedings of which were published as *The Nature of Confession: Evangelicals and Postliberals in Conversation*. At that conference, Lindbeck stated that he thought evangelicals were more likely than any other group to carry the project of postliberalism forward.[79] George Hunsinger noted at the same conference that evangelicals and postliberals have much to offer each other. He said that Lindbeck has looked to Barth and Hans Urs von Balthasar because they both read scripture as a narrative but yet do not reject historical criticism. It is because of their approach to scripture that Lindbeck finds dialogue with them "possible— perhaps even desirable," according to Hunsinger.[80] Hunsinger suggests that

79. George Lindbeck, George Hunsinger, Alister McGrath, and Gabriel Fackre, "A Panel Discussion," in *The Nature of Confession: Evangelicals and Postliberals in Conversation*, ed. Timothy R. Phillips and Dennis L. Okholm (Downers Grove, IL: InterVarsity, 1996), 253.

80. George Hunsinger, "What Can Evangelicals & Postliberals Learn from Each Other? The Carl Henry–Hans Frei Exchange Reconsidered," in Phillips and Okholm, eds., *Nature of Confession*, 150.

some evangelicals might fall into that camp as well. Additionally, if evangelicals have something to offer postliberals on this front, postliberals have something to offer evangelicals as well. Hunsinger argues that evangelicalism has produced some notable biblical scholars in recent decades, but that it has not produced any truly distinguished theologians. He attributes this to a lack of interest in theological method, and it is here that postliberalism could offer resources to evangelicalism.[81] It is perhaps thus particularly interesting that both Stanley Grenz and Kevin Vanhoozer (both of whom are covered in chap. 5) examine Lindbeck's work when discussing theological methodology, though their interpretations of him differ.

Why all of this commentary on postliberalism and evangelicalism? Evangelicals often offer one interpretation or understanding of Lindbeck that is at odds with another interpretation of Lindbeck. Vanhoozer (notably) reads Lindbeck as a relativist who has pluralist leanings when it comes to salvation. Others, though, read Lindbeck as more of an exclusivist who insists on the finality of Christ for salvation. Part of the dispute seems to circle around whether Lindbeck speaks within the cultural-linguistic milieu of Christianity or whether, when he speaks about the finality of Christ, he does so standing outside any particular milieu, speaking for all people. The answer to this question is not entirely clear, as indicated by the different interpretations of Lindbeck offered by thinkers such as Vanhoozer and Jeannine Hill Fletcher.

Paul Knitter offers Lindbeck's work as a model that moves beyond the traditional positions of exclusivism, inclusivism, and pluralism found in the Christian theology of the world religions. This will be discussed in greater detail in chapter 8, but, in short, Lindbeck's work leads to a model that seeks a clearer middle position between particularity and universality.[82] Knitter sees Lindbeck's position as part of what he calls the "acceptance" model, which understands Lindbeck as acknowledging the reality of other faiths and calling for members of differing faiths to be good neighbors to one another, respecting religious difference.[83]

Conclusion

It is clear that conversation and debate about postliberalism will continue. Although the promised follow-up to Lindbeck's *The Nature of Doctrine* has yet

81. Ibid.
82. Paul F. Knitter, *Introducing Theologies of Religions* (Maryknoll, NY: Orbis Books, 2002), 173.
83. Ibid., 184–85.

to be published, postliberalism is an important movement for postconservative evangelical theologians like Grenz and Vanhoozer and for theologians interested in interreligious dialogue like Knitter and Hill Fletcher. For these reasons and others, Lindbeck's work remains on many systematic theology reading lists and will continue to influence theological work for some time.

5

Evangelical Theologies

In the period after the Reformation, Protestant theology became systematized in ways that were not necessarily conducive to the growth of one's lived religion. The Pietist movement rose as an alternative to this, emphasizing daily, lived religion and one's connection and devotion to God. Today, evangelicalism also emphasizes one's lived religion in the form of a personal relationship with God and a life of piety. While a number of key features unite evangelicals, there are also distinctive approaches to evangelical theology and a lively debate about evangelical theological method. Among the methodologically significant thinkers are Millard Erickson, Stanley Grenz, Kevin Vanhoozer, and Clark Pinnock.

MILLARD ERICKSON

Millard Erickson is an ordained Baptist minister and has served as the pastor of two churches and the interim pastor of more than thirty churches. He was professor of theology and academic dean at Bethel Seminary for many years. At the time of this writing, Erickson is a professor of theology at Baylor University's Truett Seminary and Distinguished Professor of Theology at Western Seminary in Portland, Oregon.[1]

Theology, for Erickson, is a set of statements that delineate fundamental ideas about the nature of God and reality. Such statements treat questions about God's action in the world, human anthropology, and the ways in which human beings come into relationship with God.[2]

1. Biographical information on Erickson was taken from his faculty page at Western Seminary.
2. Millard J. Erickson, *Introducing Christian Doctrine*, ed. L. Arnold Hustad (Grand Rapids: Baker, 1992), 15.

Theology arises out of a careful study of scripture. Although there may be some insight gained from other sources, the content of theology is to be taken primarily from scripture.[3] Theology must also be systematic in that it should organize the totality of what the biblical text teaches on a given topic, rather than considering individual books separately from one another.[4] In addition to being biblical and systematic, Erickson holds that theology must be done in the context of human culture. This means that theology must relate the teachings found in scripture to the data found in other disciplines that deal with the same subject matter. Erickson rounds out his discussion of characteristics by asserting that theology must be both contemporary and practical. This means that theology must be stated in a way that is understandable to the contemporary person. Further, theology must be relevant to the everyday life of the contemporary person, rather than merely offering a set of data.[5] In his later book, *The Evangelical Left*, Erickson backs off from this assertion, suggesting that the Bible is the only source for theology and that it should be read in a way that looks for propositional truths.[6]

Theology, Erickson writes, must in some way be a science in that it must have some of the traditional criteria of scientific knowledge. These include a definite object of study, a method for investigating the subject matter and verifying assertions, objectivity in the sense that the study deals with external phenomena that are accessible to investigation by others, and a coherence among the propositions of the subject matter such that the content forms a clear body of knowledge rather than a set of loosely connected facts.[7]

Although Erickson acknowledges that several other starting points have been suggested for the study of theology, including natural theology, tradition, and experience, he reiterates that his study of theology will begin with scripture. His statements about scripture as a starting point and theology as science raise the question of his approach to theology. Erickson lays out a theological method in several steps. The first step, he writes, is to collect the necessary biblical materials. This involves an identification and interpretation of all relevant biblical passages dealing with the topic being considered. Interpretation involves using

3. Erickson writes, "Theology is biblical. It takes its primary content from the Old and New Testament Scriptures. While additional insight may be obtained by the study of God's creation, or what is sometimes referred to as the book of God's work, it is primarily God's Word that constitutes the content of theology" (ibid., 16).

4. Ibid.

5. Ibid.

6. See Millard J. Erickson, *The Evangelical Left: Encountering Postconservative Evangelical Theology* (Grand Rapids: Baker, 1997), 29, 47, 53. See also Stanley J. Grenz, *Renewing the Center: Evangelical Theology in a Post-Theological Era*, 2nd ed. (Grand Rapids: Baker Academic, 2006), 141.

7. Erickson, *Introducing Christian Doctrine*, 17.

tools such as concordances, commentaries, the biblical texts in the original languages, and grammars and lexicons.[8]

The goal of this work is, according to Erickson, to determine what the author of the biblical text was saying to the original audience. This kind of work will involve examining various types of biblical materials, but he argues that didactic passages of scripture will be the most often used and the most easily interpreted parts of scripture, because meaning in them is often quite clear.[9] Narrative passages, although more difficult, are also important; these often serve, for Erickson, as illustrations of doctrinal truths.[10]

Once the relevant biblical materials are assembled, it is important to bring them together into a coherent whole. Although there is significant diversity in the biblical texts, the assumption of the theologian should be in favor of their overall unity. Areas of disagreement should be interpreted in light of substantial agreement among the various biblical authors, according to Erickson.[11] Once this has been done, it is important to determine what the coherent whole really means. Erickson writes that although scripture is, by far, the primary source of doctrinal construction, it is not the only source. Creation, church history, and human history can also be sources for theological reflection.[12]

All of these sources together (but again primarily scripture) help the theologian to identify the essence of doctrine. Once "the abiding essence or permanent content" of doctrine is determined, it is critical for the theologian to express it in a way that is accessible to the contemporary person.[13] Erickson follows Paul Tillich's method of correlation so far as to acknowledge that the doing of theology requires identifying questions from contemporary society as the starting point for a presentation of the Christian message. At the same time, he writes, "We must not allow the non-Christian world to set the agenda completely, for in many cases it may not ask or even recognize the existence of the most important questions."[14]

8. Ibid., 19.
9. Ibid.
10. Ibid. This is a notion reflected by many within evangelicalism, to the point that numerous people have noted that evangelicals have a strong tendency to spend a great deal of time reading and preaching on the Pauline Epistles while spending far less time on the vast majority of the material found in the Gospels.
11. Ibid., 19–20.
12. Ibid., 20–21.
13. Ibid., 21.
14. Ibid. Although Erickson acknowledges Tillich's method of correlation and the idea that theology must be intelligible to the contemporary person, his actual method is clearly quite different from Tillich's.

Erickson, at least in the early stage of his work, has clearly moved beyond the notion of theology suggested by very conservative evangelical thinkers insofar as he acknowledges the importance of nonbiblical sources for theology and seeks to a degree to formulate theology in a way that responds to contemporary questions. At the same time, Erickson is careful to state numerous times that scripture must be the primary source of revelation, and he doesn't appear to give a significant amount of authority to the other sources he accepts. Further, his stress on didactic passages of scripture and his description of narrative as more difficult to interpret place him in the company of many evangelical theologians who see revelation (particularly the biblical text) as a series of propositional truths.

STANLEY GRENZ

If one were to choose one term or concept that runs through the heart of Stanley Grenz's theology, it would be community. The believing community plays a central role in Grenz's theological work, and without it, his work would not fit together well.

In *Revisioning Evangelical Theology*, Grenz sets out to identify ways in which evangelical theology must be reconsidered in the contemporary, postmodern context. In addition to calling for reconsiderations of evangelical identity and spirituality, Grenz calls for a reconsideration of various elements of evangelical theology. He calls for a revisioning of several elements of theology, including the nature and task of theology and the sources for theology, and seeks to identify the integrative motif of theology.[15]

In this book, Grenz identifies a problem within evangelical theology. Certain versions of evangelical theology treat the Bible as a collection of facts to be organized, just as the physical sciences collect and organize facts about things found in nature. This is the crux of the problem that Grenz will eventually come to call "foundationalism," the broad claim that some beliefs anchor others and the theological claims must be anchored on a foundation. An identification of this problem immediately raises the question of how to go about solving it, and Grenz offers several suggestions.[16]

---

15. *Revisioning Evangelical Theology* was published in 1993. Grenz passed away in March 2005. His final book, *The Named God and the Question of Being*, was published in November 2005.

16. It is important to point out that Grenz does not want to discard everything that may be implied by biblical propositionalism. He writes, "Despite its shortcomings, evangelical propositionalism capsules a fundamental insight. Our faith is tied to the truth content of a divine revelation that has been objectively disclosed. . . . The difficulty with evangelical propositionalism, therefore, is not its acknowledgment of a cognitive dimension of revelation and consequently of the statements of

What runs through all of his suggestions is what will become a leitmotif throughout his career: the argument that if theology is going to rightly convey the biblical message in the contemporary context, it is critical that theologians shed the modern outlook and turn to the community outlook that he sees as basic to the people of God as depicted in the Bible.[17] This new kind of theology requires a new understanding of epistemology.[18] Grenz argues that knowing and experiencing the world can happen only from within a conceptual framework. This framework is mediated by the social community in which we participate.[19] Community is an important strand in Grenz's thought particularly because it is offered as a response to the two central critiques he makes of most evangelical theology. As discussed, Grenz is critical of biblical propositionalism, and he identifies this kind of theology as taking a foundationalist approach. Additionally, he is very concerned about rampant individualism not only within secular society but also within evangelical circles as evidenced by the lack of any kind of developed ecclesiology within most of them; as a result, he offers his communitarian approach as a remedy for an atomistic view of human beings.[20]

---

theology" (*Revisioning Evangelical Theology: A Fresh Agenda for the 21st Century* [Downers Grove, IL: InterVarsity, 1993], 72). Rather, the problem with it is that evangelical theologians who place primary importance on propositions misunderstand the social nature of theological discourse. Evangelical theology, Grenz argues, has been captive to the emphasis on the individual knower that has characterized Western thinking in the modern period (ibid., 73).

17. Ibid.

18. Certainly Grenz is not claiming that his call for a communal orientation to theological work is something wholly new in the Christian tradition, but rather that it is new to evangelical theology insofar as evangelical theology has tended toward both individualism and an underdeveloped (if not nonexistent) ecclesiology.

19. Grenz, *Revisioning Evangelical Theology*, 73–74. Grenz writes, "Foundational to our self-identity, religion claims, is religious experience—an experience of or encounter with the divine. This experience, as well as the conceptual framework that facilitates it, is mediated by the religious community—through its symbols, narratives and sacred documents—in which we participate" (ibid., 74). In other words, Grenz here is arguing that at the root of the human being's knowing anything about God is some kind of experience, while at the same time seeking to be clear that this is not the same kind of religious experience he sees in liberal Protestantism. The difference between the two is whether the religious experience is that of the individual or that of the community. Although communal experience can be interpreted in very different ways by the various individuals involved, it is fundamentally corporate in nature. Further, Grenz points out that this is consistent with the biblical understanding of religious experience in that the goal of any human-divine encounter is to constitute a community of people in covenant with God. This is an important distinction, as Grenz clearly rejects any reliance on individual religious experience, which he sees as the legacy of Protestant liberalism.

20. Grenz also devotes a chapter in *Revisioning Evangelical Theology* to revisioning the church. He writes,

> Evangelicals today are unsure not only about the link between baptism and joining the church, but whether congregations should continue formal membership at all. The questioning of the traditional understanding of church membership is evident in the current phenomenon of "church hopping." Many people no longer see themselves as permanent members of a

While the earlier, scientific understanding of evangelical theology led to theological work being carried out by the isolated scholar seeking to work through and systematize the various propositions found in the Bible (as can be seen to a large degree in Erickson's theology), Grenz's communal understanding leads to a very different picture of that task. Grenz's proposal sees theology as having its ultimate end in the life of the believing community. "The biblical narrative builds the conceptual framework by which the community views itself and its experience of the world. Theology, in turn, functions within the context of the Christian community by reflecting on its conceptual framework and belief structure."[21]

Not only is theology to be done in this communal context, but it is the very task of the faith community, and there is no other reason needed to engage in the discipline than one's presence and participation in the faith community. Because of this, Grenz argues that theology is "the faith community's reflecting on the faith experience of those who have encountered God through the divine activity in history and therefore now seek to live as the people of God in the contemporary world."[22] As a result, the task of theology is to assist the contemporary believing community to both proclaim and live the message that God in Christ broke into human history for the sake of human salvation.[23]

This avenue is promising, but the question of how this is practically worked out still remains. It is important to consider three critical issues in *Revisioning Evangelical Theology* to fully understand how Grenz's communitarian outlook permeates his entire theological proposal.

The Nature and Task of Theology

Grenz writes that theology functions in much the same way that church doctrine does in George Lindbeck's classic, *The Nature of Doctrine*, as discussed in chapter 4. In developing his theological approach, Lindbeck sees doctrine as serving a regulative function.[24] For the individual believer, the community provides a cultural and linguistic framework that shapes life and thought. Rather

---

particular congregation, but flit from one church to another.... For some time the doctrine
of the church has been the neglected stepchild of evangelical theology. (Ibid., 164–65)
For a lengthy treatment of ecclesiology by Grenz, see Stanley J. Grenz, *Theology for the Community
of God*, 2nd ed. (Grand Rapids: Eerdmans, 2000), 461–570.

21. Grenz, *Revisioning Evangelical Theology*, 74–75.

22. Ibid., 75–76.

23. Ibid., 77.

24. Ibid. Grenz cites Lindbeck, *Nature of Doctrine*, 18. There Lindbeck writes that church doctrines, in the cultural-linguistic model, have a regulative function. This means that their significance is found not in the way they serve as expressive symbols or truth claims but in the way they are used in the community as "authoritative rules of discourse, attitude, and action."

than being shaped by the experiences of its constitutive individuals, the communal reality itself shapes the subjectivities and experiences of its members.[25]

To take Lindbeck's idea further, Grenz argues that theology "systematizes, explores, and orders the community symbols and concepts into a unified whole—that is, into a systematic conceptual framework."[26] As a result of this, theology puts the "community symbols and concepts," or the faith beliefs of the community, into a contemporary context. This understanding, which renders theology a second-order—or interpretive—act, does not take away from the first-order truth of theological claims but rather shows that although the theologian cannot exhaustively or accurately describe reality, the theologian can say some true things about reality.[27]

For Grenz, the believing community is basic to the correct understanding of the theological task. While he does not seek to diminish the importance of doctrine for the theological task, he writes that theology must be a practical discipline that is primarily oriented toward the believing community. Participation in a particular faith community involves a commitment to a specific conceptual framework. Because faith is linked to a conceptual framework, Grenz writes, one's participation in a particular community of faith will imply a claim to truth, even if that claim is only implicit. "By its very nature, the conceptual framework of a faith community claims to represent in some form the truth about the world and the divine reality its members have come to know and experience."[28]

Because of this, theology by necessity seeks truth. It does so by being in conversation with other disciplines of human knowledge, with the ultimate aim of

---

One of the most important points Lindbeck makes about the regulative function is that rules that appear to contradict can often be reconciled without invalidating any of them. This is so because seemingly contradictory rules must be put in their proper context. Lindbeck offers the two rules of "drive on the left" and "drive on the right" as examples. The two rules are clearly diametrically opposed, yet when each is placed in its appropriate context (such as the country in which it is in force), it becomes clear how each one can both be authoritative and not contradict the other. Lindbeck argues that when doctrines are viewed as rules and interpreted in their historical contexts, it can be clear how different doctrines emerged in different communities at different historical moments and how each can stand authoritatively without calling another into question. This way of understanding doctrine (as opposed to understanding it as propositions or expressive symbols) allows for reconciliation among various doctrines without "capitulation" or the need to change doctrine. It is important to point out that this chapter will discuss only Grenz's interpretation of Lindbeck.

25. Grenz, *Revisioning Evangelical Theology*, 77–78.

26. Ibid., 78.

27. Ibid. Here Grenz would assert that we cannot claim to exhaustively describe reality but that we can know some things about reality itself. This again shows that he does uphold a unified understanding of truth and that the significance of the postmodern critique for his work deals more with seeing human beings as having limited capacities of knowledge, rather than calling into question the nature of truth itself.

28. Ibid., 79.

offering a Christian worldview that also fits together with human experience in the world.[29] Theology thus sees the human being and the world as existing in relationship to God, which results in a fuller vision of God qua God and God's purposes in the world.[30] The logical extension of this assertion is that theology's practical dimension is in no way separated from or competing with its theoretical dimension. Every aspect of the theological task contributes to theory and the life of the community as they together make up one interconnected whole.[31]

Grenz also wants to be clear about the potential limitations of theology. While theology seeks to offer a description and account of reality from the perspective of faith, no theological system should be seen as encompassing reality in its fullness. Because theology seeks to say something about God, human beings, and creation, it inherently will never be able to give an exhaustive account of reality. At the same time, it is important to acknowledge that the human mind can know something about reality.[32]

Theology performs the function of an "intermediator,"[33] according to Grenz, in that it works to bring the affirmation of the Christian faith to the contemporary context. The community of faith is called to be faithful in history, but its constitutive members are frequently challenged by the intersection of their faith and the surrounding culture. The theologian's task is to help the community of faith rightly and effectively relate the Word of God to the varied and changing flow of human thought and life. In other words, theology must always be contextual. Grenz notes, "Theology is always *in transitu*, and the theologian is a pilgrim working on behalf of pilgrim people."[34] Although Grenz has at this point offered a basic account of the theological task, it is critical to examine the sources Grenz suggests for theological work.

29. Wolfhart Pannenberg's influence, though not directly noted by Grenz at this point in his argument, seems apparent. See Grenz, *Reason for Hope*, 13–15. Theology seeks truth, but it seeks a truth that coheres with the way in which humans experience the world. Grenz's insistence that the theological task seeks truth is also important. More than once, Grenz makes comments about taking up the work of Lindbeck but is clear that he doesn't want to fully do this. Although Grenz probably would read Lindbeck somewhat differently than Vanhoozer, he does want to make more connections between theology and the search for some kind of ultimate truth than Lindbeck would. See also Wolfhart Pannenberg, *Basic Questions in Theology* (Philadelphia: Fortress, 1970), 1:41–42; Pannenberg's introduction to *Revelation as History* (New York: Macmillan, 1968), 18–19; Dulles, *Models of Revelation*, 58–60. Pannenberg also discusses this idea in *Systematic Theology*, 1:230–57.

30. Grenz, *Revisioning Evangelical Theology*, 79. On this point Grenz cites Douglas F. Ottati, "Christian Theology and Other Disciplines," *Journal of Religion* 64 (1984): 182.

31. Grenz, *Revisioning Evangelical Theology*, 79.

32. Ibid., 82.

33. Ibid., 83.

34. Ibid.

The Sources for Theology

As stated earlier, one of the central critiques made by Grenz of mainstream contemporary evangelical theology is that much of it tends toward a propositionalist approach to theology that sees the Bible as a collection of facts to be reassembled into lists of proof texts for various doctrines. Although Grenz does not deny the critical and primary role of scripture in Christian theology, he calls on theologians to use additional sources in their work.

Grenz ultimately identifies three normative sources for theology, which he places in a hierarchical order. First in importance is the biblical message, the theological heritage of the church is second, and the thought forms of the contemporary context are third. Although scripture is to be approached in a different manner in Grenz's proposed theology, the high view of scripture central to classical evangelical theology (and traditional Protestant theology as a whole) remains. He writes that the Bible is of first importance and is the primary norm for theology.[35] According to Grenz, theologians should not spend their time engaging in lengthy prolegomena that seeks to establish the reliability of the Bible through discussions about fulfilled prophecies and the Bible's own claims about itself. Setting aside the question of whether these endeavors are actually helpful, Grenz writes that they are simply unnecessary. Rather, the theologian should assume the authority of the Bible on the basis of the relation of theology to the faith community.[36]

With the Bible established in Grenz's work as the first and primary pillar of theological work, we now turn to an examination of the second and third pillars.[37] The second pillar or norm for theological work connects to the first. Good theological work requires not just an explication of the biblical texts considered apart from the two-thousand-year history that separates the contemporary person from the writing of the New Testament. Rather, it is important for the theologian to give consideration to the corpus of Christian teaching that developed in the early church and has been transmitted and developed from one

35. Ibid.
36. Ibid., 94.
37. Grenz's use of "pillars" is interesting. Pillars are somewhat different than foundations in that they can represent the importance and interdependence of multiple sources in theological reflection. This is seen in some Anglican understandings of theological method that see scripture, tradition, and reason as three legs of a stool. The implication for this metaphor is that removing any of the three legs will result in the stool's inability to stand. At the same time, the Protestant proclivity to give scripture the trump card, so to speak, raises the question of whether the pillar analogy works in Grenz's thought. If scripture is the first and primary pillar, does it rise above the other pillars? If so, does scripture serve as a foundation of sorts? The answer to this question is somewhat unclear; however, the significance of the metaphor for Grenz is that he is arguing that scripture must be taken along with several other sources in theological reflection.

generation of Christians to the next, as this is ultimately a consideration of how the church has interpreted scripture throughout its history.[38] At the same time, Grenz is careful to point out that the Christian tradition developed in particular cultures and that the use of tradition as a norm must be nuanced.[39] Further, the tradition must be seen as ultimately subject to the judgment of scripture.[40]

Grenz notes that the church's theological history is significant for theology today in that it can warn of potential pitfalls and suggest promising directions. Further, particular formulations in the tradition have stood the test of time and have become "classic" statements of theological truth and have a particular ongoing significance for the church.[41] These classic statements are in part what enable theologians to forge new ground. Without them and without a respect for tradition as a norm in theological work, the theologian would be left to begin the theological task anew each generation, working to reestablish doctrines that have already been established in the past.

The third pillar or norm for theology is the contemporary context. Because Grenz has already argued that the task of theology is to offer a reflection on the Christian faith that is contextual, he holds that theologians must consider the work of various disciplines of human learning and seek to show the relevance of Christian faith for the human quest for truth.[42] While the church's social-historical context cannot have any kind of sole determining influence for theology (that role, if given to any theological norm, would be given to scripture), it does present particular problems and issues that the believing community must consider and explain in order to say something relevant to the surrounding culture. At many points throughout history, the church has taken categories and concepts from society in order to express the Christian understanding of its faith commitment.[43] Grenz sees the many ways this has been done in the past as showing that theologians have a continuing task to be aware of the contemporary culture in their theological work. The remaining question on this issue concerns exactly how the theologian ought to do this.[44]

38. Grenz writes, "Theological history, therefore, serves as a reference point to us as we, like our forebears, seek to grapple with the meaning of the scriptural message and our loyalty to the triune God in the context in which we live as the people of God" (*Revisioning Evangelical Theology*, 96).
39. Ibid., 95.
40. Ibid., 97.
41. Ibid., 96.
42. Ibid., 97.
43. Ibid., 98–99.
44. Ibid., 99. There seem to be two claims operating here. The contemporary context, for Grenz, involves both information gleaned from academic disciplines such as the social sciences and questions that arise in the contemporary context (as might be described by Tillich in the first volume of his *Systematic Theology*). Is the contemporary context a source or norm? Grenz would likely argue that it is insofar as information from the social sciences should be taken into account in the process

To answer this question, Grenz argues that the Christian message of God acting in Christ involves the creation of a new identity of the redeemed person participating in a redeemed society and existing in community with both creation and creator. Within any culture, the church will be a specific group of people with a specific worldview, but at the same time the church's task is that of being an inclusive group of people that conveys its worldview in culturally understandable categories so that its boundaries can be broadened to encompass all who share its loyalty to Christ.[45]

Grenz argues that the threefold source of theology that he has offered suggests a way by which works of systematic theology can be evaluated. A theology can be evaluated on the basis of its faithfulness, or lack thereof, to the three theological norms outlined above. As a result, Grenz argues that in evaluating a particular theology, one must ask, "To what extent does this theology articulate the biblical kerygma, reflect the faith of the one people of God, and speak to the historical-cultural situation in which the faith community seeks to proclaim the good news and live as the people of God?"[46] In offering this account of the normative sources for theology, Grenz has strongly stated that all three are necessary for the theological task rather than just one.[47]

Community as Theology's Integrative Motif

Because Grenz specifically critiques foundationalism, it is important to understand the nuance of his claim about the role of the community, as some have suggested that this is simply a different foundation. Although some Reformed epistemologists make arguments that lead to an assertion that the church is basic to theology,[48] Grenz wants an argument that makes more distinctions than this, for apart from that, an argument that the church is basic would in effect set up a new "foundationalism of the church."[49] In one sense, the church itself is not

---

of theological construction. It would not directly serve as a norm or source insofar as it provides questions for theology to address.

45. Ibid., 100.

46. Ibid., 101.

47. Presumably, to be faithful to the contemporary context means that theological work should be comprehensible to the contemporary person (as Karl Rahner and others have suggested) and that it should adequately address questions that arise from the contemporary context (as Tillich and others have suggested).

48. Here Grenz writes that some Reformed epistemologists, such as Alvin Plantinga and Nicholas Wolterstorff, argue that to be human means to be situated in a particular community such that communities play an indispensable role in shaping human conceptions of rationality as well as the religious beliefs that are deemed basic and to which humans appeal to test new claims (ibid., 209). In this way, the church becomes "basic" to theological work.

49. Grenz, *Renewing the Center*, 222.

basic for theology but rather for "the specifically Christian experience-facilitating interpretive framework, which in turn is connected to the gospel, and by extension to the biblical narrative."[50] In another sense, though, the church is basic for theology, and it is this very assertion that can help evangelical theology to resist the foundationalism of modern theology in both its liberal and conservative forms. This is so because theology has classically been understood as "faith seeking understanding." The very existence of the faith community, Grenz says, leads naturally to a reflection on the faith of that community, which is what we call theology.[51]

As a result, theology does not need a lengthy prolegomenon. Rather, it arises out of the life of the faith community. The very existence and presence of the Christian community leads to theological work. Because of the communitarian nature of theology, community can readily be established as theology's integrative motif. This means that theological work should be undertaken with community (or more specifically, as Grenz says, "persons-in-relationship") as the central organizing concept in light of which significant theological issues can be considered.[52]

In addition to the argument that theology comes from the very existence of the community, in that it is the faith of the community that is reflected on, theological work must be undertaken with an aim toward the good of the community, according to Grenz. If theology is the work of the community seeking to understand its faith, then its goal must turn back to the community and answer critical questions about the faith of that community. Grenz writes, "A central task of theology is to express communal beliefs and values as well as the meaning of the symbols of the faith community. Theological construction has as its goal that of setting forth an understanding of the mosaic of beliefs that lies at the heart of a particular community."[53] As a whole, theology should offer the community a particularly Christian way of understanding of the world.[54] Additionally, theology should be for the community by offering guidance to the community on how to fulfill its Christian calling. The community is ultimately called to be the image of God, and theology should take part in calling and directing the community toward that goal as expressed in the biblical text.[55]

---

50. Ibid.
51. Ibid.
52. Ibid., 222–23.
53. Ibid., 223.
54. Grenz cites Karl Barth here, writing, "As a result, Christian theology is by its very nature 'church dogmatics,' as Karl Barth describes it. As church dogmatics, as the faith of the community seeking understanding, theology is inherently communitarian" (ibid.). Grenz does not refer to a specific comment in Barth's work but rather the title of his entire project.
55. Ibid., 224.

Grenz connects the idea of the Christian community to the idea of the Triune God, writing, "Theology is by definition the study of God. . . . *Christian* theology speaks about the God known in the Christian community. And the God to whom the Christian community bears witness is the triune God. The only true God, Christians declare, is social or communal. Christian theology is inherently communal, therefore, because it is the explication of the Christian understanding of the God who is the triune one."[56] This assertion reveals why, in the end, theology must be inherently communitarian. Christian theology is the study of God. It is connected to the Bible in that the Bible contains the narrative of God fulfilling God's divine purposes. Grenz sees the ultimate goal of the work of God as the establishment of a community made up of "a redeemed people, living within a redeemed creation, enjoying the presence of the triune God."[57]

The most significant point of development in *Renewing the Center*, in continuity with his earlier *Revisioning Evangelical Theology*, is Grenz's focus on community as a hermeneutical key for theological work. Not only must biblical texts be read from within the context of the believing community, but also community is the very goal of reading the text, according to Grenz.[58] As he has made clear before, this community is not restricted to a group of local individuals, nor is it even restricted to the believing community presently living. Rather, this community is one faith community that spans the history of Christianity. As a result, a full consciousness of reading the biblical text in community will take the theological heritage of the church seriously.[59] This is an important lesson to keep in mind for those within evangelicalism who would seek a "tradition-free" interpretation.[60]

56. Ibid., 223–24.

57. Ibid., 224. Grenz cites Paul D. Hanson, *The People Called: The Growth of Community in the Bible* (San Francisco: Harper & Row, 1986), 510.

58. Grenz writes, "The Spirit's goal in appropriating the biblical text is to fashion a community that lives the paradigmatic biblical narrative in the contemporary context. The goal of reading the text, therefore, is to hear the Spirit's voice and to be formed into that community. Consequently, reading the text is a community event" (*Renewing the Center*, 216).

59. Ibid., 216–17. In addition to restating his position that tradition, or the church's theological heritage, plays an important (though secondary) role in theology, Grenz makes a second key point about the role of tradition. Because the theological task should be undertaken with a realization that it is part of a larger task that has taken place over the course of centuries, it is also important to remember that those Christians who came before the contemporary period also aimed to read the Bible in a Christian manner. While this process progresses over time, theologians today must always remain mindful that they should seek to be in "hermeneutical fellowship" with all the people of God. This leads to what Grenz calls a truly "catholic" reading of the text, even when such a reading leads to a point of difference from earlier thinkers.

60. Of course, a "tradition-free" interpretation is impossible, as Hans-George Gadamer's work *Truth and Method* affirms. This statement reminds me of an assertion a professor at Wheaton College

The Nature of the Community

Thus far, Grenz has spent a considerable amount of time discussing the importance of the community and the communitarian turn in contemporary theology.
This discussion raises a further question regarding the nature of the community.
Grenz acknowledges that asking questions about the nature of the community
in the evangelical context can be problematic. George Marsden expresses this
problem best in writing, "One of the striking features of much of evangelicalism is
its general disregard for the institutional church."[61] If the new evangelical theology
is going to take the role of the community in theological hermeneutics seriously,
it first needs to gain greater clarity on what this community should look like.
As Grenz puts it, "Evangelical theology must recapture a credible ecclesiology."[62]

There has been significant disagreement in evangelical circles about the nature of the church, in part because making a determination about that issue
has never been important for a movement that is made up of loose associations.
Grenz likens the structure of evangelicalism, particularly in North America, to
that of a parachurch organization.[63] This nature of evangelicalism has led to a
neglect of any serious discussion on the doctrine of the church. As Grenz writes,
"Evangelical leaders routinely display no indication that they have given serious,
extended attention to questions about the nature of the church. D. L. Moody,
to cite one extreme example, had no doctrine of the church whatsoever," in the
estimation of his biographer, James Findlay.[64]

In order to begin work on an evangelical ecclesiology that would move beyond the parachurch mentality described above, Grenz proposes returning to
the classic notions of the marks of the church as developed and discussed by
the Reformers. While the Reformers did not reject the practice of describing the
true church as "one, holy, catholic, and apostolic," they did object to the way in
which these descriptors were used by Roman Catholic theologians at the time,
particularly in their assertion that these were marks of a visible institution.[65]

---

made: "It is an arrogant thing to despise church history." That this needed to be said indicates a
tendency among some evangelicals to do just that.

61. Grenz, *Renewing the Center*, 296. He quotes George M. Marsden, *Understanding Fundamentalism and Evangelicalism* (Grand Rapids: Eerdmans, 1991), 81.

62. Grenz, *Renewing the Center*, 296.

63. Ibid., 297. "Parachurch organization" refers to an organization that carries out one or more
functions of a church without being formally tied to any particular church. One example of this
is Young Life, a national organization that sets up local youth ministries. Young Life does many
of the things that a local church youth group might do, but it has no formal ties to any particular
local church or national denomination, and its employees and volunteers come from a range of
churches and denominations.

64. Ibid.

65. Ibid., 317.

The Reformers did not strongly emphasize the adjectives "one, holy, catholic, and apostolic." Rather, in asking what determined a true church, they turned to other characteristics that they felt better answered this question. The true church, for the Reformers, could be found anywhere the Word of God was rightly preached and the sacraments rightly administered.[66]

This focus on Word and sacrament allows for a universal and local component, though it is important to note that the universal component is primarily invisible in nature, while the local component is visible. The universal church can be seen as the community of communities, but this does not imply a uniformity among the individual communities.[67] While there is not uniformity, there is a shared commonality that marks each community as specifically Christian.[68] In the end, the community is fundamentally local, but it must also be seen as more than that. The focus on Word and sacrament turns first to the local church in that it looks for visible communities in particular places in which the Word is rightly preached and the sacraments rightly administered. At the same time, the church "transcends any one local congregation and all local congregations."[69] In this way, the church can be said to have an important universal component even if it is fundamentally local.

In discussing the nature of the church, Grenz again shows the relationship between the Bible and the community in his thought: the church is the community specifically constituted by the biblical narrative of God at work since creation. Those in the community receive an interpretive framework in the Bible through which they find both their individual and corporate identities as those who are "in Christ."[70]

66. Ibid. Here Grenz adopts John Calvin's classic statement from *Institutes of the Christian Religion*: "Wherever we see the Word of God sincerely preached and heard, wherever we see the sacraments administered according to the institution of Christ, there we cannot have any doubt that the Church of God has some existence" (trans. Henry Beveridge [Grand Rapids: Eerdmans, 1989], 4.1.9). This is slightly different from Luther's classic statement about marks of the church: "In this Christian church, wherever it exists is to be found the forgiveness of sins, that is, a kingdom of grace and true pardon. For in it are found the Gospel, baptism, and the sacrament of the altar in which the forgiveness of sins is offered, obtained, and received. Moreover, Christ and his Spirit are there. Outside this Christian church there is no salvation, or forgiveness of sins, but everlasting death and damnation" (*Luther's Works*, ed. Jaroslav Pelikan and Helmut T. Lehmann, 55 vols. [St. Louis: Concordia; Philadelphia: Fortress, 1955–72], 37:368). This quotation was excerpted in a very helpful article on Luther's ecclesiology: Eugene F. A. Klug, "Luther's Understanding of 'Church' in His Treatise *On the Councils and the Church* of 1539," *Concordia Theological Quarterly* 44 (January 1980): 28.

67. Further, although Grenz describes the church as a "community of communities" primarily, in his thought, the universal church can include individuals who are not part of any visible community.

68. Grenz, *Renewing the Center*, 320–21.

69. Ibid., 327.

70. Ibid., 323–24.

In *Renewing the Center*, Grenz's understanding of the nature of the church both looks back to *Revisioning Evangelical Theology* (1993) and anticipates *The Social God and the Relational Self* (2001). Echoing his earlier work, Grenz notes that the community is fundamentally tied to both the past and the future in that it is a community of memory and hope.[71] Anticipating his later work, Grenz argues that the church's truest identity is found in its participation in "the fountainhead of community," the Triune God. When Christians come together in fellowship, it is a shared participation in the community of the persons of the Trinity. Further, the church as a missional community finds its central ends in the Triune God.[72] Grenz writes, "Christians declare that the touchstone of community is the eternal triune life and God's gracious inclusion of humans in Christ by the Spirit, constituting them as participants in the perichoretic trinitarian life."[73]

Grenz's Call for a "Generous Orthodoxy" in Moving Forward

In articulating his own proposal for evangelical theology, Grenz offers a statement from Hans Frei: "My own vision of what might be propitious for our day, split as we are, not so much into denominations as into schools of thought, is that we need a kind of generous orthodoxy which would have in it an element of liberalism . . . and an element of evangelicalism."[74] Grenz follows this up with his own statement: "Viewed from one perspective, this volume is an extended call to evangelicals to take seriously a concern evident within Frei's vision. These pages have emerged out of a sense that the time is ripe to reflect on the type of theological program that might result in a 'generous orthodoxy' after the manner that Frei wished to see."[75]

Grenz's call is to return to an evangelical "center," though he cautions his readers against misunderstanding the idea of a center. Noting Martin Marty's critique that the Protestant center in the United States has often been elitist

---

71. Ibid., 324. Later Grenz argues that baptism and the Eucharist evoke both the past and the future in the life of the church:

> Baptism and the Lord's supper are visual sermons in that they recount in a dramatic, symbolic manner the Christian declaration that "God was in Christ reconciling the world unto himself" (2 Cor. 5.19 KJV). To this end, these practices serve as visual memorials, recalling Christ's accomplished work on behalf of all humankind. . . . Baptism and the Lord's supper bring not only the narrative past, but also the eschatological future into view. These acts symbolically announce the promise that God will one day bring the divine creative work to completion, but more importantly, that this completion constitutes the true identity of the believer, the believing community, and even all creation. (Ibid., 326)

72. Ibid., 331, 330.

73. Ibid., 332.

74. Ibid., 333. He cites Hans Frei, "Response to 'Narrative Theology': An Evangelical Appraisal," *Trinity Journal* 8 (1987): 21.

75. Grenz, *Renewing the Center*, 333.

and exclusionary,[76] Grenz argues that the idea of the center should not be understood in Constantinian terms that would see the church as both closely identified with the state and enmeshed in Western civilization.[77] The call in Grenz's book to renew the center cannot be understood as a "return" of evangelical Christianity to the political, social, or cultural center of the nation. Rather, "the 'center' that is to be renewed is a *theological center*, and the quest to renew the center involves restoring a particular *theological* spirit to the center of the church. The renewing of this center has as its goal primarily the renewal of the church, even though, of course, such renewal can and should naturally spill over into society."[78]

A renewed evangelical center will focus on the gospel, be oriented toward doctrine, and be universal in its vision and scope.[79] Although all of these characteristics are necessary, because this is a call to a renewed *theological* center, it is important to ask what kind of theological hermeneutics should be used. This question will be addressed below in a summation of Grenz's theological hermeneutics.

KEVIN VANHOOZER

Kevin Vanhoozer teaches systematic theology at Trinity International University, and his book *Is There a Meaning in This Text?* made him a significant player in evangelical theological conversations. Like Grenz, Vanhoozer is concerned about the role foundationalism has played in evangelical theology, but his response is different.

76. Grenz writes,
Speaking of the wider, and predominantly white, Protestant "center" that in his estimation persisted into the mid-twentieth century, Marty declares, "Its members and alumni ran the universities, business and corporate life, and civic and political affairs in almost all but the hugely Catholic metropolitan areas. They overwhelmingly dominated *Who's Who in America* listings, had influence on what was in the textbooks and taught in the schools, gave birth to and then dominated many if not most voluntary associations on the philanthropic and reform fronts, made the news in the dailies and weeklies, and were the subjects of most curiosity for their ecclesial endeavors—not the least of all because they controlled the media that quickened and satisfied curiosities." (Ibid., 339–40; citing Martin E. Marty, "The Shape of American Protestantism: Are There Two Parties Today?," in *Reforming the Center*, ed. Douglas Jacobsen and William Vance Trollinger [Grand Rapids: Eerdmans, 1998], 94)

77. Grenz, *Renewing the Center*, 340. He cites Rodney Clapp, *A Peculiar People: The Church as Culture in a Post-Christian Society* (Downers Grove, IL: InterVarsity, 1996), 17.

78. Grenz, *Renewing the Center*, 341–42 (emphasis in original). Kevin Vanhoozer also calls for a renewal of theology in the church in *The Drama of Doctrine: A Canonical-Linguistic Approach to Christian Theology* (Louisville: Westminster John Knox, 2005).

79. Grenz, *Renewing the Center*, 344–54.

First Theology: God, Scripture, and Hermeneutics and the Construal of Scripture

In one of the essays found in Vanhoozer's *First Theology*, Vanhoozer considers the starting point for theology, asking whether it is properly identified as God or scripture.[80] He claims that considering scripture apart from God and considering God apart from scripture both seem to lead to dead ends. In order to appreciate Vanhoozer's position, we need to recognize at least two key claims he makes. First, he wants to position himself between both foundationalists and nonfoundationalists, and second, he develops a notion (following David Kelsey) of "construing scripture." Before looking at these, we can say briefly that Vanhoozer's theological method is a postfoundationalist method that seeks to take texts seriously in their own contexts, while also moving past a foundationalist reading of scripture that sees it as a collection of propositional truths.

Postfoundationalism

Vanhoozer suggests two ways of moving beyond foundationalism in theological study: "nonfoundationalism" and "postfoundationalism." After describing these two positions, he argues for the latter as his own.

In advancing his argument, Vanhoozer writes that "theological *scientia*" is uneasily situated between the modern ideal of an autonomous reason, where interpreters are able to transcend history, class, and culture through an "objective" reading of texts, and its postmodern inversion, where interpretation is nothing more than the projection of a particular community's interests and biases. Although theology finds itself between these two positions, Vanhoozer argues that absoluteness and relativity are not the only choices available.[81]

Foundationalism and nonfoundationalism represent the two extremes between which theology finds itself, and it is between these two extremes that Vanhoozer seeks to place his own postfoundationalist view. Vanhoozer writes that postfoundationalism seeks to hold on to notions of truth, objectivity, and rationality, while at the same time seeks to hold to an idea of human reason as provisional, contextual, and fallible.[82] In this view, knowledge is neither immedi-

---

80. Kevin J. Vanhoozer, *First Theology: God, Scripture, and Hermeneutics* (Downers Grove, IL: InterVarsity, 2002), 29.

81. Vanhoozer, *The Drama of Doctrine*, 293.

82. Ibid. On this point Vanhoozer cites F. LeRon Shults, *The Postfoundationalist Task of Theology: Wolfhart Pannenberg and the New Theological Rationality* (Grand Rapids: Eerdmans, 1999), 58. It is also important to point out that in the following footnote, Vanhoozer writes, "Wolfhart Pannenberg represents yet a third type of postfoundationalism that, while deserving of attention, is beyond the scope of this present study to investigate further" (*Drama of Doctrine*, 294n85). Pannenberg's view is in contrast to Scottish Common Sense Realism that holds that human beings

ate nor unquestionable but is rather mediated via an interpretative framework. No set of data, Vanhoozer writes, is ever foundational, because data is always framework filtered and theory laden. Despite this, because of what Vanhoozer calls "aspectival realism," some filters allow true knowledge of reality to get through.[83] Vanhoozer affirms a realist position while conceding that what we know is filtered by our own frameworks.

This raises the question of the role of the canon in a Christian theology that Vanhoozer has described both as "postfoundationalist" and as "canonical-linguistic." Vanhoozer argues that the canon is a foundation for this type of theology, and yet it is not the kind of foundation that characterizes classical foundationalism.[84] What, then, is the nature of scripture? Vanhoozer writes that in nonfoundationalist accounts of knowledge, with which he strongly disagrees, the emphasis is placed on a web or mosaic of beliefs in which no one belief is more important than any other. In such accounts, it is the believing community rather than a set of beliefs that is considered basic insofar as the web or mosaic might ultimately be changed by traditions and communities of inquiry.[85]

Grenz and Lindbeck are both nonfoundationalists, in Vanhoozer's view, as both seek to emphasize some notion of a socially mediated web or mosaic of beliefs that serves as both a means and a measure of doctrinal knowledge. For the nonfoundationalist, the beliefs an individual holds, as well as that individual's interpretive framework, are dependent on the community in which that individual is located. The major problem with nonfoundationalism, according to Vanhoozer, is that the authority of scripture, "God's communicative action," is made simply one voice among many.[86]

Responding to Lindbeck, and differing with Grenz, Vanhoozer proposes the development of a "canonical-linguistic theology." Such a theology works with a different kind of postfoundationalism and a different notion of knowledge. Vanhoozer offers the image of following maps to describe the notion of knowledge in canonical-linguistic theology. He argues that this image is better than others because it recognizes the priority of the canonical text and its relationship to

---

can generally perceive objects directly. See Jerome B. Schneewind, "Scottish Common Sense Philosophy," in *The Cambridge Dictionary of Philosophy*, ed. Robert Audi (Cambridge: Cambridge University Press, 1999).

83. Vanhoozer, *Drama of Doctrine*, 293.

84. Ibid.

85. Ibid. Here he cites Stanley Grenz and John Franke, *Beyond Foundationalism: Shaping Theology in a Postmodern Context* (Louisville: Westminster John Knox, 2001), 47.

86. Vanhoozer, *Drama of Doctrine*, 294. It is very questionable whether this is the right reading of either Lindbeck or Grenz. As is discussed above, Grenz is careful to distinguish his own position from Lindbeck's position, and he would not accept the nonfoundationalist label for his own proposal. For a discussion of Lindbeck's position, see chap. 4.

reality over a particular person or group's use or reading of them.[87] The concept of the map calls attention to the fact that the framework for interpretation in the church must be canonical before it is communal. Vanhoozer wants to be very clear about what the map is not. He writes that scripture is not a collection of propositional truths that serve as the foundation of knowledge, but it is also not a narrative that is dependent on its place in the church's "web of belief" for its meaning and truth.[88]

Several questions can be raised about Vanhoozer's position. One of the most important questions concerns whether it is possible for the church's interpretation to be canonical before it is communal, as Vanhoozer claims. It seems unclear how the framework for the church's interpretation could be canonical before it is communal, since the canon was at least recognized if not established by the Christian community.[89] Additional questions concern the practicality of using biblical maps to direct one's Christian life. In the end, what would this practically look like? Vanhoozer addresses these concerns in *The Drama of Doctrine* by seeking to show how his canonical-linguistic approach applies to the local church.

Construing Scripture

Vanhoozer is ultimately interested in finding ways to see texts (and particularly scripture) as containing essential meaning, without understanding them as merely collections of propositional truths. The solution to the question of how to treat scripture, according to Vanhoozer, is found in David Kelsey's *Proving Doctrine: The Uses of Scripture in Modern Theology*. Kelsey argues in this text that theologians must construe scripture prior to "proving" doctrine with it. Before using scripture, theologians must make some judgment about the nature of scripture. In making judgments about the nature of scripture, though, theologians also formulate their views about God. To make a judgment about the nature of scripture is ultimately to also make a judgment about the way in which God is involved with scripture and with the Christian community that seeks to interpret it.[90]

An understanding of the relationship between God and scripture is, for Vanhoozer, the task of first theology. Ultimately, this is a variation on the hermeneutical circle: the way scripture is understood affects the way God is understood,

---

87. Ibid.

88. Ibid.

89. The difference between the church recognizing or receiving the canon and the church establishing the canon is an important one that has been the subject of much debate. This is addressed below in the section "Vanhoozer's Canonical-Linguistic Approach."

90. Vanhoozer, *First Theology*, 29. He cites David H. Kelsey, *Proving Doctrine: The Uses of Scripture in Modern Theology* (Harrisburg, PA: Trinity Press, 1999), 161. This book was originally published in 1975 as *The Use of Scripture in Recent Theology*.

just as the way God is understood affects the way scripture is understood. How does the theologian ultimately make a judgment about this relationship? Kelsey, according to Vanhoozer, argues that this is not determined by exegesis of any particular text but is rather a "'pre-text' imaginative judgment" in which the theologian seeks to express the way in which God's presence among the faithful is tied up in the way that the faithful interpret scripture.[91]

Although he finds much to commend in Kelsey, Vanhoozer makes two critiques. He first takes issue with the notion that each theologian works with one construal of scripture. This at least should not be the case, he writes, for there is no one construal that accounts for the whole of the Bible.[92] Vanhoozer also takes issue with Kelsey's notion that one's decision about the God-scripture relation must be "pre-text." To place authority on the community's pre-text judgment is to give a theological priority to the community rather than to the canon,[93] and it is at this point that the distinction between Vanhoozer and Grenz is again made clear. In determining the locus of authority, Vanhoozer is unwilling to place it in the believing community, despite the insights he sees gained by Lindbeck's proposal.

Although he expresses much appreciation for Kelsey's work, Vanhoozer suggests an alternative. He construes scripture as "a rainbow of divine communicative acts" and argues that the value of this construal is that it comes from neither a pre-text decision nor a cultural construal but from the biblical text itself. The idea of the Bible as a gathering of divine communicative acts also resists construing scripture in one way or elevating one part of scripture above another. Rather, Vanhoozer claims, this assertion gives the Bible "a multifaceted authority." The implication of this is that the Bible's "promises are to be trusted, its commands obeyed, its songs sung, its teachings believed."[94]

This idea flows from Vanhoozer's argument that the best way to construe God and scripture together is to acknowledge God as a communicative agent and scripture as God's communicative action.[95] For first theology, this suggests that

---

91. Vanhoozer, First Theology, 30. Vanhoozer continues to follow Kelsey (Proving Doctrine, 167).

92. Vanhoozer, First Theology, 30–31. He writes, "We should not read all of Scripture as myth, or as history, or as doctrine, or as any one thing only" (30, emphasis in original). Vanhoozer acknowledges that theologians do tend to gravitate toward one particular part of scripture, interpreting the whole of scripture in light of that particular part. To match various systematicians to the biblical genres they favor serves as a reminder of how easy it is to fall into reductionism, thinking that scripture can fit into any one category.

93. Ibid., 31. It is not fully clear that Vanhoozer's reading of Kelsey is accurate, but because the position Vanhoozer attributes to Kelsey is the one against which he argues, this question will not be addressed.

94. Ibid., 35.

95. Ibid.

"one can neither discuss God apart from Scripture nor do justice to Scripture in abstraction from its relation to God. For if the Bible is a species of divine communicative action, it follows that in using Scripture we are not dealing mainly with information about God; we are rather engaging with God himself—with God in communicative action."[96] First theology is then, in the end, hermeneutical theology.[97]

Vanhoozer's Canonical-Linguistic Approach

Vanhoozer argues that the canonical-linguistic approach to theology creatively retrieves the *sola scriptura* principle and connects that principle to the idea of doctrine as something that is to be practiced by the church. This theological view claims that scripture itself, and not as it is used by the church, is the norm for church practice. The use of scripture that is significant in this view is its use by God, particularly when it is used over against the church. Additionally, canonical-linguistic theology focuses on both the drama in the text and the drama that continues in the church as a response to scripture.[98] This approach on its face would then seem to address issues raised earlier concerning the way doctrine has been handled in the church without placing the *sola scriptura* principle in jeopardy in the way that, Vanhoozer claims, Lindbeck's and Grenz's approaches do.

Vanhoozer's vision for canonical-linguistic theology is that it would be what he calls "a Catholic-Evangelical Orthodoxy." It is to be evangelical insofar as it is deeply concerned with speaking and acting with others in ways that are consistent with the gospel. Evangelical theology by itself is not enough. The idea of a *catholic* theology belongs alongside the idea of an *evangelical* theology because the idea of catholicity signifies the whole people of God spread out over space, cultures, and time. The idea of catholicity qualifies the idea of evangelical in that the gospel is a particular message and catholicity defines the scope of its reception.[99] This dialogue between catholic and evangelical theology is not inharmonious,

---

96. Ibid.
97. Vanhoozer writes,
> We are now in a position to respond to our initial query: should theology therefore begin with God or Word of God? The answer is: Neither. I have argued that Christian theologians must resist this pernicious either-or and affirm instead a both-and approach: we interpret Scripture as divine communicative action in order to know God; we let our knowledge of God affect our approach to scripture. . . . Theology, then, is God-centered biblical interpretation. It follows that hermeneutical theology (doing theology by way of biblical interpretation) and theological hermeneutics (bringing Christian doctrine to bear on the principles of interpretation) are equally ultimate. I therefore propose theological hermeneutics as my candidate for first theology. (Ibid., 38)
98. Ibid., 16–17.
99. Ibid., 27.

as Vanhoozer seems to imply is the case in the vision of ecumenical dialogue in Lindbeck's model, but is rather "centered on the gospel and bounded by the canon, which is the gospel's normative specification." Further, he points out, evangelical theology, unlike ecumenical theology, aims not at unity in itself but at truth and edification. This leads to a statement of one of Vanhoozer's central assumptions in writing *The Drama of Doctrine*: "Impossible as it may sound, *doctrine is one of the principle means God uses to build up his church*."[100]

One critical component to the canonical-linguistic proposal is the way in which this kind of theology is dramatic in nature. Vanhoozer writes, "If both the subject matter of Scripture (God in self-communicative action) and the process of interpreting it are dramatic, then so too is theology, the task of bringing one's interpretation of Scripture to bear on the life of the church in the world." The dramatic component of doctrine comes in putting one's understandings of scripture into practice, because ultimately doctrinal truth is of no use unless it is appropriated. A performance of scripture that puts it into practice is the proper end of this kind of doctrine.[101]

While theologians who have taken the cultural-linguistic turn, Vanhoozer argues, tend to focus on the text as used by the believing community, canonical-linguistic theology focuses on the direction the text gives for the believing community. In the end, then, canonical-linguistic theology claims to focus not on the use of scripture in the church but on the use of scripture by the Triune God that makes it canonical.[102] This element connects scripture to the life of the church without taking the way in which the church receives scripture as authoritative. Rather, in Vanhoozer's estimation, canonical-linguistic theology connects scripture to practice by arguing that scripture, in its canonical context, is not simply to be read as propositional truth or read in the context of communal tradition, but is rather something that the people of God are to perform or live out. In this way scripture remains in its place of primacy but is given a role much greater than that in the propositionalist model Vanhoozer critiques. Vanhoozer reveals exactly this kind of preference when he writes, "Who is in a position to give an authentic interpretation of the theo-drama? Specifically, which is the proper locus of authority for theology: the biblical text or the church's use of it?"[103] As has been shown throughout this chapter, for Vanhoozer the answer will always be the biblical text as understood from the perspective of the author.

The emphasis on canonical context in Vanhoozer raises the question of who has authority to interpret the gospel and determine its origin. He concedes that

100. Ibid., 28 (emphasis in original).
101. Ibid., 21.
102. Ibid., 146, 149–50.
103. Ibid., 116.

a focus on biblical primacy raises a critical question: If the locus of authority is in the gospel, who determines what the gospel means? Further, what comes first, the gospel or the church? It is at this point that the concept of canon comes in. Vanhoozer argues that the canonical scriptures alone constitute the necessary means to preserve the identity of the gospel, and thus *sola scriptura* serves *sola euangelia*. Although postliberal theology looks to the Spirit-directed use of scripture in the church for authority, canonical-linguistic theology focuses on the Spirit-directed human testimony to Christ in the scriptures as its ultimate authority.[104]

The canon thus gives both authority and Christian identity to the church because the church is ultimately constituted by scripture. Vanhoozer writes, "The most important reason for doing theology in accord with the canon, then, is that scripture is a divine *covenant* document before it is an ecclesial constitution. The norm with which the church is to assess ongoing developments in its language, thought, and life is the Spirit speaking in the Scriptures."[105] This is connected to the dramatic component of the proposal in that the canon also serves as the norm that determines which performances of scripture are actually faithful to it and which ones diverge from it.[106]

The canon is, at the end of the day, a divine/human performance that calls for further performances in the church. It contains the communicative actions that mediate God's self-communicative act in Jesus Christ from which doctrine is to be derived. Drama is ultimately intended not to convey information but to move individuals to persuade them, delight them, and purge them of unwanted feelings.[107] This raises the question of how the script should be read. Here Vanhoozer connects canonical-linguistic theology to his hermeneutical proposal in *Is There a Meaning in This Text?* by calling for a reading that looks to the illocutionary acts of the author. The church is answerable for what it does with the script, and its responsibility is to "render" the meaning of the drama of redemption in new contexts through its corporate life.[108]

104. Ibid., 124; see also 119. This understanding of the biblical text in its canonical context implies a particular kind of relationship between the Hebrew Bible and the New Testament: Vanhoozer argues that "canonical consciousness" recognizes that both the Hebrew Bible and the New Testament belong and make sense together. The New Testament clearly recognizes itself as related to the Hebrew Bible, and as a result, the two must be read together. The relationship between the two is one of continuity, but not one of simple repetition. It is rather a continuity that transcends and transfigures.

105. Ibid., 133.

106. Ibid., 152.

107. Ibid., 180.

108. Ibid., 183–84. It is important to note that Vanhoozer argues that Lindbeck has begun to point to the illocutionary acts of the author for interpretation and that he is thus moving from the cultural-linguistic approach to something like the canonical-linguistic approach put forth in *The Drama of Doctrine*.

Because Vanhoozer has made such a clear distinction between his own canonical-linguistic theology, which he claims places the primary authority in the canon, and what he claims is the cultural-linguistic theology of Lindbeck and Grenz, which places the primary authority in the way in which the believing community reads and interprets scripture, it is important to consider the role of the believing community in Vanhoozer's approach. The members of the believing community, as a whole, are the actors in the theo-drama, and they are directed in part by the pastor, but much more significantly by the Holy Spirit. The Holy Spirit, sometimes called the "Cinderella of the Trinity,"[109] is particularly important in Vanhoozer's dramatic proposal. The Holy Spirit, who has been involved in the writing, canonizing, and interpretation of the Bible at every stage of the church's history, is active today, directing the readers of the Bible to perform it, putting it into action.[110]

Is the Christian life truly only play-acting? Vanhoozer seems to acknowledge this potential criticism when he writes that the best actors become the roles they play. Similarly, the Christian who is acting the theo-drama is not merely playing a role but is learning how to become that role. Vanhoozer writes, "The drama of doctrine has nothing to do with pretending but everything to do with participating in the once-for-all mission of Jesus Christ and the Holy Spirit. Such participation is neither play-acting nor a matter of Platonic ontology. Christian participation is rather *pneumatic*: those who participate in the theo-dramatic missions do so through union with Christ."[111] As a result, the theo-drama does not mean that its actors are simply performing a role detached from themselves. Rather, they are becoming the roles they play, roles that are very real and not merely the product of an individual's imagination.

Although he emphasizes throughout all his books the primacy of the biblical text and the need to construe the biblical text from what it claims about itself rather than from external sources, Vanhoozer would never claim to have formulated this proposal without interacting with the ideas of others. He points out that his call for a catholic and evangelical theology is connected to that of a generous orthodoxy as discussed by Frei. Frei argues that Lindbeck's proposal about the nature of doctrine does not fully make sense apart from the background context of ecumenical dialogue, because Lindbeck explains how various doctrines can be reconciled without requiring actual doctrinal change. Vanhoozer quotes Frei as stating that apart from this context "we can *'forget [Lindbeck's]*

---

109. Alister McGrath writes, "The Holy Spirit has long been the Cinderella of the Trinity. The other two sisters may have gone to the theological ball; the Holy Spirit got left behind every time" (*Christian Theology: An Introduction* [Oxford: Blackwell, 2006], 235).

110. Vanhoozer, *Drama of Doctrine*, 217.

111. Ibid., 366.

book.'"[112] Vanhoozer wants to be clear that he certainly does not want to "forget Lindbeck's book." He points out some points of overlap between his own work and Lindbeck's, noting that catholic-evangelical theology as he has envisioned it is certainly ecumenical in that it seeks to bring about dialogue among various Christian traditions.[113]

CLARK PINNOCK

Clark Pinnock's obituary in one publication noted that he was "not afraid to change his mind."[114] This is an apt statement that perhaps represents why he is an important figure on the evangelical spectrum. Pinnock was born in Toronto in 1937 and came from a family that was open to theological change. While his parents were liberal Protestants at the time of his birth, they later converted to a more conservative form of evangelicalism. Pinnock was involved with a number of notable evangelical organizations, including Youth for Christ, the Canadian Keswick Bible Conference, and InterVarsity Christian Fellowship while he was in high school and college. He graduated from the University of Toronto and then earned his PhD studying at Manchester University under F. F. Bruce. Pinnock once said that "his career goal was to help the church worship God, 'with freedom, to experience the truth of the Bible in fresh ways, and to be able to share the gospel in a more effective and natural manner.'"[115] Grenz, commenting on Pinnock's work, said that he "has been lauded as an inspiring theological pilgrim by his admirers and condemned as a dangerous renegade by his foes. Yet no story of evangelical theology in the twentieth century is complete without the inclusion of his fascinating intellectual journey from quintessential evangelical apologist to anti-Augustinian theological reformist." Pinnock saw himself as starting out on the right, moving toward the left, and finally ending up in the center.[116]

While Pinnock started his work with fairly conservative theological convictions, by the end of his lifetime he was asserting positions that were considered

112. Ibid., 28. Vanhoozer cites Hans Frei, "Epilogue: George Lindbeck and *The Nature of Doctrine,"* in *Theology and Dialogue: Essays in Conversation with George Lindbeck,* ed. Bruce Marshall (Notre Dame, IN: University of Notre Dame Press, 1990), 277–78 (emphasis in original).

113. Vanhoozer writes, "I do not wish to forget Lindbeck's book. My chosen problematic—the Scripture/tradition relationship—will undoubtedly cast its shadow over the whole book, as the doctrine reconciliation/change problematic did Lindbeck's. Nevertheless, there is some overlap: catholic-evangelical theology is ecumenical in the sense that it aims to foster a lively dialogue among Christian voices across cultures and across centuries" (*Drama of Doctrine,* 29).

114. Doug Koop, "Clark Pinnock Dies at 73," *Christianity Today,* August 17, 2010 (web only), http://www.christianitytoday.com/ct/2010/augustweb-only/43-22.0.html.

115. Ibid.

116. Ibid.

by many evangelicals to be far to the left. One of the most notable areas of debate in which he engaged late in his career was that of open theism. Open theism was a matter of frequent discussion among evangelical theologians in the early 2000s, though the subject had been broached by some long before that. Open theists argue that when one looks at the biblical narrative, there are clear points that indicate that God at times changes direction or acts in a way other than earlier proclamations might suggest. One example is found in Exodus 32. This chapter contains the story of the Israelites fashioning a golden calf to worship while Moses was on Mount Sinai. Exodus depicts God's swift response:

> The LORD said to Moses, "Go down at once! Your people, whom you brought up out of the land of Egypt have acted perversely; they have been quick to turn aside from the way that I commanded them; they have cast for themselves an image of a calf, and have worshipped it and sacrificed to it, and said, 'These are your Gods, O Israel, who brought you up out of the land of Egypt.'" The LORD said to Moses, "I have seen this people, how stiff-necked they are. Now let me alone, so that my wrath may burn hot against them and I may consume them; and of you I will make a great nation." (Exod. 32:7–10)

Moses quickly responded to this proclamation by asking God what the Egyptians might think of the annihilation of the people of Israel. He asks God to not bring about their end but to remember the promises made to Abraham, Isaac, and Jacob. The text then states, "And the LORD changed his mind about the disaster that he planned to bring on his people" (Exod. 32:14).

Open theists argue that the text isn't taken seriously when readers claim that God didn't truly change the divine will but rather planned to change course in response to the intercession of Moses. Unlike most other evangelicals, open theists say that in order to take the biblical text seriously, one must see this event, and others like it, as a genuine change in the divine will. Of course, a change wouldn't be genuine if it was anticipated in advance. As a result, open theists argue that God must not know the future.

The question that is immediately raised is how an all-powerful God cannot know the future. Classical theology has tended to place God outside time and to argue that all moments are present for God. This accounts for God's relationship with the future. Since all time is present now for God, God has knowledge of all events in human history. However, open theists purport that God is in time and experiences time in the same way that human beings do. Even if this were true, one could argue that God has exhaustive knowledge of the future. Open theists say, though, that in order to have genuine relationships with human beings, God has chosen to limit God's knowledge of the future. God does know, according to them, some future things, but God does not know the future concerning individual human beings. As a result, the exchange in Exodus 32 was a genuine one. The open theist will argue that God truly intended to destroy the Israelites, and that God truly decided to spare the Israelites as a result of the intercession of Moses.

Open theism was not received well by most evangelicals. In 2003 the Evangelical Theological Society (ETS) voted to challenge the membership status of Pinnock and another open theist, John Sanders. The basis for the challenge was the claim that Pinnock and Sanders, as open theists, could not uphold ETS's statement of faith, which includes the inerrancy of the Bible. After a vote at ETS's annual meeting, Pinnock and Sanders were able to remain members.

In *Most Moved Mover*, where Pinnock lays out his theology of God's openness, Pinnock explains his theological method. He writes, "My approach to theological method is bi-polar. I believe that theology ought to be faithful and timely and have a double thrust. I must state the truth of the Christian message on the one hand . . . and open up the truth to the present generation on the other. We want to capture the truth of the revelatory foundations, while at the same time being conscious of the contemporary situation."[117] As a result of this, "Theology, then, moves back and forth between two poles, between the eternal truth of the revelatory foundations and the temporal situation in which it is offered and received."[118] Pinnock concedes that this is not an easy task, and as a result, some theologians compromise the truth, while others ignore the role of the contemporary context in theological work.[119]

Pinnock cites four key sources for theological work: the biblical text, tradition, reason, and experience. He argues that his understanding of scripture comes within a "trilateral hermeneutic." This means that, as an evangelical, his first allegiance is to scripture rather than to the other three sources. He writes, "I hold the Bible to be the primary norm for theology in the midst of other sources."[120] The problem with traditional ways of reading the Bible, according to Pinnock, is that it is read through a particular lens. To make a comparison, he notes that Mormons read the Bible through the teachings of Joseph Smith. Similarly, traditional readers of the Bible read it through the lens of Greek philosophy,

117. Clark H. Pinnock, *Most Moved Mover: A Theology of God's Openness* (Grand Rapids: Baker Academic, 2001), 19. Pinnock explicitly references Paul Tillich, writing, "As Paul Tillich put it, theology ought to satisfy two basic needs: to state the truth of the Christian message and interpret the truth for every generation." He cites Tillich, *Systematic Theology*, 1:3.

118. Pinnock, *Most Moved Mover*, 19.

119. Ibid.

120. Ibid. Pinnock argues here that he takes scripture seriously, and perhaps more seriously than classical theists, because as an open theist he does not set aside biblical passages that seem to be at odds with the classical conception of God.

introduced into the Christian tradition in the early centuries of the church's history. Pinnock argues that his own approach is different. He writes,

> In terms of biblical interpretation, I give particular weight to narrative and to the language of personal relationships in it. Biblical history is real history and not a charade. It describes genuine personal interactions, not manipulation. I seek to recover the dynamism of biblical revelation. The story involves real drama and is a unique vehicle of truth and to the interactivity of God. It lifts up God's self-involvement in history, and, supremely, the decision to become incarnate in Jesus Christ. Too often we have privileged the non-historical and supposedly non-metaphorical propositional material. But we have to take it all into account. As McGrath puts it, returning to the narrative of scripture "offers an invaluable catalyst for the cathartic process of purging evangelicalism of the lingering influence of the Enlightenment and reaching behind the enlightenment to recover more authentically evangelical approaches to the role of scripture in Christian life and thought." The Bible offers a narrative that tells of Yahweh, the living God who seeks loving relationships with creatures that are open, dynamic, and personal. We must take seriously how God is depicted in these stories and resist reducing important metaphors to mere anthropomorphic or accommodated language. God's revelation is anthropomorphic through and through. We could not grasp any other kind. We must take it all seriously if not always literally.[121]

This passage encapsulates Pinnock's theology. He also notes that the kind of theology he opposes is the exact kind of theology opposed by Karl Rahner, Bernard Lonergan, and Stanley Grenz. This theology, he claims, is characterized by a proof-texting approach to the Bible, which takes texts out of context in support of a theological system that is already in place. The problem with this approach is that it could be used to make the Bible appear to support anything. This is because the meaning of any text can be discerned only in its broader, original context. Finally, Pinnock writes, the Bible is characterized by both diversity and dialogue. The Bible has many authors, and many authors will result in a multitude of perspectives in the search for the will of God.[122]

For Pinnock, the problem with the way that many contemporary evangelicals read the Bible is that they come to the text with a whole host of assumptions. These assumptions come from the Greek milieu of the centuries immediately following the birth of the church. As a result, the Bible is now frequently read to support an understanding of reality that is not indigenous to the text itself.

---

121. Ibid., 20. He quotes Alister McGrath, *A Passion for Truth: The Intellectual Coherence of Evangelicalism* (Downers Grove: InterVarsity, 1996), 116. He also cites Grenz, *Revisioning Evangelical Theology*, chap. 5.

122. Pinnock, *Most Moved Mover*, 21.

Additionally, taking a propositional approach to the biblical text involves removing statements in the biblical text from their original (and frequently narrative) contexts. When this is done, pieces of biblical passages can be used to support anything.

Ultimately, for Pinnock, authority in theology lies in the Bible, but the theological task can be informed by sources beyond the biblical text. While the text has authority, Pinnock does not endow various interpretations of the Bible with the same authority. His concern is that although evangelicals frequently claim to have no tradition or magisterium, they do prefer particular interpretations that are more indebted to the Greek milieu of the early church than they are to scripture itself. This is a fundamental problem, according to Pinnock.

Conclusion

What Erickson, Grenz, Vanhoozer, and Pinnock all share is an identification with evangelicalism. Even though evangelicalism is a historically complex movement that attracts people from multiple streams of Christianity, it shares some key characteristics that can be seen in each of these four thinkers. What the diverse approaches of these four figures perhaps indicates is an ongoing debate concerning what counts as evangelical. If one had the opportunity to ask Erickson, Grenz, Vanhoozer, and Pinnock about the essence of evangelical theology, they would all say something about the biblical text, but they would disagree about how to read that text. They would also say different things about other sources. This is a result of a larger disagreement about exactly what the bounds of evangelicalism are. Some thinkers would draw a broader circle than others, which makes clear that the question of boundaries is far from settled.

6

Political Theologies

Since his election in 2013, Pope Francis has received a great deal of attention for what some see as his unorthodox ways. Even prior to his election, as the archbishop of Buenos Aires, the then cardinal Jorge Bergoglio was known in part for rejecting the standard accommodations of his office. Cardinal Bergoglio, who entered the Society of Jesus in 1958, took his vows of poverty seriously. He lived in a shared apartment in Buenos Aires and took the bus rather than making use of a driver.

Since being elected pope, Francis has attracted a great deal of attention for similarly rejecting the accommodations available to him as part of his office. He is currently not living in the papal apartment, and he has made himself far more accessible to the crowds of people clamoring to see him than his two predecessors (much to the frustration of his security detail). In what has set the tone for his time as pontiff, Francis stated that in the conclave, when it became apparent that he might be elected pope, a friend of his (an archbishop from Brazil) said, "Don't forget the poor." In telling that story, Francis stated, "Ah, how I would like a church that is poor and is for the poor."[1] While this is certainly a shift in tone from that of many of his predecessors, Francis's move toward a more outspoken concern for the poor is something that resonates with a number of theologians. Those who find themselves in the stream of liberation theology would argue that Francis is doing exactly what the church should have been doing all along.

---

1. Lizzy Davies, "Pope Francis declares: 'I would like to see a church that is poor and is for the poor,'" *Guardian*, March 16, 2013, http://www.theguardian.com/world/2013/mar/16/pope-francis-church-poverty.

"Christian theology is a theology of liberation. It is a rational study of the being of God in the world, in light of the existential situation of an oppressed community, relating the forces of liberation to the essence of the gospel, which is Jesus Christ."[2] So opens James Cone's *A Black Theology of Liberation*. Liberation theology is a stream of theology that begins with the situation of specific people in specific contexts. It has roots in a number of schools of thought, and the first thing that must be noted is that liberation theology varies with the context in which it works.

JOHANN BAPTIST METZ

The origins of liberation theology are somewhat varied, just as the contexts are varied. Some important developments took place in the mid-twentieth century that led to the emergence of liberation theologies. One development was the critique of Karl Rahner's work found in Johann Baptist Metz's work. Chapter 3 discusses Rahner's theological approach and his understanding of universal human religious experience. Before the work of theology can begin, Metz argues, it is important to consider some key questions: "Who does theology? Where? Which is to say, with whom, and in whose interests?"[3]

In other words, Metz is concerned that theology speaks to particular situations on the ground and not simply the universal human experience.[4] Because Rahner's theological work starts with the pre-thematic openness to God that all human beings have, his work universalizes human experience, according to Metz. This approach to theology does not lead to a consideration of actual human experiences in context. The very questions raised above by Metz ask

2. James H. Cone, *A Black Theology of Liberation*, 20th anniversary ed. (Maryknoll, NY: Orbis Books, 1990), 1.

3. Johann Baptist Metz, *Faith in History and Society: Toward a Practical Fundamental Theology*, trans. J. Matthew Ashley (New York: Herder & Herder, 2007), 68. He goes on to say,

Is it enough to refer to the usual division of labor within the church? Is it enough to fall back on the standard subjects (professors and "specialists"), places (universities, seminaries), the usual forms of communication (books and seminars), and interests (the church's mission to teach and evangelize)? It seems to me very important that *theology* pose these questions to itself and that they not be merely imposed on it from the outside, mostly motivated by ideology critique. (Ibid.; emphasis in original)

4. Metz writes,

Besides the fundamental question of the relationship between the subject and praxis, which stands equally in need of more detailed discussion, we are especially confronted with the question of the appropriate *subjects of theology*, or, if you will, the doing of theology. That is to say, must not a practical fundamental theology cultivate in particular a sensitivity for the fact that theology does not simply elaborate and pass down subjectless themes, but must in all of them be 'interrupted' by praxis and by experience? (Ibid.; emphasis in original)

about human experiences in context rather than in abstraction. Metz's primary concern is that even though Rahner argues that explicit human knowledge of God comes from experience in the world, he has universalized this claim.

Metz argues that the historical character of Christian faith is always threatened in its identity, and that because of this, a speculative approach that generalizes experience is problematic. The only way to move forward is with a praxis[5] that looks to narrative and concrete experience rather than to universal religious experience.[6] Metz argues that Rahner's approach never places Christianity in history and, more significantly, never admits that Christianity can potentially be endangered in history. In other words, by moving toward universal human experience, Rahner has created a scenario that removes the subject from any real danger. Metz puts this particularly well when he writes, "Does not transcendentalizing the Christian subject take the edge off of the historical-apocalyptic struggle for Christianity and its identity?"[7] In Metz's view, Rahner's position doesn't seem to pay attention to actual history, despite his emphasis on knowing God and truth in history.

This critique may not be entirely fair to Rahner's position. Rahner always emphasizes that anything known at the categorical level is known through inter-actions in the world and in history. Rahner makes this clear in the opening chapter of *Foundations of Christian Faith* by writing, "Man always experiences himself both in his activity in the world and also in his theoretical, objective reflection as one to whom an historical situation in a world of things and of persons has been given in advance, given without his having chosen it for himself, although it is in it and through it that he discovers and is conscious of transcendence."[8] Rahner always emphasizes the role of the historical in his theology. One example of this is his trinitarian theology. One of the most significant critiques that Rahner makes of Augustine's trinitarian theology is that it does not account for how God is encountered in salvation history. Because of this, Rahner's theology seems to have a theoretical framework for talking about experience in the world and for moving toward practical action. Other scholars have also noted that Rahner's emphasis on the unity of love of neighbor and love of God can be understood as a claim about the unity of the mystical and political dimensions of Christian theology and that such unity allows for solidarity among human beings.[9] In addition, others have pointed out that Rahner emphasizes the importance

---

5. *Praxis* generally just means "practice." In the context of liberation theology, it means the way in which one's life is moved by the Christian gospel, with an emphasis on the ways in which human beings both are shaped by and can be shapers of their context.

6. Metz, *Faith in History and Society*, 149–50.

7. Ibid., 152.

8. Rahner, *Foundations of Christian Faith*, 42.

9. Declan Marmion, "Rahner and His Critics: Revisiting the Dialogue," *Irish Theological Quarterly* 68 (2003): 195. On these points he cites Karl Rahner, *Politische Dimensionen des Christentums:*

of individual conscience and that conscience comes to bear directly on actual political issues, such as nuclear weapons.[10]

Rahner is said to have acknowledged Metz's critique as a significant one.[11] His endorsement of Metz's *Faith in History and Society: Toward a Practical Fundamental Theology* is an interesting statement given the relationship between their theologies: "Finally we have a fundamental theology in which the spiritual and social challenge of our time is taken up and transformed in a new praxis of Christianity and theology." Regardless of any debate about Rahner's views on the person in history and actual concrete events, Metz's work was groundbreaking in that it foregrounded the importance of concrete situations. Even though Rahner writes about such situations late in life, it cannot be found in much of his earlier work.[12] This move toward actual situations opens the door to liberation theology, as does one other important development.

Vatican II

In 1958 Angelo Giuseppe Roncalli was elected pope and took the name John XXIII. His pontificate came on the heels of that of Pius XII, whose pontificate spanned nineteen years. While the proceedings of the conclave that elects a pope are secret, the common wisdom around that particular conclave was that after such a long pontificate, the cardinals were looking for someone who would serve for only a few years and who would generally maintain the status quo at the Vatican.[13] If that thinking is correct, the cardinals received far more than they bargained for from John XXIII. In 1959 John XXIII announced that a council would take place with the aim of refreshing and updating the church. In 1962 the Second Vatican Council opened.[14] While John XXIII did not live to see the end of the council in 1965, its accomplishments were very much in keeping with the direction in which he sought to take the church.

Ausgewählte Texte zu Fragen der Zeit, ed. Herbert Vorgrimler (Munich: Kösel, 1986), and John Sobrino, "Karl Rahner and Liberation Theology," *Theology Digest* 32 (1985): 257–60.

10. Marmion, "Rahner and His Critics," 199. Marmion cites Rahner's article "Nuclear Weapons and the Christian," which appeared in vol. 23 of *Theological Investigations*.

11. Roberto S. Goizueta, "Karl Rahner," in *Beyond the Pale: Reading Theology from the Margins*, ed. Miguel A. De La Torre and Stacey M. Floyd-Thomas (Louisville: Westminster John Knox, 2011), 179.

12. I have treated the question of Metz's critique of Rahner in "Relation and Person: Potential Contributions of Karl Rahner's Theology to Evangelical Trinitarian Debates," in *The New Evangelical Subordinationism? Perspectives on the Equality of God the Father and God the Son*, ed. Dennis W. Jowers and H. Wayne House (Eugene, OR: Wipf & Stock, 2012), 311–24.

13. Mark A. Noll, *Turning Points: Decisive Moments in the History of Christianity*, 3rd ed. (Grand Rapids: Baker Academic, 2012), 290.

14. Ibid.

The Second Vatican Council was a watershed moment in the history of the church. It produced sixteen official documents that addressed every facet of the church, from the formation of priests to respect for religious liberty to problems facing the modern world. While the entire council has shaped the trajectory of recent Catholic theology, *Gaudium et Spes*, the Pastoral Constitution on the Church in the Modern World, has been particularly important for liberation theology.

Gaudium et Spes

Gaudium et Spes opens with these words: "The joys and the hopes, the griefs and the anxieties of the men of this age, especially those who are poor or are in any way afflicted, these too are the joys and hopes, the griefs and anxieties of the followers of Christ. Indeed, nothing genuinely human fails to raise an echo in their hearts."[15] In this document, the council fathers showed their clear concern for the problems facing the world. In this way, *Gaudium et Spes* continued the trajectory begun by Leo XIII (1878–1903) and his successors in the tradition of Catholic social teaching.

Gaudium et Spes was promulgated in 1965, and many of the problems it points out can be directly connected to pressing events in the 1960s. It makes reference to racism, and it notes that although there had been recent growth in prosperity, much of the world faces desperate poverty.[16] *Gaudium et Spes* also notes the growth of technology and acknowledges the many ways in which technological development can shape the trajectory of society.[17] The Second Vatican Council opened in the same year that the Cuban Missile Crisis occurred, and *Gaudium et Spes* alludes to this, arguing that the horrors of war are intensified by the presence of scientific weapons. It condemned the use of such weapons and notes that if armories already in place were fully deployed, it would cause an existential threat to humanity.[18]

Medellín

The significance of *Gaudium et Spes* to both the larger project of the Second Vatican Council and the trajectory of Catholic theology since cannot be overstated. One of the key ways it shaped that trajectory lies in how it was

15. *Gaudium et Spes* 1, in *The Documents of Vatican II*, ed. Walter M. Abbott (New York: Guild Press, 1966), 199–200. Document available at http://www.vatican.va/archive/hist_councils/ii_vatican _council/documents/vat-ii_const_19651207_gaudium-et-spes_en.html.

16. *Gaudium et Spes* 4.

17. *Gaudium et Spes* 5.

18. *Gaudium et Spes* 80.

interpreted by the Latin American bishops. In 1968 the bishops of the Latin American Catholic Bishops' Conference met at Medellín, Colombia. The aim of this meeting was to discuss the ways in which the Second Vatican Council could speak specifically to the Latin American context.

At that meeting, the bishops discussed the situation of many in Latin America. They noted that the young in Latin America did not have universal access to quality education, women did not have equality with men, peasants lived in poor conditions, and workers did not have economic security. Many of those with more skilled training had left for more developed countries, and Latin American industrialists had become increasingly dependent on international businesses. The bishops' words at the end of this section are particularly apt: "We cannot ignore this phenomenon of almost universal frustration of legitimate aspirations which creates the climate of collective anguish in which we are already living."[19]

The bishops closed the opening of the document by making reference to the unjust structures that they held characterized the Latin American situation. In effect, the bishops looked at the Latin American context and saw a system that they believe was fundamentally unjust. They had to address it because the church had already made clear that the concerns and problems of this world were problems and concerns for the church. In the section of the document that focuses on doctrine, the bishops argue that the goods of creation should be allocated in a just manner. It is ultimately sin that brings about social evils like hunger and oppression, and it is to liberate human beings from this that God sent Christ into the world.[20] In order for liberation to happen, though, human beings need "a profound conversion" to the kingdom.[21]

Most scholars point to this meeting as the origin of liberation theology. Although some of what was said there was also stated in earlier church documents (typically in documents found in the corpus of Catholic social teaching), it is also the case that the bishops made some more pointed critiques toward the prevailing powers in Latin America and the larger world. The bishops argued that Latin American businesses failed to treat workers as people endowed with human dignity but rather treated them as a means to an end.[22] In response to

19. Conference of Latin American Bishops (CELAM), "Justice," September 6, 1968, Medellín, Colombia, §1. Document accessed at http://theolibrary.shc.edu/resources/medjust.htm.

20. "It is the same God who, in the fullness of time, sends his Son in the flesh, so that he might come to liberate everyone from the slavery to which sin has subjected them: hunger, misery, all oppression and ignorance, in a word, that injustice and hatred which have their origin in human selfishness" (ibid., §3).

21. Ibid.

22. "The system of Latin American business enterprises, and through it the current economy, responds to an erroneous conception concerning the right of ownership of the means of production

this problem, the bishops called on business owners to radically change their views of business.[23] Ultimately, the bishops argued that the changes that were needed could come about only via political reform. It is the role of the state to ensure that all people are able to participate and be represented in government, even if achieving this required a significant change in the ways in which government is administered.[24]

The bishops surprised many with the frankness with which they addressed the problems facing Latin America. Their message is clear about the ways in which larger forces are culpable when they refer to "international monopolies and international imperialism of money" imposed on Latin America.[25] Perhaps most important, they include the church in their analysis. The bishops acknowledge that many have complained that the members of the church hierarchy are part of the small class that controls the bulk of the resources. They further concede that there are many things about the church (including extravagant buildings, rectories, and religious houses; expensive vehicles; and ornate attire) that contribute to those complaints. They further cite taxes and tuition that support the clergy and the secrecy with which the church keeps its finances.[26] These things all give the impression that the Latin American church is a wealthy church. At the same time, the bishops are clear that this is a false impression. They note that many of the parishes in Latin America are extremely poor and that the majority of bishops, priests, and religious live simply and devote their lives to the service of the poor. This, they say, isn't something that is noticed by many people, though, and it doesn't help dissuade anyone from the overall perception that the church is a wealthy church.[27] The bishops call for the church to take up the spirit of poverty by living simple lives in solidarity with the poor.

---

and the very goals of the economy. A business, in an authentically human economy, does not identify itself with the owners of capital, because it is fundamentally a community of persons and a unit of work, which is in need of capital to produce goods. A person or group of persons cannot be the properties of an individual, of a society, or of the state" (ibid., §10).

23. Ibid.

24. Ibid., §16.

25. Conference of Latin American Bishops (CELAM), "Peace," September 6, 1968, Medellín, Colombia, §9. Document accessed at http://theolibrary.shc.edu/resources/medpeace.htm. "We wish to emphasize that the principal guilt for economic dependence of our countries rests with powers, inspired by uncontrolled desire for gains, which leads to economic dictatorship and the 'international imperialism of money' condemned by Pope Pius XI in *The Reconstruction of the Social Order* and by Pope Paul VI in *The Development of Peoples*."

26. Conference of Latin American Bishops (CELAM), "Poverty of the Church," September 6, 1968, Medellín, Colombia, §2.

27. Ibid., §3.

GUSTAVO GUTIÉRREZ

The Medellín meeting is widely recognized as the origin of Latin American liberation theology. It was followed by the release of Gustavo Gutiérrez's *A Theology of Liberation* in 1971. Gutiérrez is a Peruvian born priest who began his career ministering among the poor in Lima. For Gutiérrez, theology is fundamental to life. All believers do theology, because all believers seek to understand the faith. As a result, the work of theology is intrinsic to a life of faith.[28]

Praxis

Gutiérrez notes that theological study continues to evolve today. While in the early church, theology was understood as wisdom, and in the medieval church, theology was understood as science, theology today must be considered in the context of a critical reflection on praxis.[29]

In some ways, theology as critical reflection is not new. Gutiérrez points out that Augustine's *City of God* gives a theology of history that is based on Augustine's context and the challenges that context has posed to the church. After considering a number of historical moments, Gutiérrez points out that *Gaudium et Spes* calls on every Christian to "[discern] the signs of the times." Pastors and theologians in particular are called to examine the contemporary context and consider it in relation to the Word of God.[30] Ultimately, theology must be a critical reflection on humanity. Part of the work of theology must include a consideration of economic and social issues in the contemporary context. Because of this, theology will necessarily be a criticism of society and the church.[31]

Undergirding all Gutiérrez's claims is that theology is a reflection on pastoral action. It is in pastoral activity that the Holy Spirit can be found bringing about the action of the Christian community. Connected to this, Gutiérrez claims that theology is always linked to praxis and seeks to understand historical events with the intention of revealing and proclaiming their meaning.[32] In other words, theology is always connected to action, and theology always reads the signs of the times. Theology's role must be prophetic, which means that it must be willing to critique the prevailing powers—and this includes the church—when necessary.

Gutiérrez is sometimes accused of understanding this account of theology as something that supersedes earlier understandings of theology. He wants to

---

28. Gustavo Gutiérrez, *A Theology of Liberation*, rev. ed. (Maryknoll, NY: Orbis Books, 1988), 3.
29. Ibid., 3–5.
30. Ibid., 5–7.
31. Ibid., 9.
32. Ibid., 9–10. He writes on p. 10, "Theology as critical reflection thus fulfills a liberating function for humankind as the Christian community, preserving them from fetishism and idolatry as well as from a pernicious and belittling narcissism."

be clear that this is not the case. Theology is still wisdom and rational knowledge; now, though, wisdom and rational knowledge will have "ecclesial praxis" as their starting point and context. Theology as praxis lays the groundwork for a distinctively Latin American theology. This is a theology that should always look to the future and endow that future with hope.[33]

Gutiérrez believes that liberation is connected to development, though they are not the same thing. He notes that development deals with an improvement in living conditions. One thing that must be clear, he argues, is that development cannot be understood as simply an improvement in economic status. He cites Colin Clark, who argues that the goal of economic activity should not be wealth but rather well-being.[34] Gutiérrez suggests that development is better understood as a social process that encompasses economic, social, political, and cultural realms. These various realms are interdependent, and growth in one requires growth in the others.[35] Viewing development in this way implies a concern for human values. It also places development itself in a broader context where humanity is able to control its own destiny. This idea is directly connected to what Gutiérrez calls "liberation."[36]

Liberation

In order to understand Gutiérrez's approach to theology, it is important to understand his definition of liberation. One of the first things he points out is that the word *development* has become problematic in Latin America because policies connected to it have broadly changed. In addition to this, development typically entails poorer countries seeking out the assistance of more wealthy countries. Poorer countries eventually realize that their lack of development is not isolated but is rather the product of the overdevelopment of other countries. In order to become truly developed, poor countries need to break free of the holds that wealthier countries have on them. In other words, only a complete break with what Gutiérrez refers to as the "status quo" will allow for the kind of change needed. This break with the status quo will involve changing the way property is acquired and held, and it will also involve giving the lower classes access to power. Gutiérrez describes this as nothing less than a social revolution. The better word for these changes is liberation.[37]

One of the key assumptions that undergirds Gutiérrez's understanding of liberation is that humanity is in control of its own destiny. Human beings in

33. Ibid., 11.
34. Ibid., 14.
35. Ibid., 15.
36. Ibid., 16.
37. Ibid., 15–16.

the contemporary context are seeking two things. The first is liberation from exterior pressures that prevent fulfillment for members of some social classes, countries, or societies. Second, human beings seek an interior liberation that frees them from an interior experience of dependency on outside social forces.[38] History itself is a process of human liberation, and history has not yet reached its conclusion. As a result, Gutiérrez argues that a liberative approach will see the human being as oriented toward the future. The human being acts in the present in anticipation of tomorrow.[39]

For Gutiérrez, the biblical message depicts the work of Christ as the work of liberation. Although for much of Christian history this reality was not emphasized, Gutiérrez argues that the idea is present in the writings of Paul, who frequently speaks of the significance of freedom in Christ.[40] Sin is fundamentally a failure to love one's neighbor and, by extension, a failure to love God. In Gutiérrez's reading of the Bible, sin is the cause of poverty, injustice, and oppression. At the same time, he wants to be clear that viewing sin as the cause of these things does not mean that significant structures of society aren't at fault. Rather, behind any kind of structure of society that brings about oppression and injustice, there is a will (whether personal or collective) to reject God.[41]

Gutiérrez argues that in the past, theologies that dealt with social action didn't fully account for what he refers to as the political dimension. Rather, theology stressed individuals' private lives, and things that were political or that dealt with the church in public life were considered less important. In addition to this, Gutiérrez points out that Christians have often emphasized the parts of the gospel that are more conciliatory, while ignoring parts that are political or confrontational. There is a significant political dimension to the gospel, though, and Gutiérrez argues that the contemporary context demands that we engage it.[42]

The Integral

Gutiérrez critiques earlier approaches to theology that completely separated the human and material from the supernatural. These approaches held that the supernatural was fundamentally alien to humanity and that humanity was passive in the face of the supernatural. This view resulted in a move among some theologians toward an approach that still held that the natural and the

38. Ibid., 20.
39. Ibid., 21.
40. Ibid., 23.
41. Ibid., 24.
42. Ibid., 31–32.

supernatural were distinct, but emphasized the openness of the human spirit to God.[43]

The import of the theological moves made here is the reaffirmation of the human being moving toward God. Karl Rahner, as discussed in chapter 3, emphasizes both the universal salvific will of God toward humanity, which results in human beings having access (even if only on the subconscious level) to some element of God's grace, and the human orientation toward God. For Rahner, the human state is one that is not supernatural but is inevitably oriented toward the supernatural.[44] This is significant for Gutiérrez, because it moves from a partitioning of the supernatural and the material to an emphasis on the integral. The integral focuses on the development of the whole person rather than compartmentalizing the various facets of a human being.[45] One clear result of this is that the relationship between the church and the world, or the spiritual and material, becomes closer. No longer are these separate things that are relegated to their own specific territories. Rather, the whole person (for example) has a physical body with material needs but also has a soul with spiritual needs. Further, the work of the church now can directly address the problems of the world. Gutiérrez argues that Metz put it best when he said, "Is not the Church also world? . . . The Church is of the world: in a certain sense the Church is the world: the Church is not Non-World."[46] Above all else, these moves have one crucial result for Gutiérrez's theology—they affirm "the single vocation to salvation." What Gutiérrez means by this is that it is now clear that action done to better the conditions of people in the temporal world has spiritual value. There is no question now that work to bring about a more just world has value in the kingdom of God. Because of this, the work of liberation is directly connected to the Christian understanding of salvation.[47]

A "social revolution" is the only thing that can bring the significant changes needed to the conditions under which most people in Latin America live.[48] Gutiérrez notes (and here it is important to remember that he is writing this text in 1971) that groups have appeared in Latin America seeking to mobilize

43. Ibid., 43–44.

44. Ibid., 44.

45. He writes, "Integral vocation and integral development are expressions which tend to stress the unity of the call to salvation" (ibid., 45).

46. Ibid., 46. He quotes Johann Baptist Metz, *Theology of the World* (New York: Scribner, 1968), 93.

47. Gutiérrez writes, "This affirmation of the single vocation to salvation, beyond all distinctions, gives religious value in a completely new way to human action in history, Christian and non-Christian alike. The building of a just society has worth in terms of the Kingdom, or in more current phraseology, to participate in the process of liberation is already, in a certain sense, a salvific work" (*Theology of Liberation*, 46).

48. Ibid., 54.

the masses. These have typically taken the form of leftist guerilla groups. The situation is such that Gutiérrez can say, "In Latin America we are in the midst of a full-blown process of revolutionary ferment. This is a complex and changing situation which resists schematic interpretations and demands a continuous revision of the postures adopted."[49] Even though this is occurring, Gutiérrez argues that the realities of poverty and exploitation in Latin America call for radical change. The groups that are seeking these kinds of radical change are usually doing so under the banner of socialism, but he also points out that these movements can't be considered monolithically. There is some diversity in both strategy and tactics among these various groups.[50]

Liberation must go beyond simply breaking chains of economic, political, and social dependence, according to Gutiérrez. It must also include a move toward human beings understanding themselves as free from servitude and having the ability to shape their own futures. It fundamentally entails seeking a new humanity. This seeking of a new humanity is vital to the work of liberation (and, as will be seen, this is precisely where the Christian faith comes in). In addition to this, though, this liberation must be initiated by the oppressed.[51] This may be where some confusion comes in regarding liberation theology. Liberation theology, as Gutiérrez articulates it, will focus on those who are oppressed and seeking their own liberation. The task of the oppressed in the work of liberation is to reject the oppression that burdens them, instead becoming aware of their situation and finding ways in which to describe it. This makes them less dependent and more free, and from here they are able to begin the work of changing society. Gutiérrez is clear that coming to this state of mind is an ongoing work and not something that is mastered at any particular point. But this is the work that will ultimately bring about the liberation of the oppressed.[52]

The role of the church is to participate in this work of liberation and to live in solidarity with the poor and the oppressed. Gutiérrez wants to make clear that the church must not ally itself with the dominant forces that create the

49. Ibid., 55.

50. Ibid., 55–56.

51. Gutiérrez quotes Che Guevara: "We revolutionaries often lack the knowledge and intellectual audacity to face the task of development of a new human being by methods different from conventional ones, and the conventional methods suffer from the influence of the society that created them" (ibid., 56–57). The quote from Guevara is from "Man and Socialism in Cuba," in Venceremos! The Speeches and Writings of Ernesto Che Guevara, ed. John Gerassi (New York: The Macmilian Company, 1968), 396.

52. Citing Paulo Freire (Pedagogy of the Oppressed [New York: Herder and Herder, 1970]), Gutiérrez writes, "In this process, which Freire calls 'conscientization,' the oppressed reject the oppressive consciousness which dwells in them, become aware of their situation, and find their own language. They become, by themselves, less dependent and freer, as they commit themselves to the transformation and building up of society" (ibid., 57).

oppression that characterizes much of the Latin American churches. He is also clear that the church has already been doing this for some time. While the church sought the support of those in power earlier in its history (which he dates to the sixteenth century and the Catholic Reformation / Counter-Reformation), the Latin American church is now (along with individual Christians and small communities) seeking to be aware of its current reality and understand the things that bring it about. This has led the Latin American church to advocate liberation even though there are many who would seek to prevent this move.[53]

Liberation involves fundamental change, and therefore it requires a break from the past. While Gutiérrez acknowledges that the people calling for this were initially few in number, that count is growing and their voices are being heard more clearly in the church. This can involve multiple constituencies within the church. One of the most important groups within the church to take on this task is the laity. While lay movements in the past tended to be politically moderate, Gutiérrez notes that such groups have become more radical, particularly when those involved are younger. The by-product of this is a clash between some of these movements and the hierarchy.[54]

At the same time, there are many priests in Latin America who are labeled "subversive." Gutiérrez writes,

> Frequently in Latin America today certain priests are considered "subversive." Many are under surveillance or are being sought by the police. Others are in prison, have been expelled from their country (Brazil, Bolivia, Colombia, and the Dominican Republic are significant examples), or have been murdered by terrorist anti-communist groups. For the defenders of the status quo, "priestly subversion" is surprising. They are not used to it. The political activity of some leftist groups, we might say, is—within certain limits—assimilated and tolerated by the system and is even useful to it to justify some of its repressive measures; the dissidence of priests and religious, however, appears as particularly dangerous, especially if we consider the role which they have traditionally played.[55]

In other words, the laity has played a key role in the rise of some of the more militant groups described by Gutiérrez. This puts them at odds with a hierarchy that is too often allied with the prevailing powers in Latin America. Gutiérrez paints a more diverse picture when priests, rather than bishops, are discussed. Many priests have become more politically active and seek to live and minister in solidarity with the poor.

53. Gutiérrez, *Theology of Liberation*, 58.
54. Ibid., 59.
55. Ibid., 62.

Ultimately, Gutiérrez argues that the role of the church must be one of solidarity with the poor and oppressed in Latin America. The church cannot somehow see itself as exempt or above the reality on the ground in Latin America, because it has supported injustice both in the ways it is connected to the prevailing powers and in how it has remained silent about the abuses inflicted by those prevailing powers.[56] At Medellín, the bishops noted the situation in Latin America and described it as "institutionalized violence," which Gutiérrez states is responsible for the deaths of thousands of people.[57]

Despite talk of institutionalized or unjust violence, Gutiérrez and the Latin American clergy do not argue for a strictly nonviolent approach. Rather, they make a distinction between the "unjust" violence of the oppressor and the "just" violence of the oppressed who see no other choice but to use violence to achieve liberation.[58]

One last concept to bear in mind regarding Gutiérrez's thought is his understanding of sin. For Gutiérrez, sin is not simply an individual affront to one other person or to God. Rather, situations, systems, and institutions can be sinful. Gutiérrez characterizes sin as a social and historical reality in which relationships with God and other people are broken. This account gets us back to a more collective understanding of sin.[59] It is a more thoroughgoing recognition of how sin has affected every facet of creation rather than just one's own standing before God.

Gutiérrez's Sources

One of the distinctive features of liberation theology is its use of the findings of the social sciences. Gutiérrez cites Marx a number of times in *A Theology of Liberation* and also alludes to his work in several other places. He writes that contemporary theology makes use of conversation with Marx's work and that

---

56. He quotes the Peruvian bishops who write, "We recognize that we Christians for want of fidelity to the Gospel have contributed to the present unjust situation through our words and attitudes, our silence and inaction." He also notes that the bishops and laity in El Salvador have written, "Our church has not been effective in liberating and bettering the Salvadoran. This failure is due in part to the above-mentioned incomplete concept of human salvation and the mission of the Church and in part to the fear of losing privileges or suffering persecution" (ibid., 63).

57. Ibid., 64.

58. Ibid.

59. He writes,

But in the liberation approach sin is not considered as an individual, private, or merely interior reality—asserted just enough to necessitate "spiritual" redemption which does not challenge the order in which we live. Sin is regarded as a social, historical fact, the absence of fellowship and love in relationships among persons, the break of friendship with God and with other persons, and therefore, an interior, personal fracture. When it is considered in this way, the collective dimensions of sin are rediscovered. (Ibid., 103)

Marx's work has helped theology to understand what its own work might mean for the positive change of this present world.[60] Gutiérrez envisions a fundamental change in life as human beings currently know it. This would include changes in the private property system, access to power for those who are marginalized, and a "social revolution" that would bring about "a new society, a socialist society," or would at least allow for the possibility of such a society.[61]

One of the things that concerns some critics of liberation theology is its use of a thinker who so thoroughly critiques the notion of religion. There are ways to make critiques about religion without denying the importance of life-giving faith. At the same time, Marx is famous for referring to religion as "the opium of the people."[62] This statement is often taken out of context as a simple dismissal of religion as a whole. Here is the longer statement Marx made about this:

> Religious suffering is, at one and the same time, the expression of real suffering and a protest against real suffering. Religion is the sigh of the oppressed creature, the heart of a heartless world, and the soul of soulless conditions. It is the opium of the people. The abolition of religion as the illusory happiness of the people is the demand for their real happiness. To call on them to give up their illusions about their condition is to call on them to give up a condition that requires illusions. The criticism of religion is, therefore, in embryo, the criticism of that vale of tears of which religion is the halo.[63]

Clearly, Marx is not simply dismissing religion. Rather, he seems to be saying that religion is used as a way to keep the people who are oppressed from seeing the injustice of their situations. This does not mean that Marx is friendly to religion, but what this does mean is that Marx's statement about religion as an opium seems to be less about faith in a divine being and more about the ways in which religion can be used to keep those who are marginalized from protesting their status. This is exactly the kind of critique Gutiérrez wants to make about the role of the church in oppression. The key distinction between Gutiérrez and Marx is that Gutiérrez is far more interested in how a thoroughgoing faith in the liberating work of Christ can bring about the social changes that they both agree are needed. Marx is certainly uninterested in how Christian faith might bring about change (because he ultimately doesn't believe), but his vision of change is something that resonates with Gutiérrez.

60. Ibid., 8.
61. Ibid., 17.
62. Karl Marx, "A Contribution to the Critique of Hegel's Philosophy of Right," *Deutsch-Französische Jahrbücher*, February 1844.
63. Ibid.

In addition to scripture and the findings of the social sciences, Gutiérrez also refers to the Christian tradition. Unsurprisingly, he cites *Gaudium et Spes* frequently and also refers to other documents from the corpus of Catholic social teaching, including *Mater et Magistra, Pacem in Terris, Populorum Progressio, Sollicitudo Rei Socialis, Quadragesimo Anno,* and others. He also cites the work of contemporary Catholic theologians such as Karl Rahner, Edward Schillebeeckx, and Johann Baptist Metz. Finally, he cites significant historical figures such as Augustine, Thomas Aquinas, and Bartolomé de Las Casas.

Most importantly, Gutiérrez emphasizes the need to start one's theological work with the on-the-ground situation. While many twentieth-century theologians discuss whether one's work should start with God, the biblical text, or universal human experience, it is Gutiérrez who turns to the particular for his work. He is not alone, nor is liberation theology alone, as will be seen as this chapter moves to black theology and when the next chapter considers feminist theologies.

Black Theology

Historical Background

African Americans have had a particularly challenging history in the United States. People of African descent were forcibly brought to the United States via the middle passage from the sixteenth century into the nineteenth century. The institution of slavery in the United States lasted several decades after the formal ending of the slave trade. While scholars debate whether slavery was a contributing factor to the Civil War, President Lincoln's Emancipation Proclamation in 1863 ended slavery in the states that had seceded from the Union (note that this did not include Kentucky, Maryland, and Missouri, all of which had slavery but also remained part of the Union). The Thirteenth Amendment to the US Constitution, which was passed by Congress in January 1865 and ratified by the states in December 1865, formally ended slavery and involuntary servitude.

While African Americans in the South made some significant progress during the period of Reconstruction immediately after the Civil War, the end of Reconstruction brought the rise of the black codes, the growth of oppressive sharecropping, and the transition into the Jim Crow period. It is hard to overestimate the impact that the Jim Crow period had. With so many students today born well after the civil rights movement, it is easy to think of the Jim Crow period as a time in which schools, housing, and lunch counters were segregated and that was the extent of the problem. An honest look at history, though, reveals that the period was characterized by a system that dehumanized an entire group of people on the basis of skin color.

One of the most tragic features of this time period was the reality of frequent lynching. The NAACP undertook an anti-lynching campaign in 1920. Part of this campaign involved flying a flag outside its New York City headquarters that read, "A man was lynched yesterday." This flag remained flying until 1938. Sadly, it was not the end of lynching that brought the flag down but rather the threat of the NAACP losing its lease.[64]

Although lynching was a frequent occurrence during the Jim Crow period, it is still hard to have it included in US history curricula for secondary schools. James Lowen documents this problem, noting that showing a photo of a lynching can often lead to a particular text being rejected for use in public schools in certain states.[65] Even more disturbing is that even a quick glance at any one of the many photos of lynchings shows the white people present posing for the camera. They were typically dressed up and had their children with them. This says something powerful about how children were being taught about race and how those being photographed did not fear any serious reprisal for their actions.

The Sin of Ham

Both during the period of slavery and after it, many white Christians claimed theological justification for the systems under which African Americans lived. The root of such argumentation lies in the discussion of the sin of Ham in Genesis 9. According to Genesis, after Noah and his sons came out of the ark, Noah planted a vineyard. After drinking some of the wine that he made, Noah became drunk and passed out in his tent without any clothing. Ham (whose son was Canaan) saw Noah's nakedness and told his brothers about it. His brothers Shem and Japheth covered Noah with a garment without themselves seeing his nakedness.

When Noah awoke, he became aware of what Ham had done. He spoke in no uncertain terms about this, saying,

> Cursed be Canaan;
>> the lowest of slaves shall he be to his brothers.

According to the text, he also said,

> Blessed by the LORD my God be Shem;
>> and let Canaan be his slave.

64. Library of Congress Exhibition, "NAACP: A Century in the Fight for Freedom," https://www.loc.gov/exhibits/naacp.

65. James Lowen, *Lies My Teacher Told Me* (New York: Touchstone), 2007.

> May God make space for Japheth,
>   and let him live in the tents of Shem;
>   and let Canaan be his slave.[66]

This is an odd story. Most modern readers of the Bible would not read this passage and jump to questions about race. A couple of contextual notes make sense of this story. First, for a son to see his father in Noah's state was to fail the father. Ham's role should have been to cover Noah and not tell anyone else about the incident. Ham compounded his sin by telling his brothers. Shem and Japheth do their proper duty by covering their father so that no more shame is brought on him. Some scholars have suggested that there is also some kind of sexual transgression involved in Ham's actions because Genesis 9:24 states that Noah knew after waking what his son had done to him. Further, this story takes on ethnographic import, with Noah cursing not Ham himself but Ham's son Canaan.[67]

The next chapter of Genesis tells us that Ham's descendants include Cush, Egypt, Put, and Canaan (Gen. 10:6). That means that the Hamites generally live to the south but also include Canaan, which was once a province of the Egyptian Empire. This means that Canaan will, centuries later, be associated with Africa in the minds of some biblical interpreters. Although the text itself never claims that Ham has dark skin, Ham and his descendants are eventually associated with Africa.

Early interpreters of the biblical text assumed that the flood mentioned in Genesis 7–9 was a global phenomenon that ended the human race, save for Noah, his wife, and their sons. As a result, all human beings were understood as tracing their ancestry to Ham, Shem, and Japheth. Because Ham was associated with Africa, he was believed to be the father of all people of African descent. This was a common view at the time that African slavery was growing, and as a result, Noah's curse of Ham was used to justify the slave trade.[68]

The origin of this interpretation of the biblical text may be rabbinic Judaism. Some statements in the Midrash, Talmud, and later medieval texts seem to indicate that God cursed the descendants of Ham with dark skin and lives of slavery. The Midrash on Genesis, which dates to the fifth century, makes reference to Ham coming from the ark with dark skin, and the Babylonian Talmud, which dates to the sixth century, makes a similar statement.[69] Despite this, the

---

66. This story is found in Gen. 9:18–27. The quotation is from Gen. 9:25–27.
67. *Harper Collins Study Bible*, ed. Harold Attridge (San Francisco: HarperSanFrancisco, 1997), notes on 9:22–24 and 9:25–27.
68. Edwin M. Yamauchi, "The Curse of Ham," *Criswell Theological Review* 6, no. 2 (Spring 2009): 45.
69. Ibid., 49.

evidence is not as clear as it might appear. Remember that Noah cursed Canaan in the text. While Canaan and Cush are both sons of Ham, the biblical text and later rabbinic sources clearly depict Cush as the forefather of people from Africa. Rabbinic literature follows the biblical text in seeing Canaan, rather than Ham, as the one who was cursed.[70]

How, then, did the curse of Canaan become theological justification for the institution of slavery? Because the context of James Cone's theology (see next section) is in the United States, it is important to understand how the curse of Ham was understood among the early Americans. Although British sailors were involved in the slave trade beginning in the mid-sixteenth century, slaves were first brought to the British colonies in the early seventeenth century. In 1644 a group of Boston merchants began to organize trips to Africa for the procurement of slaves. The slave trade grew quickly in the British colonies. Between 1680 and 1700, more than three hundred thousand slaves were brought into the colonies.[71]

The earliest use of Genesis 9 to justify slavery is found in the 1670s, though some have argued that this type of argument played a minor role until the period immediately prior to the American Civil War. One can find numerous writers in the antebellum South who cite the sin of Ham as justification for the slave trade. Interestingly, the most influential proponent of this view was Josiah Priest, a preacher from New York, rather than a person from the South. Priest wrote,

> God, who made all things, and endowed all animated nature with the strange and unexplained power of propagation, superintended the formation of two sons of Noah, in the womb of their mother, in an extraordinary and supernatural manner, giving to these two children such forms of bodies, constitution of natures, and complexion of skin, as suited his will. Japheth he caused to be born white, differing from the red color of his parents, while he caused Ham to be born black, a color still further removed from the red hue of his parents than was white.[72]

Another influential preacher described those of African descent as "descendants of Ham, the beastly and degraded son of Noah."[73] A recent study has also found at least fifty documents from the antebellum South that cite Noah's curse

---

70. Ibid., 50. Yamauchi cites Ephraim Isaac, "Genesis, Judaism, and the 'Sons of Ham,'" *Slavery & Abolition* 1 (1980): 17. He also points out that Talmudic literature was not generally read by the general Jewish population, much less any non-Jewish population. As a result, its influence would have been nonexistent for other readers of the biblical text.

71. Yamauchi, "Curse of Ham," 55.

72. Ibid. Yamauchi cites L. Richard Bradley, "The Curse of Canaan and the American Negro," *Concordia Theological Monthly* 42, no. 2 (1971): 102, as the source of this quotation, which originally comes from Priest's *Bible Defense of Slavery*.

73. Yamauchi, "Curse of Ham," 56. He quotes Thornton Stringfellow, *Slavery: Its Origin, Nature and History Considered in the Light of Bible Teachings, Moral Justice, and Political Wisdom* (New York:

as the central justification for slavery. As the abolitionist movement grew, so did the voices of those who would use the biblical text to justify the oppression of an entire group of people.[74]

JAMES CONE

James Cone was born to a family in the Deep South, spending his childhood in the 1940s and 1950s in Bearden, Arkansas. Cone sees Bearden and the church he attended while growing up as foundational for his vocation. While writing, Cone imagines the people of Bearden around his desk, calling him to speak for his people.[75]

Cone's experience in Bearden gave him two key insights. It exposed him to the harsh realities of the Jim Crow period, and it instilled a faith that maintained his own dignity even in the midst of the unjust Jim Crow context. The side-by-side experience of the injustice of the Jim Crow system and his own deep faith created a tension for Cone that remains unresolved for him. Growing up, Cone says, he spoke with his brothers about their own suffering in light of Christian faith, as if these questions were new rather than perennial problems for the faith.[76]

The faith of the church is what sustained the community, according to Cone. He writes, "God was that reality to which the people turned for identity and worth because the existing social, political, and economic structures said that they were nobody. How were they to know that they were somebody when their humanity was not recognized by the existing arrangement, and when it appeared that they were powerless to do anything about it?"[77] Cone notes that in the eyes of God, African Americans are children of God who are not defined by their white oppressors. Although African Americans in this context were not valued in society, they were valued in the church.[78]

As Cone undertook his studies, he became increasingly convinced of the justice of the African American cause. It didn't matter what white pastors and politicians said about Christian love or the importance of law and order. The problem was that if he rejected the words of the pastors, he didn't have a theological framework in which to advocate for the African American cause. Cone

---

J. F. Trow, 1861), as cited by James O. Buswell III, *Slavery, Segregation and Scripture* (Grand Rapids: Eerdmans, 1964), 16.

74. Yamauchi, "Curse of Ham," 56.

75. James H. Cone, *My Soul Looks Back* (Maryknoll, NY: Orbis Books, 1986), 17.

76. Ibid., 18.

77. Ibid., 23.

78. Ibid.

writes, "The apparent irrelevance of theology created a vocational crisis in me, and I did not know what to do about my future as a theologian. I began to develop an intense dislike for theology because it avoided the really hard problems of life with its talk about revelation, God, Jesus, and the Holy Spirit." The solution for Cone was not far away. "When the murderers of humanity seize control of the public meaning of the Christian faith, it is time to seek new ways of expressing the truth of the gospel."[79]

Cone says that his anger grew as he saw African American pastors denounce black violence and say nothing about the violence of white people against African Americans. Such pastors called on people to embody Jesus by turning the other cheek rather than to fight against injustice. The turning point for Cone came in 1966, when he read the National Conference of Black Churchmen's statement about Black Power in the *New York Times*.[80] That statement addressed questions of Black Power in the context of the black church. From this point on, Cone saw a way forward.

Black Theology and Black Power

Cone's theological work began with the writing of *Black Theology and Black Power* in 1969. In that book he sought to argue that Christianity, rather than having no relevance to the African American struggle, had at its heart the theme of liberation against oppression. In *Black Theology and Black Power*, Cone argues that while civil rights leaders like Martin Luther King Jr. did much to show that the Christian faith calls for the equality of all people, they did not go far enough, because "they did not liberate Christianity from its cultural bondage to white, Euro-American values."[81]

In a later book, Cone would compare the visions of America found in King's thought and Malcolm X's thought.[82] Malcolm X ended up being an important figure for Cone. Malcolm X referred to Christianity as "the white man's religion," and he called on African Americans to find a religious tradition that came out of their own cultural history. He states, "Brothers and sisters, the white man has brainwashed us black people to fasten our gaze upon a blond-haired, blue-eyed Jesus! We're worshipping a Jesus who doesn't even *look* like us!" This was not the only problem identified by Malcolm X. He also wrote, "The white man has taught us to shout and sing and pray until we *die*, to wait until *death*, for some

79. Ibid., 43.
80. Ibid., 44.
81. James H. Cone, *Black Theology and Black Power*, 2nd ed. (Maryknoll, NY: Orbis Books, 1989), vii.
82. See James Cone, *Martin and Malcolm and America: A Dream or a Nightmare* (Maryknoll, NY: Orbis Books, 1992).

dreamy heaven-in-the-hereafter, when we're *dead*, while this white man has his milk and honey in the streets paved with gold dollars here on *this* earth!"[83]

In other words, Malcolm X argued that Christianity is a tool of the white oppressor to keep African American people compliant. They were expected, according to Malcolm X, to praise God in this life, despite their oppression, and to wait until the next life for their salvation. Meanwhile, white people were able to live well off the backs of African American laborers. For Malcolm X, there was nothing redeeming about Christianity for the African American.

Cone writes that he initially tried to ignore Malcolm X's claims on this point. He saw himself as a follower of King, and he didn't want to "disturb the theological certainties that [he] had learned in graduate school."[84] Surrounding events pushed Cone to action. He writes that the growth of urban unrest and the rise of Black Power meant that he could no longer ignore Malcolm X's "devastating criticisms of Christianity," particularly as they were being reinforced by other prominent leaders.[85]

In light of that critique, Cone was left with one of two options. He could accept the critiques of Malcolm X and others and abandon Christianity, or he could work to show that Christianity has ongoing relevance for the African American community. *Black Theology and Black Power* is Cone's attempt to do the latter. In it, he argues that the Christian faith is not antithetical to the Black Power movement. Rather, Black Power is the message of Christ to Cone's own context. As a result, Cone argues, the problem is not Christ or Christ's message. The problem is the church. Cone argues that without the church making an effort to identify with the poor as Jesus did, the church stands as something that is antithetical to Christ. The ultimate call of the church is to be prophetic. To be prophetic, the church must demand a fundamental change in the order of society that attacks racism in all of its forms.[86] Ultimately, black theology, for Cone, must take account of the black condition and the suffering of black people. If it does not, theology asks those who are black to accept an identity imposed on them and contrary to what they know reality to be.[87]

A Black Theology of Liberation

A Black Theology of Liberation followed *Black Theology and Black Power* in 1970. In this book Cone seeks to take the theological perspective developed in

---

83. Malcolm X quoted in Cone, *Black Theology and Black Power*, viii.
84. Ibid.
85. Ibid.
86. Ibid., 1–2.
87. Ibid., 117.

his first book and examine how it understands major Christian doctrines. Before considering some of the central doctrines to the Christian faith, Cone spends some time examining the sources and norms for theology. He argues that black theology carefully considers the black experience, characterized by humiliation and suffering. Any attempt to talk about God must take this experience seriously.[88] In addition to this, it must also consider black history, defined by Cone as how those of African descent were brought to what is now the United States and how they have been treated. This history must also include black resistance against white oppression. Although most people think Black Power is new, it isn't, Cone writes, just as black theology is not new. Black theology came about when "the black clergy realized that killing slave masters was doing the work of God. It began when the black clergy refused to accept the racist white church as consistent with the gospel of God."[89] An additional source for black theology is black culture, which is the black "soul" that both reacts to the oppression and suffering imposed by whites and affirms black value. Cone writes that this source involves the many forms of creative expression in the community.[90]

In addition to the sources specific to the black experience, Cone addresses sources more traditionally found in Christian theology, including revelation, scripture, and tradition. He describes revelation as a particular event in human history. Knowing revelation is knowing how God has acted in human history. Further, revelation is a "black event" insofar as it encompasses the ways in which those who are black seek liberation.

As can be seen across Cone's work, scripture is crucial to black theology.[91] The biblical text is crucial to understanding the gospel, according to Cone. Cone takes a quasi-Barthian approach to the relationship between revelation and scripture, saying that the Bible isn't the revelation of God; the only revelation of God he recognizes is Jesus. At the same time, the Bible is a witness to revelation, and as a result, it must take a central role in Christian understandings of God. Scripture is not infallible, though, because the biblical text does not have divine authorship. Cone holds that arguments about infallibility can distract from the central place of liberation in the biblical narrative. He argues that questions

88. Cone, *Black Theology of Liberation*, 23.

89. Ibid., 25–26. It is important to note that Cone points out that it was not only American whites that participated in the slave trade, and certainly we can find historical instances of slavery that long predate the transatlantic slave trade. For Cone, though, what sets apart slavery in America was the attempt by its proponents to define nonwhites as nonpersons.

90. He writes, "Black theology must take seriously the cultural expressions of the community it represents so that it will be able to speak relevantly to the black condition. Of course, black theology is aware of the danger of identifying the word of human beings with the word of God, the danger Karl Barth persuasively warned against in the second decade of this century" (ibid., 27).

91. Ibid., 29–31.

of authorship and historicity are not important when compared to whether scripture can be used to confront and combat oppression.[92]

Cone also talks about the place of tradition in black theology. He defines tradition as "the theological reflection of the church upon the nature of Christianity from the time of the early church to the present day."[93] Tradition is utterly inescapable for the Christian, according to Cone, because the New Testament wouldn't have been compiled apart from it. Cone understands tradition as crucial to the theological task, but he also wants to be clear that black theology is not uncritical of it. He specifically notes that in the Western church, the conversion of Constantine raises questions about whether the church could stay true to its original charge. Cone further writes that this historical moment was a precursor to the decline in Christianity seen today.[94] The church was seen for much of its history as an institution that keeps order, and therefore it has been an institution that has mostly worked against the oppressed. The Protestant Reformation did not bring about much change. Martin Luther sided with the German princes in the peasant revolt and saw the state as the servant of God, even while the state was persecuting some of its weakest members. While Cone also critiques John Calvin and John Wesley for effecting little change for the oppressed (and specifically notes connections among "Calvinism, capitalism, and slave trading"), he does note that the Anabaptists were different. These reformers, according to Cone, were closer to the true message of Christianity because they identified themselves with the oppressed.[95]

If tradition is questionable (and Cone seems clear that it is), one must ask how it fits into black theology, if it fits at all. Cone suggests that there are rare moments across the church's tradition when the church seems to take seriously the ethical implications of Christ's gospel. The problem, Cone indicates, is that the definition of tradition is up for debate. He refers to "what is often called tradition,"[96] and what he means by this is the common Western narrative of church history, which focuses on Christianity under the Roman Empire, Christianity in Europe, Christianity in North America, and the modern missionary movement coming out of Europe and North America. This is the narrative that many intend to call to mind when speaking about tradition or the history of the

---

92. Here Cone writes, "Efforts to prove verbal inspiration of the scriptures result from the failure to see the real meaning of the biblical message: human liberation! Unfortunately, emphasis on verbal infallibility leads to unimportant concerns. While churches are debating whether a whale swallowed Jonah, the state is enacting inhuman laws against the oppressed" (ibid., 31).

93. Ibid., 33.

94. Ibid.

95. Ibid., 33–34.

96. Ibid., 34.

church. The problem is that it leaves large swaths of nonwhite Christians out of the picture. When black theology speaks of tradition, it is primarily speaking of a different set of narratives. According to Cone, it looks primarily to the history of the black church in the United States and only secondarily to the history of white, Western Christianity. He writes,

> [Black theology] believes that the authentic Christian gospel as expressed in the New Testament is found more in the pre-Civil War black church than in its white counterpart. Richard Allen, Daniel Payne, and Highland Garnet are more important in analyzing the theological implications of black liberation than are Luther, Calvin, and Wesley. This is partially true because they are black but more importantly because inherent in their interpretation of the gospel is political, economic, and social liberation. These men recognized the incompatibility between Christianity and slavery. While the white church in America was rationalizing slavery by recourse to fallacious exegesis, black ministers were preaching freedom and equality.[97]

In addition to examining sources, it is important to consider norms for theology. Cone's norm for black theology sounds somewhat similar to Gutiérrez's norm and also resonates with norms examined in prior chapters.[98] If theology is going to speak to human beings, its content must be relevant to the conditions faced by human beings. Here Cone is not referring to universal or generic human experience. Rather, he sees theology as embedded in various contexts, and theology must be able to speak to those contexts. Black theology must, as a result, relate itself to the situation faced by black people today. He writes, "Blacks have heard enough about God. What they want to know is what God has to say about the black condition. Or, more importantly, what is God doing about it? What is the relevance of God in the struggle against the forces of evil which seek to destroy black being? Those are the things which must shape the character of the norm of black theology."[99] Cone wants to be clear, though, that revelation is an important component of this norm. Black theology must not articulate a norm that ignores revelation but must rather examine the encounter between the black community and God.[100]

97. Ibid., 34–35.
98. Cone gives a helpful illustration regarding norms for theology. He writes, "Sometimes it is possible to perceive the norm of a particular theology by an evaluation of the selection and analysis of its sources; but this is not always the case, because most theologies share common sources. As I have pointed out, the difference between Barth and Tillich does not lie in their choice of sources. The crucial difference is in their use of sources, which is traceable to their theological norm" (ibid., 35).
99. Ibid., 36.
100. Ibid., 37.

Ultimately, for Cone, the norm for black theology is the black Christ, who comes seeking liberation. In order to understand how Cone approaches his theological work, it is crucial to understand his account of Christ.

God in Cone's Thought

In order to fully understand Cone's account of Jesus, it is important to first briefly look at his understanding of God. In what is arguably his most significant work, *A Black Theology of Liberation*, Cone spends some time parsing out his understanding of whiteness and blackness. He argues that while some people have argued that God is "concerned about blacks," the reality is that God himself is black.[101] Anyone who truly seeks God must become black as well. To do this, one must find himself or herself living in solidarity with the oppressed and working to bring about liberation.[102] Cone argues that understanding the blackness of God is a necessary corrective to tendencies to focus on the love of God at the expense of the righteousness of God. He writes that while most theologians agree on the idea that God is love, there is far less agreement on how the wrath of God can be related to the love of God.[103] Most theologians, he claims, attempt to resolve this problem by reading the wrath of God through the lens of the love of God. The problem with this, Cone writes, is that it fails to give a full account of the righteousness of God, and it reduces the love of God to "mere sentimentality."[104]

The question for black theology, according to Cone, is not whether love is important for understanding God but whether love itself can be rightly understood apart from the biblical view of God's righteousness. Cone's own answer to this is that wrath is a prerequisite for love. He asserts that downplaying or ignoring the wrath of God weakens what should be understood as one of the central images of God in the biblical text. As he puts it, "A God without wrath does not plan to do too much liberating."[105] God's love for the oppressed implies the righteous condemnation of everything racist, Cone claims. This righteous condemnation requires the wrath of God.[106]

101. Ibid., 65.
102. Ibid.
103. Ibid., 67.
104. Ibid. Here Cone makes interesting use of Marcion, who is remembered as a heretic by the tradition of the church. Cone writes that Marcion famously tried to resolve the juxtaposition of the wrath of God and the love of God by positing two different gods. Cone argues that if we simply try to resolve the wrath/love problem by reading wrath through love, we have essentially taken up a Marcionite approach. The only difference between this approach and Marcion's approach, Cone claims, is that Marcion is more honest about what he is doing.
105. Ibid., 69.
106. Ibid. This insight also appears to be an important corrective for popular evangelical conceptions of God, which often focus on God's love, God as friend, etc.

Christ in Cone's Thought

With this understanding of Cone's view of God, we can now turn to Cone's claims about Jesus. Cone's vision of Jesus is of one who comes preaching the kingdom of God. When he describes the contents of Jesus's preaching in *God of the Oppressed*, he emphasizes the Magnificat as well as other passages in Luke that seem to emphasize the social dimension of the gospel.

While Cone identifies the story of Jesus's temptation as Jesus's rejection of a "political," revolutionary messiahship, he says that most interpreters of this story miss the underlying significance of this move, which is that Jesus rejects any role that would separate him from the poor. The mission of Jesus, according to Cone, is "one of Lordship and Servanthood together [which establishes] justice through suffering."[107]

Cone answers Adolf von Harnack's famous question about the essence of Christianity with the words "Jesus Christ." Because Christ is at the center of the gospel, Cone argues, it is necessary to read his life and work through the lens of the black perspective. This is because, according to Cone, knowledge of Christ isn't simply about the being of Christ. Rather, Christology is ultimately the answer to an existential question. Cone locates Christology in praxis, writing, "We know who [Jesus] is when our own lives are placed in a situation of oppression, and we thus have to make a decision for or against our condition. To say no to oppression and yes to liberation is to encounter the existential significance of the Resurrected One. He is the Liberator par excellence whose very presence makes persons sell all they have to follow him."[108]

It is important to be clear about Cone's understanding of the boundaries within which we can actually speak of Jesus. He states that when we ask about the significance of Jesus for our times, we have to address the historical and resurrected Jesus. In other words, we have to focus on both the historical Jesus and the meaning of the resurrection for the contemporary context. Cone argues that it is impossible to faithfully depict Jesus without addressing both of these issues.[109] A critical implication of this claim for Cone is that our understanding of Jesus today must be tied to the actual, historical Jesus. This is a clear refutation of any appeal to a Jesus of the people or Jesus of the context that is divorced from the actual historical reality of Jesus. He writes, "We are not free to make Jesus as we wish him to be at certain moments of existence. He *is* who he *was*, and we know who he was through a critical, historical evaluation of the New Testament Jesus. Black theology takes seriously Pannenberg's comment that

---

107. James H. Cone, *God of the Oppressed*, rev. ed. (Maryknoll, NY: Orbis Books, 1997), 68–69.
108. Cone, *Black Theology of Liberation*, 119–20.
109. Ibid., 119.

'faith primarily has to do with what Jesus was.'"[110] As one considers the historical Jesus, one must also make points of contact with the contemporary context. To look at the contemporary significance of the resurrection, one must still ask the question of how this historical Jesus is connected to black persons (to use Cone's descriptor). To do this, one must ask about the relevance of Jesus to the contemporary black community. That relevance is to be found in liberation.[111]

In Cone's thought, Jesus is the liberator, and his central work is liberation. Jesus's mission was to become a slave, an oppressed one himself, so that he could "open the realities of human existence that were formerly closed to man."[112] It is in an encounter with Jesus that the human being knows both the work of God in history and how human beings fit into it. Cone argues that this is clear enough in the Gospel accounts of Jesus (he points particularly to Luke 4:18–19 and Mark 1:14–15) but that we fail to fully grasp the meaning of the message because of a gap between the biblical context and the contemporary context.[113]

In addition to describing Jesus as liberator, Cone sees Jesus as the black Christ, and he appeals directly to the New Testament to make this claim. A failure to see blackness as that on which one's Christology hangs is a denial of the New Testament message, he claims. Jesus, in Cone's thought, is one who reveals to the oppressed what is necessary for liberation. If this is the case, Cone argues, then Jesus is black. As a result, Cone's understanding of what it means to be black is directly tied to his understanding of liberation, and both of these ideas make up the core of his whole theological project.[114]

Of particular interest in Cone's various examinations of Jesus is his use of Luke's Gospel. This is seen as early as *Black Theology and Black Power*, where Cone raises the question of the content of the gospel of Jesus and finds its answer in the early part of the Lukan story about the rejection at Nazareth. In this story, Jesus enters the synagogue and reads from a scroll of Isaiah, and it is this text that Cone says defines Jesus's ministry: "The Spirit of the Lord is upon me, because he has anointed me to bring good news to the poor. He has sent

110. Ibid. On this point he cites Wolfhart Pannenberg, *Jesus—God and Man*, trans. L. L. Wilkins and Duane A. Priebe (Philadelphia: Westminster, 1968), 11 (emphasis in original).

111. Cone writes,

No matter how seriously we take the carpenter from Nazareth, there is still the existential necessity to relate his person to black persons, asking, "What is his relevance to the black community today?" In this sense, unlike Pannenberg, we say that the soteriological value of Jesus' person must finally determine our christology. It is the oppressed community in the situation of liberation that determines the meaning and scope of Jesus. We know who Jesus *was* and *is* when we encounter the brutality of oppression in his community as it seeks to be what it is, in accordance with his resurrection. (*Black Theology of Liberation*, 119)

112. James H. Cone, *Black Theology and Black Power*, 34.

113. Ibid., 35–36.

114. Cone, *Black Theology of Liberation*, 120.

me to proclaim release to the captives and recovery of sight to the blind, to let the oppressed go free, to proclaim the year of the Lord's favour."[115] This under-standing of liberation is further reinforced in Luke 7 when messengers from John the Baptist come to ask Jesus if he is the one to come. The response to this question is, "Go and tell John what you have seen and heard: the blind receive their sight, the lame walk, the lepers are cleansed, the deaf hear, the dead are raised, the poor have good news brought to them" (Luke 7:22).[116]

Cone's interpretation of this passage is crucial: "This is not pious talk, and one does not need a seminary degree to interpret the message. It is a message about the ghetto, and about all other injustices done in the name of democracy and religion to further the social, political, and economic interests of the oppres-sor. In Christ, God enters human affairs and takes sides with the oppressed."[117]

Black and White in Cone's Thought

Many readers who encounter Cone for the first time find his work shocking. Students reading the work of Cone may wonder whether Cone is putting for-ward a racist theology. It is important to keep one thing in mind: Cone does not use black and white to speak solely about skin color. When Cone writes, "Black theology must realize that the white Jesus has no place in the black community, and it is our task to destroy him,"[118] he is writing about a particular construal of Jesus that he sees as being fundamentally unfaithful to the core of the gospel.

Black and white, in Cone's thought, ultimately have to do with one's associa-tion with the oppressor or the oppressed. If the fundamental sin is racism, as Cone claims it is,[119] liberation in Christ means ending racist systems. Throughout his writings, Cone uses the terms *black* and *oppressed of the land* in tandem with each other. The black experience is the experience of oppression, and when Cone makes that claim, he is making it for the specific black experience in the United States (which is what he ultimately wants to speak to), but he also hints in some places that he is not referring exclusively to the black experience. He writes, "'Where Christ is, there is the Church.' Christ is to be found, as always, where men are enslaved and trampled under foot; Christ is found suffering with the suffering; Christ is in the ghetto—there also is his Church."[120] Because of this,

115. Cone, *Black Theology and Black Power*, 35. Here he quotes Luke 4:18–19.
116. Ibid., 36.
117. Ibid.
118. Cone, *Black Theology of Liberation*, 38.
119. "Preaching in its truest sense tells the world about Christ's victory and thus invites people to act as if God has won the battle over racism. To preach in America today is to shout, 'Black Power! Black Freedom!'" (ibid., 67).
120. Ibid., 66.

it is also true that following Christ is not primarily about church attendance. Cone says that where one is on Sunday morning does not define whether one is a Christian. He says that Christ was crucified between two criminals, not on an altar between candles. So also Christ is not in affluent, suburban churches but in the "ghetto, fighting the racism of churchly white people."[121]

Cone is clear that black theology will make some breaks with traditional Western theology. He notes that some traditional theological concerns should be set aside by black theology because they are unrelated to the reality of oppression. While black and white may not always literally refer to skin color, certainly sometimes they do. Cone acknowledges that while black theology seeks to proclaim liberation in Christ for the oppressed, "it will be difficult for white theologians to participate in this reality—because of their identification of unreality. Creative theological reflection about God and God's movement in the world is possible only when one frees oneself from the powers that be. The mind must be freed from the values of an oppressive society."[122] As a result, the church is about the work of liberation. The church is supposed to be where Christ is, in the "ghetto," fighting injustice and oppression. Because God is black, the church must also become black with God. And while those who, because of race or socioeconomic status, look like the oppressor may want to become black with the church to fight injustice, it will be very hard for most of them to actually do that.

Conclusion

The starting point of the person on the ground unites liberation thinkers from disparate contexts. Liberation theologies approach Christian theology from the standpoint of the oppressed and marginalized, and they all have an ultimate aim of action. To merely contemplate the nature of God without ever moving to action in the here and now is insufficient for liberation theologians. Good theology, for them, always ends in action and is always concerned with the experiences of actual people, rather than the human being generally construed. These concerns will also be seen clearly in the work of feminist scholars, who also work under the broader umbrella of liberation theology, in the next chapter.

121. Ibid.
122. Ibid., 20.

7

Feminist Theologies

In the introduction to her *Woman's Bible*, Elizabeth Cady Stanton (1815–1902) writes,

> From the inauguration of the movement for women's emancipation the Bible has been used to hold her in the "divinely ordained sphere," prescribed in the Old and New Testaments. The canon and civil law, church and state, priests and legislators, all political parties and religious denominations alike have taught that woman was made after man, of man, and for man, an inferior being, subject to man. Creeds, codes, scriptures and statutes, are all based on this idea. The fashions, forms, ceremonies and customs of society, church ordinances and discipline all grow out of this idea.[1]

Stanton's work is an attempt to grapple with the biblical text and consider the ways in which it has had a particular impact on women. Her conclusion critiques the perspective of the biblical text on women. She writes, "The Bible in its teachings degrades Women from Genesis to Revelation."[2]

Stanton is not alone in arguing that the Bible has been an instrument of the oppression of women, and she is not alone in claiming that the problem is in the biblical text itself and not just in its interpretation. Feminist theology is an attempt to respond either positively or negatively to those claims. While feminist theology can be done from any number of religious perspectives, feminist

---

1. Elizabeth Cady Stanton and the Revising Committee, *The Woman's Bible*, 1898. This is from the first lines of the introduction. Accessed at http://www.sacred-texts.com/wmn/wb/.

2. "The Woman's Bible," Internet Sacred Text Archive, http://www.sacred-texts.com/wmn/wb/.

Christian theology seeks to address the experiences of women and the relationship between those experiences, the biblical text, and Christian tradition.

First-Wave Feminism

While Stanton was not the first woman to raise these kinds of questions in the Christian tradition, she is a good place to start. In the United States, the abolitionist movement in the early and mid-nineteenth century involved a number of people who identified as Christian, many of them women. In the process of arguing for the equality of nonwhite people, it is perhaps unsurprising that the women involved in the movement started to think seriously about the equality of women and men.[3] While one might have hoped that a number of male abolitionists would also come to see the logic of this move, most of the men in the movement remained uninterested in issues of women's rights.

Stanton was an abolitionist who also sought to address the ways in which the Bible was used to support the subordination of women. *The Woman's Bible* came about as the result of collaboration with other colleagues. Together with Stanton, Lucretia Mott (1793–1880) and Susan B. Anthony (1820–1906) are the best-known proponents of the first wave of feminism.[4] Stanton, Mott, and Anthony were instrumental in the calling of the Seneca Falls Convention in 1840. The convention was attended by more than three hundred people and led to a declaration of the equality of men and women and of a political strategy to seek equal opportunities for women. The Seneca Falls meeting marks the beginning of the suffragist movement.[5] This first wave of feminism was primarily made up of white, middle-class, well-educated women. Despite its roots in the abolitionist movement, some were concerned that progress on gaining the vote for women would serve as a hindrance to efforts to gain the vote for African American men.[6]

Although the focus of the suffragists was seeking the vote for women, their unconventional ways meant that they challenged gender stereotypes that went beyond the question of granting the vote to women. They undertook public campaigns for change, which challenged the common idea at that time that a woman's place was in the home. This meant that when women spoke in public, they were defying traditional gender norms that saw them as the weaker sex.[7]

3. Anne M. Clifford, *Introducing Feminist Theology* (Maryknoll, NY: Orbis Books, 2001), 11.
4. Ibid.
5. Charlotte Krolokke and Anne Scott Sorensen, *Gender Communication Theories: From Silence to Performance* (Thousand Oaks, CA: Sage, 2006), 3.
6. Ibid.
7. Ibid., 5.

Although first-wave feminists largely argued for the legal equality of men and women, there were some who argued that women were inherently morally superior to men. This perspective understood patriarchy as something that was illegitimate, even though it defined society in such a way that women were marginalized and dominated. The individuals who held to this view of women's moral superiority argued that men and women deserved equal treatment in general but that women should also be acknowledged for their particular strengths and the ways in which those strengths contribute to society.[8]

The period from the 1920s to the 1950s witnessed a decline in women's rights. Women had achieved the right to vote, but much of the ground gained by women in the first part of the twentieth century was lost. During this period of time, the number of women in the workforce declined, as did the number of women who earned advanced degrees. Although women's participation in the workforce did grow during World War II (because of a shortage of men in the labor market), these women were expected to return to the domestic realm as soon as men returned from the war and were able to enter the workforce again.

Second-Wave Feminism

One of the most important texts for second-wave feminism was Betty Friedan's *The Feminine Mystique*, published in 1963. Friedan's text identified "the problem that has no name," the vague experience of dissatisfaction felt by many privileged (or relatively privileged) women in postwar Western countries. Friedan argued that the dissatisfaction experienced by such women could be attributed to their lack of social power and political influence.[9] One well-known slogan of second-wave feminism is "The personal is political," and this sums up the movement well. Second-wave feminism emerged in postwar Western societies amid a whole host of other movements, including the antiwar, civil rights, Black Power, and the gay and lesbian movements. What these movements all shared was a concern about the oppression of the marginalized by the privileged.[10] In theory, these movements should have readily found common cause and worked together. However, women often found themselves at the bottom of the ladder. Their voices were used as needed, but they were not given roles of great significance, and as a result they again experienced oppression.[11]

8. Ibid., 5–6.
9. Ibid., 11.
10. Ibid., 8–9.
11. Ibid., 9.

In response to their failure to achieve equality, some women began to create what were called "consciousness-raising groups." These groups were composed of women only and were an attempt to give a voice to women by providing a space for them to share their experiences and also critique the reality that created the experiences in the first place. It was from these kinds of groups that the phrase "consciousness raising" and the slogans "The personal is political" and "Sisterhood is powerful," which are now so well known, arose.[12]

When many people think of second-wave feminism, they fail to understand the nuance involved in the movement and instead treat it like a monolith. Second-wave feminists do not speak of one voice, however, and it is important to understand the distinctions among a few key types of second-wave feminism.

Types of Second-Wave Feminism

Maria Riley's analysis of second-wave feminism identifies four major types of feminism: liberal feminism, cultural feminism, radical feminism, and socialist feminism. Liberal feminism is perhaps the opposite of what some might think when hearing the term *liberal*. Liberal feminism uses the term *liberal* in the same way that liberalism was understood in the nineteenth century. Liberal feminism generally seeks equal rights for women, equal pay for equal work, equal protection under the law, and the like, but does so from within the current political system. Most important for liberal feminism is a stress on social equality that is fleshed out in equal political and economic rights for women. Anne Clifford connects liberal feminism to the kind of feminism seen during the first wave of feminism. These tactics can include promoting legislation that ensures equal pay for equal work and seeking new leadership positions in various industries that have historically been closed to women. Finally, liberal feminism calls for individual freedom for women, which includes the right of women to make their own decisions about their reproductive health.[13]

A second type of second-wave feminism is cultural feminism, which Clifford points out is sometimes called "romantic feminism" or "reform feminism."[14] If the emphasis of liberal feminism is the fundamental equality of men and women and the ability of women to do the same tasks that men are able to do, cultural feminism approaches the entire problem from a different angle. Cultural feminism argues that there are genuine differences between women and men. It

12. Ibid.

13. Clifford, *Introducing Feminist Theology*, 21–22. She cites Maria Riley, *Transforming Feminism* (Kansas City: Sheed & Ward, 1989), 46, for the fourfold breakdown of second-wave feminism.

14. Clifford, *Introducing Feminist Theology*, 22.

focuses on attributes that are traditionally associated with women and argues that it is this very set of traits that can improve society. As a result, cultural feminism has as one of its core assumptions that women are morally superior to men (and this is often connected to women's maternal role).[15] Clifford writes that cultural feminism has its roots in a reaction against the Industrial Revolution and a romanticization of the domestic role of women. Cultural feminists often stress women's traits in contrast to the aggressiveness and competition of the broader post–Industrial Revolution culture. As a result, cultural feminism characterizes women as less competitive and driven, and more likely to be nurturing and peacemaking.[16]

While these two approaches work within existing systems and assume that change can come without overthrowing current political, social, or economic schema, two additional approaches envision much more thoroughgoing change. Radical feminism certainly supports the interests of liberal feminism, but it wants to take the project much further. While liberal feminists seek changes that would bring greater social, political, and economic equality to women, radical feminists want to root out every type of male domination. For the radical feminist, this cannot fully happen within the current system; instead, radical, systemic change is necessary. Radical feminists argue that patriarchy is the cause of all the major problems faced by the broader world. In order to solve such problems, patriarchy must be rooted out. For this to happen, women must be freed from male control in every area of life. While some may question the extent to which this can go, radical feminism asserts that it even rises to the level of personal relationships between men and women. Some radical feminists go so far as to argue that the traditional understanding of romantic relationships between men and women inherently involves the oppression of women, because women are left to be the passive recipients of male attention. Other radical feminists look at the traditional understanding of the family and raise questions about the true place of women in families when inevitably their primary role is reproduction.[17]

Another approach that seeks to go beyond the current system is that of socialist feminism. Socialist feminism seeks to bring the insights of Marxism into an account of women's suffering under patriarchy. For the socialist feminist, the oppression women face is not simply caused by men. Rather, socialist feminists understand the oppression of women as part of a broader economic class struggle. Further, they argue that it is precisely those who are in economic power who make decisions about the distribution of society's benefits and burdens. Within

15. Ibid.
16. Ibid.
17. Ibid., 23–24.

the capitalist system in the West, it is white men who control the economic system. Women are oppressed in large part because they are primarily valued by a capitalist system for their role in reproduction in the private sphere. Because that is work that does not produce capital, it is considered to be less important than the economically productive work done by men in the public sphere.[18] Socialist feminists take issue with both liberal and radical feminists. They question the goals of the liberal feminists, which seem to be closely associated with the goals of well-educated, economically privileged women. At the same time, they do not think that radical feminists understand the problems faced by women correctly when they see them only along the lines of sex and not along the lines of race or class.[19]

The types of feminism found in second-wave feminism represent varying sources, assumptions, and goals. At the same time, second-wave feminism as a whole tends to represent the interests and concerns of well-educated, white, middle- and upper-class Western women and seems less relevant to women of color in the West and women from the non-Western world. Many second-wave feminists assumed that their concerns were the concerns of women everywhere. However, just as there are as many liberation theologies as there are contexts, there are as many feminist theologies as there are diverse groups of women with unique interests and concerns.[20]

Third-Wave Feminism

Third-wave feminism (which overlaps in time with second-wave feminism) is attentive to difference. It acknowledges that women come from particular contexts, and it holds that one's particular context will have an effect on one's theological context. Because of this, third-wave feminism represents the diversity of women across the globe. One example of third-wave feminism is womanism. Alice Walker coined the term *womanist* in the 1970s. A womanist is an African American feminist. The term *womanist* is preferred to *feminist* by this group to make clear that the struggles faced by African American women are often different from the struggles addressed by white women. Walker writes, "Womanist is to feminist as purple is to lavender."[21] In addition to womanism, the term

18. Ibid., 24.
19. Ibid., 24–25.
20. Ibid., 25.
21. Alice Walker, *In Our Mother's Gardens: Womanist Prose* (New York: Harcourt Brace-Jovanovich, 1983), xi–xii, quoted in Clifford, *Introducing Feminist Theology*, 25. Clifford writes that the term comes from the popular folk term *womanish*, which refers to young women who are assertive and not subservient. Clifford writes, "When an African American woman identifies herself as a womanist,

mujerista was given by Ada Maria Isasi-Díaz to refer to Latina feminist theology. The third wave also includes various Asian feminisms, African feminisms, and Native American feminisms. What the third wave makes clear is that one cannot do thoroughgoing feminist work without paying attention to difference.[22]

In addition to looking to diverse backgrounds, third-wave feminism also turns to concerns about ecology. This is often referred to as "ecofeminism." Feminists who take up ecological concerns argue that the same systems that oppress women also oppress and exploit the environment to the detriment of both nonhuman animals and marginalized people. These thinkers argue that any move toward the liberation of women is incomplete without an accompanying move toward the liberation of the earth.[23]

Patriarchy

One term that is central to any conversation about feminism is *patriarchy*. Patriarchy is commonly understood as a system in which privileged men oppress women. It is important to point out, however, that patriarchy can involve the marginalization of men, and it can involve women as oppressors.[24] Indeed, Delores Williams argues that it is hard for white women to legitimately critique patriarchy. This is because, according to Williams, African American women are oppressed not only by men but by white women as well. While white women are oppressed by patriarchy, they also enjoy white privilege.[25] For this reason, Elizabeth Schüssler Fiorenza has suggested a shift away from "patriarchy," which is focused on the distinction between men and women as the oppressor and the

she proclaims who she is as a woman and as black in a world that places little value on either status. She also affirms her gifts and talents as a black woman who has something of value to contribute to the well-being of her people, female and male" (ibid., 25–26).

22. Clifford quotes bell hooks (*Feminist Theory from Margin to Center* [Boston: South End Press, 1984], preface) and adds her own statement in a particularly apt way: "African American author bell hooks has expressed well why attending to these differences is important: 'Much feminist theory emerges from privileged women who live at the center, whose perspectives on reality rarely include the knowledge and awareness of the lives of women and men who live at the margin.' The experience of being a woman is inseparable from being the kind of woman one is" (ibid., 27).

23. Ibid., 23.

24. Gloria Albrecht points out in her book *Hitting Home: Feminist Ethics, Women's Work, and the Betrayal of Family Values* (New York: Continuum, 2004) that privileged women in the workforce often achieve their work-life balances only through the work of marginalized women who must leave their own children to work in the homes of the privileged women.

25. Kwok Pui-lan, "Feminist Theology as Intercultural Discourse," in *The Cambridge Companion to Feminist Theology*, ed. Susan Frank Parsons (Cambridge: Cambridge University Press, 2002), 29. She cites Delores S. Williams, "The Color of Feminism: Or Speaking the Black Woman's Tongue," *Journal of Religious Thought* 43, no. 1 (1986): 48.

oppressed, to the term *kyriarchy*, which comes from the Greek word for lord, *kurios*, to make clear the complexity of oppression.[26]

Types of Feminist Theology

Clifford gives three helpful categories within which to understand feminist theology. These categories can be understood as falling on a spectrum. The first group that Clifford names is that of the "reformist Christian feminist theologians." These are theologians who approach the biblical text and the Christian tradition with the assumption that the biblical text in itself is fundamentally liberating for women. As a result, the changes this group seeks are relatively modest and do not require the reworking or overthrowing of current church structures. This group will acknowledge that liberation has not been the experience of most women. That reality is a result of patriarchal interpretations of the biblical text throughout much of the Christian tradition. As a result, the problem lies not in the biblical text itself but rather in the way fallible human beings in a patriarchal context have read and interpreted the Bible.[27]

The other end of the spectrum is made up of what Clifford refers to as "revolutionary feminist theologians." These theologians often identify with radical feminism and have the opposite assumption from the reformist Christian feminist theologians. For these thinkers, the fundamental problem is not only the Christian tradition but also the patriarchal biblical text that has driven that tradition for over two millennia. The revolutionary feminist theologians hold that the biblical text and the Christian tradition are irredeemably patriarchal. As a result, there is nothing redeeming for women either in text or tradition. These thinkers argue that the best way forward for women seeking liberation is to move beyond Christianity and seek new religious forms.[28]

26. Kwok, "Feminist Theology," 29. She notes that kyriarchy refers to the rule of emperor/master /lord/father/husband over his subordinates. She cites Elisabeth Schüssler Fiorenza, *Jesus: Miriam's Child, Sophia's Prophet; Critical Issues in Feminist Christology* (New York: Continuum, 1994), 14.

27. Clifford, *Introducing Feminist Theology*, 33. Clifford points out that Catholic thinkers who fall into this category have a deep respect for both the Catholic tradition and its institutional authority, but they also call for the greater inclusion of women in church structures. For those readers who are familiar with the egalitarian-complementarian debates in contemporary evangelicalism, reformist Christian feminists will sound similar to egalitarians. These thinkers argue that the problems of women's secondary status can be resolved with better translations and interpretations of the biblical text.

28. Ibid., 32–33. Clifford traces the origins of this line of thinking to the work of Matilda Joslyn Gage (1825–93), who worked closely with Anthony and Stanton. Gage spent a great deal of time researching ancient Near Eastern cultures and out of that argued for goddess worship as a means to elevate the status of women in both religious and secular contexts. She argued that women would never be liberated so long as they remained identified with Christianity and the Bible.

Between these two groups is a large and diverse middle group that Clifford calls the "reconstructionist Christian feminist theologians." These thinkers neither claim that the Bible is fundamentally free from patriarchy, nor do they claim that the Bible is so entrenched in patriarchy that there is nothing redeemable for women. Rather, they argue that the biblical text comes out of a patriarchal context and therefore contains sections that are deeply problematic. At the same time, reconstructionist thinkers argue that there is a liberating core to the biblical text, and that the text and tradition have evidence of women's voices that may have been silenced or downplayed because of the patriarchal setting. Reconstructionist Christian feminist theologians are interested in retrieving and emphasizing the liberating core of the biblical text. They do not hesitate to point out places in the biblical text that are the product of a patriarchal context, and they insist that part of the task of doing this is to carefully attend to the experiences of women. By doing this work, they argue that they can articulate a Christian theology that is aware of its patriarchal heritage and that seeks to be a more liberating force for women and other oppressed peoples.[29] Many feminist theologians fit in the reconstructionist category. Because of this, and because of their particular approach to the biblical text, it is important to look at two important feminist thinkers, Elizabeth Johnson and Delores Williams.

ELIZABETH JOHNSON

Elizabeth Johnson (b. 1941) grew up in Brooklyn, New York, in an observant Catholic family. She joined the Congregation of the Sisters of St. Joseph (CSJ), an order of religious sisters based on Long Island, when she was a young adult. The Second Vatican Council was convened relatively early in her vocation, and although she was at that point teaching in an elementary school, the council intensified her interests in academic theology, which ultimately led to her work in higher education. When Johnson was in college, she chose theology as her minor area of study because she had questions about the reality of suffering and its relationship to God. Her college studies were primarily built on the foundation of Thomas Aquinas's *Summa Theologiae*. Although commentators on the work of Thomas take his ideas in various directions, Johnson's study was primarily focused on Thomas's text itself, rather than the work of later

---

29. Ibid., 33–34. Clifford writes, "What makes a reconstructionist theology Christian? The short answer is Jesus. The somewhat long answer is the gospel vision of release from bondage for a new creation—the realization of the reign of God, proclaimed by Jesus, the Christ, in word and deed" (ibid., 34).

commentators. Johnson found herself fascinated with Thomas's vision of reality.[30] The Second Vatican Council turned her attention again to theology, and she found herself captivated with the documents that came out of the council, particularly *Gaudium et Spes*. As she began to undertake advanced study of theology, Johnson's interests in questions about God remained, but they were accompanied by other urgent questions. As she considered the work of Karl Rahner, Johann Baptist Metz, and Edward Schillebeeckx, as well as Karl Barth, Dietrich Bonhoeffer, and Wolfhart Pannenberg, as aids to questions about God, she also became deeply interested in both Latin American liberation theology and feminist theologies from various parts of the world. Most recently, Johnson has been interested in comparative theology and ecological theology.[31]

Johnson noted that her congregation was living the standard religious life in the mid-1960s. This included strong authority at the top of the order, a strict schedule of keeping the hours, a full habit worn by the sisters, limits put on human relationships, and a distance from the world. The sisters were expected to have a commitment to the saving of souls in a church that needed renewal, and the council was a distant event that had little to do with daily life. At the same time, the 1960s were under way. They brought the death of John F. Kennedy, the civil rights movement, the war on poverty, and the rebellion of a younger generation against the ways of an older one. Johnson writes,

> In contrast to what our vow preparation was teaching, I kept thinking that if God created and loved this world, then shouldn't those of us radically seeking God in religious life be in the forefront of engagement with this world? Wouldn't final vows box me into a narrow life of perfection when the evolving, struggling world needed to be embraced with the love of God? Wouldn't I be denying the divine call that I felt in my own spirit? And so I struggled.[32]

One day Johnson was given a draft version of a document from the council on which the bishops had not yet voted. She read the document, which opened with the statement, "The joys and the hopes, the griefs and the anxieties of the people of this age, especially those who are poor or are in any way afflicted, these too are the joys and hopes, the griefs and anxieties of the followers of Christ." These were the opening words of *Gaudium et Spes*, which called for a deep

---

30. Elizabeth A. Johnson, "Forging Theology: A Conversation with Colleagues," in *Things New and Old: Essays on the Theology of Elizabeth A. Johnson*, ed. Phyllis Zagano and Terrence W. Tilley (New York: Crossroad, 1999), 91–123.

31. Ibid.

32. Elizabeth A. Johnson, "Worth a Life," in *Vatican II: Fifty Personal Stories*, ed. William Madges and Michael J. Daley (Maryknoll, NY: Orbis Books, 2012), 238.

involvement in the world on the part of the church. This was the spirituality that made sense to Johnson.

The document was important to her in many ways, but she notes that one part was of particular importance: the emphasis on human dignity. The document affirmed that every human being was created in the image of God, which gives the foundation for seeing all people as fundamentally equal and worthy of respect. Further, discrimination, be it on the basis of one's sex, race, color, social condition, language, or religion, was condemned. Johnson writes, "On that hot summer day, my young questing spirit intersected with this Council document and found its life-long direction. In the decades since then, much has changed in myself, my religious community, the church, and the world, but the power of *Gaudium et Spes* to inspire and challenge me has not waned." For Johnson, this call was worth her life.[33]

Eventually continuing her study of theology, Johnson earned a PhD from the Catholic University of America in 1981. She taught there for ten years before she moved to Fordham University, where she became Distinguished Professor of Theology. She has been involved in a number of key committees in the church, including ecumenical dialogues and dialogues on science and religion, and has been a consultant to the US Catholic Bishops' Committee on Women in Church and Society.

Out of this experience with *Gaudium et Spes* and her subsequent work in theology, Johnson has developed a centrist feminist perspective that has stayed rooted in the teachings of the Catholic Church while also challenging its understanding of the role of women in the church. Of particular interest to this examination of Johnson's feminist thought are her theology of God and her theology of Christ.

Language for God

In her most well-known book, *She Who Is*, Johnson opens by emphasizing the importance of using right language about God. She argues that Christians throughout church history have had a vested interest in using right language about God. As evidence of this, Johnson notes that many of the controversies in the early church dealt with questions about how to talk about God. This is important for one key reason: speech to and about the mystery that surrounds human lives and the universe itself is a key activity of a community of faith. In that speech, the symbol of God functions as the primary symbol of the whole religious system, the ultimate point of reference for understanding experience,

33. Ibid., 239.

life, and the world. Hence the way in which a faith community shapes language about God implicitly represents what it takes to be the highest good, the profoundest truth, the most appealing beauty.[34] In other words, the way in which human beings speak about God reveals what they believe about the most fundamental things of life. Because of this, it is immensely important to get this language about God right.

If the symbol of God works to show how a faith community understands God and ultimate reality, then it follows that one must be very careful about how God is portrayed. The problem identified by Johnson is that the Christian tradition has not correctly understood how to interpret God. Language about God in the Christian tradition has been overwhelmingly male. One critical way in which this is problematic is that it suggests that God is actually a human being rather than a divine, transcendent being. Johnson states,

> While officially it is rightly and consistently said that God is spirit and so beyond identification with either male or female sex, yet the daily language of preaching, worship, catechesis, and instruction conveys a different message: God is male, or at least more like a man than a woman, or at least more fittingly addressed as male than as female. The symbol of God functions. Upon examination, it becomes clear that this exclusive speech about God serves in manifold ways to support an imaginative and structural world that excludes or subordinates women. Wittingly or not, it undermines women's human dignity as equally created in the image of God.[35]

This type of speech, for Johnson, subordinates women and lends itself to an inappropriate anthropomorphizing of God.

The solution to this problem is to incorporate female imagery into one's God-talk. Johnson argues that making this move will not only question the dominance of male imagery for God in the tradition but will also reinforce the divinity and nonhuman nature of God.[36] Some may object that if the biblical text offers language of God that casts God in male terms, this must be the only appropriate way to talk about God in Christian theology. In response to this kind of critique, Johnson argues that there is no timeless speech about God in the Judeo-Christian tradition. All language about God arises from cultural contexts and is influenced by those contexts. Citing Thomas Aquinas, she argues that language about God need not be restricted to language found in the biblical text.

---

34. Elizabeth A. Johnson, *She Who Is: The Mystery of God in Feminist Theological Discourse* (New York: Crossroad, 2002), 3–4.

35. Ibid., 4–5.

36. Ibid., 5.

Rather, as long as the terms are consistent with the overall scriptural picture of God and present faith experience, new language is fully appropriate.[37]

Above all, the theologian must bear in mind that God is beyond all understanding. Johnson writes, "The historical open-endedness of talk about God is due not only to its location in time, place, and culture, which is the case with all human speech, but to the very nature of what we are talking about. The reality of God is mystery beyond all imagining. So transcendent, so immanent is the holy mystery of God that we can never wrap our minds completely around this mystery and exhaust this divine reality in words or concepts."[38] Johnson writes,

> If God is not intrinsically male, if women are truly created in the image of God, if being female is an excellence, if what makes women exist as women in all difference is participation in divine being, then there is cogent reason to name toward Sophia-God, "the one who is," with implicit reference to an antecedent of the grammatically and symbolically feminine gender. SHE WHO IS can be spoken as a robust, appropriate name for God. With this name we bring to bear in a female metaphor all the power carried in the ontological symbol of absolute, relational liveliness that energizes the world.[39]

The Maleness of Jesus

It is also important for feminist thought to address the question of Jesus. In doing this, Johnson makes clear that the historical fact of Jesus's maleness is not a problem. The problem with the tradition's understanding of Christ is that Christ has been interpreted from within a patriarchal framework. Jesus's maleness is a historical reality, and it is as important to who he was historically as his race, class, culture, and religion. The problem arises when the historical

37. Johnson writes,
   In one of those myriad interesting little discussions that Aquinas carries on in the formal framework of the *quaestio*, he deals luminously with the legitimacy of this historical development. The question at hand is whether it is proper to refer to God as "person." Some would object that this word is not used of God in the scriptures, neither in the Old Testament nor in the New. But, goes his argument, what the word signifies such as intelligence is in fact frequently applied to God in scripture, and so "person" can be used with confidence. Furthermore, he muses, if our speech about God were limited to the very terms of scripture itself, then no one could speak about God except in the original languages of Hebrew and Greek! Broadening the argument, Aquinas defends the use of extra-biblical language about God on grounds of historical need: "The urgency of confuting heretics made it necessary to find new words to express the ancient faith about God." In conclusion, he clinches the argument with an exhortation to appreciate this new language: "Nor is such a kind of novelty to be shunned; since it is by no means profane, for it does not lead us astray from the sense of scripture." (Ibid., 6–7)
38. Ibid., 7.
39. Ibid., 242–43.

fact of his maleness is elevated to be something fundamental to his identity as the Son of God.[40]

Misusing the maleness of Jesus happens in several ways. The historical reality of Jesus's maleness is used to support male images of God. Further, his maleness is used to reinforce the superiority of men over women in the church. The assumption is that because Jesus was male, maleness is normative, while the experience of women is outside that norm. In addition to that, the assumption of the normativity of maleness puts the salvation of women into question.[41]

The Catholic Church argues that women cannot be ordained because, as women, they cannot symbolically represent Christ in the way men do. To understand the problem with this, Johnson evokes an ancient Christian controversy, Arianism. Arius believed that Christ was not of the same substance with God the Father but was rather a creation of God that stood higher than human beings but lower than God. The early church declared this view to be heretical at the Council of Nicaea in 325 and again at the Council of Constantinople in 381 and the Council of Chalcedon in 451. Arianism continued to thrive in the Roman Empire for some time after the Council of Nicaea. Apollinaris, a follower of Athanasius, the great theological opponent of Arius, wanted to articulate a theology that would definitively exclude the possibility of Arianism. To do this, Apollinaris argued that Jesus had a human body but that the Son provided the soul or intellect. In other words, Jesus had a human body but a divine mind. The church fathers argued that anything that was not assumed by Christ was not actually redeemed by Christ. In effect, if Christ did not have a human soul or intellect, the souls or intellects of human beings are not redeemed by Christ. Christ redeems that which he takes on, but not that which is outside his own humanity. Apollinaris was condemned by Pope Damasus I (366–84) and refuted by the Cappadocian Fathers. Because of this and the objections of other theologians, Apollinaris's christological views were condemned as heretical at the Council of Constantinople in 381.[42] His ideas are also clearly excluded in the 451 Definition of Chalcedon.

This controversy becomes immediately relevant to Johnson's understanding of Christ and the faulty understanding of Christ that she sees implicit in the Catholic Church's teachings on the ordination of women. The church's argument against the ordination of women is twofold. First, Christ chose men to

40. Elizabeth A. Johnson, "Redeeming the Name of Christ," in *Freeing Theology: The Essentials of Theology in Feminist Perspective*, ed. Catherine Mowry LaCugna (San Francisco: HarperSanFrancisco, 1993), 118–19.

41. Ibid., 119.

42. Justo L. González, *A History of Christian Thought: From the Beginnings to the Council of Chalcedon* (Nashville: Abingdon, 1987), 349, 351.

make up the twelve apostles, and the apostles followed suit when founding their churches. The Catholic Catechism says,

> Only a baptized man validly receives sacred ordination. The Lord Jesus chose men to form the college of the twelve apostles, and the apostles did the same when they chose collaborators to succeed them in their ministry. The college of bishops, with whom the priests are united in the priesthood, makes the college of the twelve an ever-present and ever-active reality until Christ's return. The Church recognizes herself to be bound by this choice made by the Lord himself. For this reason the ordination of women is not possible.[43]

Second, the church argues that women cannot represent Christ in offering the sacraments in the same way that men can. Christ was incarnate as a male human being, and so women cannot stand in for Christ in the sacraments in the way that men can. Avery Dulles writes,

> The Congregation for the Doctrine of the Faith and the popes have appealed to the "iconic" argument to suggest reasons why Christ chose to reserve the priest-hood to men. The argument is that the ministerial priest has to represent Christ, especially in the Eucharist, which is the sacrament that preeminently "expresses the redemptive act of Christ, the Bridegroom, toward the Church." The words of institution are no mere narrative about the past; they are performative speech-acts whereby Christ himself, through the priest, accomplishes the sacramental sacrifice. The shift to the present tense and the first person singular are therefore essential. Uttering the words, "This is my body . . . this is my blood," the priest puts on the very person of Christ. In order for him to be identified with Christ as Bridegroom, it is fitting for the priest to be of the male sex.[44]

Johnson argues that this line of thinking leads theology back down the road to Apollinaris. By arguing that only men can properly represent Christ in offer-ing the sacraments, the church has essentially affirmed that there are two types of human nature: male human nature and female human nature. If one's sex is something essential to one's human nature, then there are now two different types of humanity. If this is the case, then it raises the question about whether female humanity is redeemed. Reminding us of the maxim of the Eastern fathers, Johnson notes, "That which is not assumed is not healed." In other words, if women are unable to serve as the image of the Bridegroom, there is a significant question about whether Christ is able to represent women in human salvation,

---

43. *The Catechism of the Catholic Church*, 2nd ed. (New York: Doubleday, 1995), para. 1577.

44. Avery Cardinal Dulles, "Priesthood and Gender," in *Church and Society: The Lawrence J. Mc-Ginley Lectures, 1988–2007* (New York: Fordham University Press, 2008), 212.

whether that salvation comes as a substitutionary death, a ransom, or a renewing of the image of God. If female humanity is separate from male humanity, and a male savior has come to offer redemption, are women adequately represented in salvation?[45]

The clear answer to this question in the minds of Johnson and others is that women are clearly intended to be included in salvation. If that is the case, then it must be the case that women can image Christ in offering the sacraments. To be clear, no Catholic theologian who opposes the ordination of women would actually claim that women are outside salvation. The point Johnson wants to make is that that line of thinking is the logical outcome of claims like the one made by Dulles.[46]

Johnson makes clear that the historical reality that Jesus was male is not a problem for feminist theologians. She writes,

> The fact that Jesus of Nazareth was a man is not in question. His maleness is constitutive of his personal identity, and as such, it is to be respected. His sex is intrinsic to his historical person as are his race, class, ethnic heritage, culture, his Jewish religious faith, his Galilean village roots, and so forth. The difficulty arises, rather, from the way this one particularity of sex, unlike the other historical particularities, is interpreted in sexist theology and practice. Consciously or unconsciously, Jesus's maleness is lifted up and made essential for his christic function and identity.[47]

Christ as Wisdom

Johnson suggests that the way out of a sexist construal of Christ is to look to the imagery of wisdom. The imagery of Christ as Wisdom (Sophia) was one of many ways in which first-century Christians described him. Despite this, it is one of the more neglected images today. Johnson points out that Wisdom is found in both the Old Testament and the intertestamental literature. Wisdom, she writes, "is a complex female figure who personifies God's presence and creative action in the world."[48]

One example of Wisdom in scripture is her depiction in Proverbs. Proverbs is styled as a father instructing a son on taking a particular path. The son (the reader) can choose to follow the path of wisdom or folly. Woman Wisdom shows up in the first chapter but is more fully described in the eighth and ninth chapters of the book. There Wisdom is said to call out to people to learn to live the

---

45. Johnson, "Redeeming the Name of Christ," 118–20.
46. Ibid.
47. Ibid., 118–19.
48. Ibid., 120–21.

good, moral life. Additionally, Wisdom says that she was created by Yahweh at the beginning of the work of creation and played a role at creation. In both chapters eight and nine, Wisdom is said to live at a high point in the city. In its ancient Near Eastern context, this is a clear indicator of Wisdom's deity. As a result, Lady Wisdom in Proverbs is a personification of God.

Wisdom is directly tied to Christ in Johnson's work. She writes that there are clear parallels between how Judaism spoke of Wisdom and how the early Christians spoke of Christ. Making a connection between Christ and Wisdom was, for the early church fathers, a way to extend their understanding of Christ's work in the world by seeing him at work prior to the incarnation. Perhaps most important, Johnson suggests that an understanding of Christ as Wisdom is prior to any understanding about Christ as the Son of God. She writes, "The identification of the human being Jesus with divine Sophia, God's gracious nearness and activity in the world, moved thought to reflect that Jesus is not simply a human being inspired by God but must be related in a more personally unique way to God. Jesus came to be seen as God's only begotten Son only after he was identified with Wisdom."[49]

This move has a number of theological implications. Johnson points out that the Wisdom tradition is interested not only with major events in salvation history but also with the everyday lives of the people of God. This is significant because most individuals meet God not in mighty events of salvation history (e.g., Moses's reception of the law at Mount Sinai) but in their common activities. Because the entire world is God's creation, one cannot compartmentalize sacred and nonsacred parts of life. Rather, the whole of life is to be one where God is encountered. The Wisdom tradition makes this clear.[50]

Another theological payoff of associating Christ with Wisdom is that Wisdom gives language to interpreting Christ that is not strictly masculine. To see how this plays out, Johnson turns to the ministry of Jesus, emphasizing its inclusive nature and Jesus's association with those on the margins of society. The relationships Jesus built were characterized by mutuality rather than the oppression so familiar to marginalized people.[51]

One of the most important things about the image of Wisdom, according to Johnson, is that unlike traditions surrounding the Mosaic law and the temple, Wisdom was a tradition that was not controlled by any one group. Wisdom does not live in the temple, so to speak, but lives in the world, where anyone can find her. Because Wisdom has this more democratic appeal, it opens the doors to

49. Ibid., 121.
50. Ibid.
51. Ibid., 123.

the experiences of women (which are not often valued in traditional religious circles) and allows them to have religious significance as well.[52]

How does Wisdom recast our understanding of Jesus? Throughout Jesus's ministry, the affirmation of those who are at the lowest levels of society is central. Johnson draws this together well:

> Through his ministry, Jesus unleashes a hope, a vision, and a present experience of liberating relationships that women, the lowest of the low in any class, as well as men, savor as the antithesis of patriarchy. Women interact with Jesus in mutual respect, support, comfort, and challenge, themselves being empowered to acts of compassion, thanksgiving, and boldness by Spirit-Sophia who draws near in him. Although long neglected by the later tradition, these women engage in feminist interpretation in significant ways. They befriend, economically support, advise, teach, and challenge Jesus, break bread with him and evangelize in his name. Others receive the gift of his healing, being empowered to stand up straight beyond physical or mental suffering, spiritual alienation, or social ostracism. One woman whose name has been forgotten by patriarchal tradition prophetically anoints his head in an act that commissions him towards his death.[53]

For Johnson, then, it is of crucial importance that our own communities follow the pattern identified by Jesus rather than the old patterns by which patriarchal society was characterized.

DELORES WILLIAMS and Womanism

Delores Williams is one of the most well-known proponents of womanism. Williams writes that womanism is a concept that allows African American women to identify with both the African American community and feminism. Williams writes, "What then is a womanist? Her origins are in the black folk expression, 'You acting womanish,' meaning, according to Walker, 'wanting to know more and in greater depth than is good for one . . . outrageous, audacious, courageous and willful behavior.'"[54] Williams also notes that Walker insists that a womanist is someone who is committed to the entire community, whether male or female. As such, there should not be separation "except for [matters of] health."[55]

52. Ibid., 122.
53. Ibid., 123.
54. Delores S. Williams, "Womanist Theology: Black Women's Voices," in *Feminist Theology from the Third World: A Reader*, ed. Ursula King (Maryknoll, NY: Orbis Books, 1994), 77.
55. Ibid., 78.

The Intents of Womanist Theology

According to Williams, Christian womanist theological methodology is informed by four things: a multidialogical intent, a liturgical intent, a didactic intent, and a commitment both to reason and female imagery and metaphorical statements in the work of theology.[56] What this means is that womanism is committed to dialogues with multiple groups on gender, race, society, politics, and religion. Womanism is distinguished from white feminism precisely because it takes the African American experience into account. Similarly, womanism is distinct from the black theology of James Cone in that it pays particular attention to the experiences of women. The womanist seeks dialogue with any group that addresses the well-being of oppressed peoples. Williams is careful to point out that even in such dialogue, the womanist must have an eye toward the oppression of African American women, children, and men via systemic injustices.[57]

To have a liturgical intent means that womanism has relevance for the black church. While womanism works with and within the black church, though, womanism also offers it challenges. Williams notes that womanism will challenge the theology, liturgical practices, and actions of the black church. Of this Williams says, "Womanist theology will consciously impact *critically* upon the foundations of liturgy, challenging the church to use justice principles to select the sources that will shape the content of the liturgy."[58] For Williams, womanism will call the church to ask how the ways in which it thinks, lives, and acts portray blackness, women, and marginalized peoples.[59]

One thing that all the theologians in this volume share in common is that they believe that the role of theology is to have some sort of good news to proclaim to the world. Williams makes this same assertion when she claims that womanism is intended to have a didactic intent. Womanist theology, according to her, should teach Christians in particular something about the moral, or Christian, life. This should have its foundation in an ethics that has an eye

---

56. Ibid., 83.
57. Williams writes,

  The genocide of culture and peoples (which has often been instigated and accomplished by Western white Christian groups or governments) and the nuclear threat of omnicide mandate womanist participation in such dialogue/action. But in this dialogue/action, the womanist also should keep her speech and action focused upon the slow genocide of poor black women, children, and men by exploitative systems denying them productive jobs, education, health care, and living space. Multidialogical activity may, like a jazz symphony, communicate some of its most important messages in what the harmony-driven conventional ear hears as discord, as disruption of the harmony in both black American and white American social, political, and religious status quo. (Ibid.)

58. Ibid.
59. Ibid., 84.

toward marginalized groups. This also means that the sources for womanist theology will be particular to the experience of African American women, such as African American folk wisdom (and here Williams specifically mentions Brer Rabbit literature) and African American women's moral wisdom that seeks to address how Christians should live in this world. Although tensions might exist between teachings from these sources and teachings that have been put forth in "traditional" or Eurocentric Christian theology, womanist theology has a role to play in teaching the church to listen to these earlier, ignored voices.[60]

One thing that Williams mentions that is often lost in theological conversations is the role of the Spirit. Noting that the spirit is important in Walker's writings, Williams makes a connection from Walker to the black church, pointing out that in the black church an appraisal of the value of a given service isn't about the liturgy or about effective preaching but whether the spirit is working and present. Talking about spirit is important for Williams because it offers a way for womanist thinkers to approach the biblical text. Womanists can find stories in the biblical text in which marginalized people (and particularly women) have encounters with God. Further, the salvation story, for the womanist thinker, can be understood to begin with the revelation of Christ to Mary, a poor woman in a backwater area.[61]

The most important element of Williams's discussion of womanist God-talk is diversity. She writes,

> Christian womanist responses to the question, "Who do you say God is?" will be influenced by these many sources. Walker's way of connecting womanists with the spirit is only one clue. The integrity of black church women's faith, their love of Jesus, their commitment to life, love, family, and politics will also yield vital clues. And other theological voices (black liberation, feminist, Islamic, Asian, Hispanic, African, Jewish, and Western white male traditional) will provide insights relevant for the construction of the God-content of womanist theology.[62]

In her most well-known work, *Sisters in the Wilderness*, Williams writes about the relationship between womanist God-talk and black liberation theology. She states that African American women have often in history used their religious convictions to cope with daily life. She also notes that African American women have shared experiences with African American men, both in experiencing oppression and relating those experiences in the context of the community.[63]

60. Ibid.
61. Ibid., 85.
62. Ibid., 86.
63. Delores S. Williams, *Sisters in the Wilderness: The Challenge of Womanist God-Talk* (Maryknoll, NY: Orbis Books, 1993), 143.

Williams identifies three key ways in which womanist theology can come into conversation with black theology: a non-liberative thread, identification-ascertainment, and the wilderness experience. Each of these ways is significant in her thought and invoke questions of theological methodology.

A Non-Liberative Thread

Williams notes Cone's claim that the biblical witness depicts God acting as liberator on behalf of all oppressed people, and then she argues that the problem with this claim is that it is not actually borne out in the biblical text. She argues that there is a "non-liberative" thread running through the biblical text. If one reads the text with an eye toward stories about non-Hebrews, this thread becomes clear. One of the strongest pieces of evidence for this is the story of Hagar and Sarah as told in Genesis and as mentioned in Galatians. Williams says, "In the Genesis stories about Hagar and Sarah, God seems to be (as some Palestinian Christians today suggest about the God of the Hebrew testament) 'partial and discriminating.' God is clearly partial to Sarah. Regardless of the way one interprets God's command to Hagar to submit herself to Sarah, God does not liberate her."[64] Not only does God not liberate Hagar, but God also does not outlaw slavery in the Mosaic law. Instead, there are clear provisions in Exodus for how the male slave is to be part of Israel's rituals. In addition to that, while the covenant code provides for the freedom of a male slave after the seventh year, there is no such provision for female slaves.[65]

Williams also notes that God tells the ancient Israelites that they may not enslave their brothers, but they may enslave men and women from other nations. She cites Leviticus 25:44–46, which states,

> It is from the nations around you that you may acquire male and female slaves. You may also acquire them from among the aliens residing with you, and from their families that are with you, who have been born in your land; and they may be your property. You may keep them as a possession for your children after you, for them to inherit as property. These you may treat as slaves, but as for your fellow Israelites, no one shall rule over the other with harshness.

What this text indicates, along with Leviticus 19 and others, is that God is perhaps not opposed to the slavery of non-Israelites. Williams writes, "The point here is that when non-Jewish people (like many African-American women who

64. Ibid., 144–45.
65. Ibid., 146.

now claim themselves to be economically enslaved) read the entire Hebrew testament from the point of view of the non-Hebrew slave, there is no clear indication that God is against their perpetual enslavement."[66] This reality makes it hard for Williams, and others, to fully endorse Cone's claim that the biblical text depicts God as a liberator for all people.

This is an important distinction between the thought of Williams and many liberation theologians. Latin American liberation theology, black theology, and several other theologies of liberation take up the Exodus narrative and understand it as paradigmatic for the ways in which God works to liberate oppressed peoples.[67]

Williams also points out that this isn't something exclusive to the Old Testament, noting that in Matthew 10 Jesus commanded the disciples to go nowhere among the gentiles but to instead minister only to Jews. She notes the connection between the Genesis account of Sarah and Hagar and the way in which Paul invokes that story in Galatians 4. Paul writes that Hagar bore children for slavery, while Sarah bore children of the promise, who are given the freedom so eloquently described in Galatians 5.[68] Ultimately, while Cone argues that the power of scripture lies in how it can be employed as "a weapon against oppressors,"[69] Williams argues that a scripture that seems to have equivocal messages about slavery (depending on the social location of the slave/potential slave), or silence about the liberation of those who were non-Israelite, does not seem to be an effective tool for liberation.[70]

While she may disagree with Cone's argument that the Bible can be used as a tool for liberation, Williams notes that Cone is correct to hold that it is the community of faith that should influence how its theologians make use of the Bible. Her concern here is that black theologians and the faith communities around them have closely allied themselves in their minds with the oppressed Israelite slaves in Exodus rather than those who were marginalized and even destroyed (e.g., the Canaanites) in scripture. Williams's words are apt here: "Have they, in the use of the Bible, identified so thoroughly with the theme of Israel's election that they have not seen the oppressed of the oppressed in scripture? Have they identified so completely with Israel's liberation that they have been blind to the awful reality of victims making victims in the Bible?"[71]

---

66. Ibid.

67. Ibid., 147. Several Native American liberation theologians also reject the use of Exodus as paradigmatic and alternatively claim that they are identified with the Canaanites rather than the Israelites.

68. Ibid. See Gal. 4:21–31 and Gal. 5.

69. Ibid. She quotes Cone, *Black Theology of Liberation*, 31.

70. Williams, *Sisters in the Wilderness*, 147–48.

71. Ibid., 149.

Identification-Ascertainment

Williams argues that the only way for black liberation theologians to come into dialogue with womanist theologians is to look for "what has been made invisible" in the text and understand ways in which their work might have contributed to the silencing of other voices. Positively put, Williams calls for a hermeneutic of "identification-ascertainment" that looks at the subjective, communal, and objective responses to scripture. The subjective response involves the theologian determining which events and characters in the biblical text evoke resonance. The communal response involves asking the same question, but about the community of faith rather than just the individual theologian. Taking these first two steps allows the theologian to identify areas of potential bias when considering the biblical text. After this has been done, the theologian is to examine the biblical text with an eye toward both the characters and stories that evoke resonance and the characters and stories that do not evoke resonance.[72]

The Wilderness Experience

Williams also addresses the place of experience in black liberation theology. Black liberation theology emphasizes the black experience as a crucial component of theological reflection. According to Williams, the problem is that, in much black liberation theology, this emphasis is limited in its scope. The experience of black women is not explicitly (or often even implicitly) taken into account. Taking the experiences of black women into account will broaden the understanding of the overall black experience in the United States.[73]

Williams notes four key components to an understanding of the black experience in black liberation theology. The first component is the horizontal experience, which focuses on relations between black and white groups, particularly in the context of the United States. The second component, the vertical encounter, focuses on the relationship between God and an oppressed people. It is here where clear connections between experience and the exodus account is clear. The third component involves transformations of consciousness. Transformations of consciousness can be positive when they involve an oppressed group becoming more aware of its self-worth and value. Negative transformations of consciousness occur when an oppressed group internalizes the dominant narratives that produce and reinforce its marginalization. A final component

72. Ibid.
73. Ibid., 153.

is the epistemological process. This element looks at how one interacts with theological data in light of the first three elements.[74]

While James Cone, Cecil Cone, James Deotis Roberts, and other black liberation thinkers emphasize the importance of black experience and stress that it is an experience that comes in a particular context, there is a piece missing to their analysis. James Cone argues that one's own awareness is shaped by one's context, and as a result, "epistemological realities" are truly different for black and white people. Williams quotes Cone: "The social environment functions as a mental grid in deciding what will be considered as relevant data for a given inquiry."[75] For Williams, the problem with this is that while black liberation theologians stress the social contexts of human consciousness, they fail to take the additional layer of gender into account. A particular kind of history has been ignored, according to Williams. She writes,

> [There is] another kind of history to which black theology must give attention if it intends to be inclusive of black women's experience. This is "women's re/production history." It involves more than women birthing children, nurturing and attending to family affairs. Though the events and ideas associated with these realities do relate, "women's re/production history" has to do with whatever women think, create, use and pass on through their labor for the sake of women's and the family's well-being.[76]

In other words, within the experiences of black women is a microcosm of the black experience itself. By ignoring the voices and experiences of black women, black liberation theologians have essentially cut themselves off from what is potentially one of the most valuable resources at their disposal.

Williams suggests the paradigm of the wilderness experience as the best way to describe the black experience in the United States today. In looking to the wilderness experience, Williams looks to the figure of Hagar. She notes that Hagar and African American women have much in common, with their similar experiences in the wilderness as the most significant point of contact. The narrative of Hagar in the Hebrew scriptures depicts a woman who, in the end, has no one but God to whom she can appeal. Similarly, Williams points out, the narratives of many African American slave women mention "how they would slip away to the wilderness or to 'the haystack where the presence of the Lord overshadowed' them."[77] Sojourner Truth, in her "Ain't I a Woman?"

74. Ibid., 154. Williams notes that this fourth element is particularly important to Cone's work.
75. Ibid., 156. She quotes Cone, *God of the Oppressed*, 52.
76. Williams, *Sisters in the Wilderness*, 158.
77. Ibid., 108. She quotes Old Elizabeth, "Memoir of Old Elizabeth, a Colored Woman," *Six Women's Slave Narratives*, ed. Henry Louis Gates Jr. (New York: Oxford University Press, 1988), 7.

speech, notes that when she cried out as her children were sold into slavery, no one but Jesus heard her.[78] Like Hagar, many African American women have no one to cry out to but God.

Williams gives the following illustration of the wilderness experience from a workshop she attended:

> One woman turned to another and said, "Tell the group about your wilderness experience." The woman began to tell about her experience in her last parish. A few members of the congregation had all but successfully turned the rest of the congregation against her. Her ministry was about to be destroyed, she said. But she, alone, "took her situation to God as she fasted and prayed." Finally God "came to her," giving her direction. This was a positive turning point and her ministry survived to become one of the most outstanding in the district.[79]

The biblical story is similar. Hagar leaves all that she knows and goes into the wilderness. She manages to escape from Sarah, whose treatment of her is quite bad, but it is her religious experiences that sustain her when it seems all but certain that she and her child are doomed. Williams writes, "For both Hagar and the African-American women, the wilderness experience meant standing utterly alone, in the midst of serious trouble, with only God's support to rely upon."[80]

This type of experience ultimately results in a "risk-taking" faith. In Hagar's story, she actually names God, something that no one else in the Hebrew scriptures does. In doing this, Hagar affirms that this God who cares for her is her God. Similarly, many African American women have taken significant risks in the struggle for liberation. Harriet Tubman worked to lead numerous slaves to freedom, despite having a bounty placed on her while doing it. Williams writes that Tubman is said to have relied solely on God, looking to no one else for help. Because of this, Williams calls Tubman and Hagar, and many others, "sisters in the wilderness" who are struggling for liberation in the midst of desperate circumstances.[81]

It is this understanding of the wilderness experience that needs to become present in black liberation theology. There are several critical reasons why this is the case in Williams's mind. Perhaps most important, the wilderness experience is fundamentally inclusive of men, women, and families. Also, the wilderness experience shows the role of the human being in survival and community

78. Williams, *Sisters in the Wilderness*, 108.
79. Ibid., 108–9.
80. Ibid., 109.
81. Ibid.

building. It also shows that there is more to the black experience than the term
black experience, with its negative connotations, suggests. The wilderness experience emphasizes intelligence and ingenuity on the part of those who are in need
of liberation. Williams points out that "black experience says very little about
the black initiative and responsibility in the community's struggle for liberation,
and nothing about internal tensions and intentions in community building and
survival struggle."[82] Further, the wilderness experience is both sacred and secular. Finally, Williams argues that in a Christian theological context, wilderness
experience gives a point of contact for black liberation theologians, womanist
theologians, and feminist theologians. She writes,

> While black liberation theologians lift up the exodus/liberation tradition as foun-
> dational, they have forgotten to give serious attention to the wilderness experience
> in the exodus story, in which the ex-slaves grumbled against God and wanted
> not to bear responsibility for the work, consciousness, and struggle associated
> with maintaining freedom. While some feminist theologians claim the prophetic
> tradition significant for the biblical foundations of feminist theology, they give
> little or no attention to the way in which the wilderness figures into the work of
> making the prophet and making the people. Womanist theologians can invite
> feminist, black liberation and other interested theologians to engage with them
> in the exploration of the question: What is God's word about survival and quality
> of life formation for oppressed and quasi-free people struggling to build com-
> munity in the wilderness?[83]

For Williams, it is precisely in the wilderness experience that the intersecting yet
divergent approaches to theology of the non-liberative thread and identification-
ascertainment can converse.

Atonement

A final issue addressed by Williams concerning methodology is one of doctrine. She holds that it is one of the crucial responsibilities of the womanist thinker to examine the relationship between Christian doctrine and black
women. One clear example that she gives is the way in which the Christian
tradition has thought about salvation. Traditionally, salvation involves God
redeeming a fallen humanity through the work of Christ on the cross. Williams
specifically mentions this in the context of substitutionary atonement, presumably because that has been the dominant model in the West.[84]

82. Ibid., 160.
83. Ibid., 161.
84. Ibid., 162.

This model of the atonement makes Jesus "the ultimate surrogate figure," according to Williams, because on the cross he stands in the place of human beings. Because of this, Williams argues that surrogacy becomes sacred. It is at this juncture that she wants to ask if this image works for black women. While surrogacy may sound like a positive thing if it involves God in Christ standing in for human beings and making human salvation possible, Williams points out that surrogacy is an all-too-familiar experience for black women, and that, in their context, surrogacy has always been exploitative. She writes, "It is therefore fitting and proper for black women to ask whether the image of a surrogate-God has salvific power for black women or whether this image supports and reinforces the exploitation that has accompanied their experience with surrogacy. If black women accept this idea of redemption, can they not also passively accept the exploitation that surrogacy brings?"[85]

Substitutionary atonement raises a number of theological issues that Williams confronts. One potential problem in this theological view is the role that the Father played in determining what the Son would endure. Was Jesus's work on the cross both free and voluntary, or did the Father mandate it? Of equal importance to that question is the question of other models of the atonement. Williams points out that even though the substitutionary atonement has been a dominant view, other views of salvation were prevalent in earlier periods of church history. The ransom theory, for example, involves God paying a ransom to regain control of humanity from Satan, rather than Christ paying the debt of a fallen humanity to a wrathful God. That the model of substitutionary atonement originally rose in the medieval context of feudalism makes it even more historically problematic for Williams.[86]

Conclusion

While feminist theologies are deeply diverse, they are all united by a common starting point. Johnson, Williams, and many others seek to do the work of Christian theology from the standpoint of the experiences of women. This leads them to ask questions about both traditional readings of the biblical text that privilege the experiences of white men and the ways in which those readings have influenced theology and practice throughout the history of Christianity. This interest in the realities facing people on the ground is something that unifies these thinkers with the liberation theologians in the previous chapter.

85. Ibid.
86. Ibid., 162–63.

8

Theologies of Religious Pluralism and Comparative Theology

Christianity has always existed in the context of conversation with other traditions. At its inception, it was located in a Greco-Roman world characterized by religious diversity. Whether a person ascribed to one or more of the various philosophies that were offered, to one of the numerous mystery religions that had sprung up, to Judaism, or to any number of indigenous religions throughout the Mediterranean world, living in the Greco-Roman world meant that one was surrounded by religious variety.

During the medieval period, Christianity was the dominant religion in most (though not all) of Europe. Despite this, Christians were engaged in active conversations with other faiths. This engagement produced some positive results, such as the masterful theological work of Thomas Aquinas, which would have been impossible without his interaction with thinkers such as the Jewish philosopher Maimonides and the Islamic philosopher Averroës. It also produced some negative results; for example, Jews living in Europe during this time were often poorly treated. Like much of its history, Christianity's contemporary context makes it impossible to think about doing the work of theology without considering what intersecting points there may be with other faiths.

Theologies of Religious Pluralism

In the modern era, improvements in communication and transportation technology have meant that Christians are continuing to live in contexts of religious diversity and are growing in an awareness of the many faiths around
the world. This reality presents problems for Christian theology, according to
Ian Markham. One problem is epistemological. Markham argues that with an
increasing awareness of other religions, many people have raised the question
of how one knows that Christianity is the truth. Christianity has held that it is
a true description of reality and that its understanding of God and salvation is
necessary for one to be saved. With 68 percent of the world's population ascrib-
ing to something other than Christianity, does this mean that those individuals
stand condemned before God?[1]

These kinds of questions are often raised in the context of a theology of religious pluralism. Theologies of religious pluralism seek to account for questions
of salvation in the context of a religiously diverse world. A spectrum of positions
can be found among various theologies of religious pluralism. Pluralism itself
is commonly seen as one end of a spectrum, with exclusivism on the other end
and inclusivism in between the two.

One well-known proponent of pluralism, John Hick, argues that there is
a single god that each religious tradition accesses in its own way and that is
revealed in all the major religions of the world. Hick's initial way of putting
this could work quite well for the Abrahamic faiths and could potentially be
compatible with Hinduism, but it fails to work with Buddhism. To nuance his
views further, Hick went on to speak of the major religious traditions as access-
ing "the real," a single reality that stands behind all of these traditions.[2] One
of the first questions raised about this type of position concerns the claims in
religious traditions that seem to exclude or potentially exclude other traditions.
Hick offers a straightforward answer to this: any doctrine or claim that excludes
other traditions must be reconsidered. For Hick, who originally comes from a
Christian context, one can no longer claim that Christ is God incarnate, if his
pluralist hypothesis is correct. What one would need to say instead is that Christ
is one who shows us God.[3]

If pluralism is at one end of the spectrum, exclusivism is at the other end.
Markham claims that exclusivism is generally characteristic of conservative
forms of religion. Exclusivism relies on commitments to truth and revelation

---

1. Ian Markham, "Christianity and Other Religions," in *The Blackwell Companion to Modern
Theology*, ed. Gareth Jones (Oxford: Blackwell, 2004), 406–7.
2. Ibid., 407–8.
3. Ibid., 409.

and rejects the notion that all the religions access the same reality. Exclusivism's understanding of revelation is that it is something that comes from God.[4] Christian exclusivists argue that Christ is the ultimate revelation of God as God incarnate and that it is the Christ event that uniquely brings about the possibility of human salvation. In addition to this, exclusivists argue that salvation is limited to those who have made some kind of conscious profession of faith in Christ. Of course, the major difficulty with this position was noted above: With 68 percent of the world adhering to a religious tradition other than Christianity, what does an exclusivist position demand that one say about salvation for those individuals?

The position that has attempted to offer some kind of middle ground is inclusivism. Markham argues that many Christians are drawn to inclusivism because of questions about the unevangelized. If the exclusivist position is correct, how is this a just situation for those who have never heard of Christ or his church? Inclusivists argue that people of other faiths may be saved even though salvation itself comes only via the life and work of Christ.[5]

Karl Rahner is the best-known proponent of inclusivism. His understanding of the anonymous Christian was discussed in chapter 3, but here it is also important to note that his understanding of the anonymous Christian was influential on Vatican II and on the current *Catechism of the Catholic Church*. The wording found in the current catechism makes the position fairly clear: "Those who, through no fault of their own, do not know the Gospel of Christ or His Church, but who nevertheless seek God with a sincere heart, and, moved by grace, try in their actions to do his will as they know it through the dictates of their conscience—those too may achieve eternal salvation."[6]

Dominus Iesus, a document promulgated by the Vatican's doctrinal office, makes these statements:

> Nevertheless, God, who desires to call all peoples to himself in Christ and to communicate to them the fullness of his revelation and love, "does not fail to make himself present in many ways, not only to individuals, but also to entire peoples through their spiritual riches, of which their religions are the main and essential expression even when they contain 'gaps, insufficiencies and errors.'" Therefore, the sacred books of other religions, which in actual fact direct and nourish the existence of their followers, receive from the mystery of Christ the elements of goodness and grace which they contain. . . . Theology today, in its reflection on the existence of other religious experiences and on their meaning in God's salvific

4. Ibid.
5. Ibid., 412.
6. *Catechism of the Catholic Church*, para. 847.

plan, is invited to explore if and in what way the historical figures and positive elements of these religions may fall within the divine plan of salvation. In this undertaking, theological research has a vast field of work under the guidance of the Church's Magisterium. The Second Vatican Council, in fact, has stated that: "the unique mediation of the Redeemer does not exclude, but rather gives rise to a manifold cooperation which is but a participation in this one source."[7]

What these statements make clear is that the Catholic Church is operating within a framework in which salvation is possible only through Christ and yet salvation may be available to adherents of other faiths. What is more remarkable is that there is a clear openness in the text to the idea that other faiths may in certain ways convey salvific truth. Rahner argues that this is the only way to reconcile the notion that Christ is the only path to salvation with the reality that there are many people in the world who do not profess faith in Christ.[8] Markham concurs, arguing that the strongest argument for inclusivism is inevitable for Christians when they consider the millions who have never heard of Christ and all the people who died before the rise of Christianity. When those things are considered, he claims, it must be the case that God can save some people apart from any explicit faith in Christ.[9]

Markham makes one final point that is worth considering. He argues that pluralist positions are inevitably actually inclusivist. He points out that Hick posits a "real" that is accessed indirectly by all the major world religions. That "real" is not fully articulated in any of the religious traditions, but all of them access it. If that is the case, Markham argues, then Hick is simply suggesting one particular view of the real to which all religions inadequately point. Since that "real" is the source of any concept of salvation or truth, pluralists are essentially articulating inclusivism rather than actual pluralism.[10]

7. *Dominus Iesus* 1.8; 3.14. Document available at http://www.vatican.va/roman_curia/con
gregations/cfaith/documents/rc_con_cfaith_doc_20000806_dominus-iesus_en.html.

8. Karl Rahner, *Karl Rahner in Dialogue*, ed. Paul Imhof, and Hubert Biallowons (New York: Crossroad, 1986), 135.

9. Markham, "Christianity and Other Religions," 413.

10. His words here are important:

Even a pluralist, at this point, operates as an inclusivist. Pluralists insist that religious believers may imagine that they are encountering a particular God described in their tradition, as, say, a Trinity, but in point of fact they are encountering a Real which transcends all particular descriptions. If the pluralist hypothesis is true, then it means that the vast majority of adherents of most religions are mistaken and the "symbol system" (i.e., the vocabulary embedded within a particular world-view) of pluralism is what the orthodox are really discovering. A commitment to the truth of pluralism, ironically, makes the pluralist a kind of inclusivist. (Ibid., 414)

Note that Markham argues that this applies only to truth and not soteriology (the theological understanding of the work of Christ/human salvation), though it could be argued that it applies to both.

This critique of pluralism should not suggest that inclusivism is without its own problems. Many people have suggested that inclusivism from a Christian perspective comes across as arrogant or condescending of other traditions. The claim of inclusivism could suggest that adherents of other faiths actually agree with Christian beliefs, even though they do not explicitly know that they do.

These categories (pluralism, exclusivism, and inclusivism), while initially helpful to describe the issue, do not adequately offer solutions to the question of religious difference. The problem, according to Jeannine Hill Fletcher, is that they do not get beyond the impasse of sameness or difference. She argues that although these three positions have some distinct characteristics, all three of them fail to allow the religious "other" to be genuinely different. In both exclusivism and inclusivism, the religious other is always considered in relationship to Christianity, and pluralism does not truly allow for any distinctiveness among the traditions as something to be valued.[11] Hick makes clear that any theological position that does not fit with the pluralist perspective must be reinterpreted in such a way that it is not opposed to any element of the pluralist project. One example he gives of this coming from the Christian tradition is to see Christ as one who "shows us God" rather than one who is God.[12] Hill Fletcher argues that Christ remains normative for the Christian pluralist, even though that claim is explicitly denied. She claims that while the inclusivist position argues clearly for the normativity of Christ, the pluralist still uses Christ as a norm by which to consider religious difference.[13]

If that is the case, what is one to do about religious difference? If these categories do not adequately answer our questions, have other attempts been made to articulate categories that do? Paul Knitter, in his book *Introducing Theologies of Religions*, articulates these models somewhat differently, though it is clear that these models are still operating with exclusivism, inclusivism, and pluralism in the background. Knitter describes four models: the replacement model, the fulfillment model, the mutuality model, and the acceptance model.

Knitter's description of exclusivism comes in the form of the replacement model. The total replacement model described by Knitter and most often associated with conservative Christians sees no value in other religions. Knitter argues that Karl Barth lays the groundwork for this particular model, though Barth was not a fundamentalist Christian.[14] The way in which Barth accomplishes this is interesting: he ultimately argues that religion is unbelief because it is a

---

11. Jeannine Hill Fletcher, "Shifting Identity: The Contribution of Feminist Thought to Theologies of Religious Pluralism," *Feminist Studies in Religion* 19, no. 2 (2003): 9.

12. Markham, "Christianity and Other Religions," 409.

13. Hill Fletcher, "Shifting Identity," 89.

14. Knitter, *Introducing Theologies of Religions*, 23.

human attempt to grasp the nature of God.[15] This might seem to be a logical fit with the kind of exclusivism that comes out of more conservative versions of Christianity if Barth were making that critique only against non-Christian religions. The key thing to realize is that Barth is not doing this. Rather, Barth's claims about religion as unbelief are directed just as much at Christianity as they are at non-Christian religions. In fact, Barth is particularly harsh in his judgments against Christianity as religion.[16]

Despite Barth's claims about religion as unbelief, he does in other places argue that Christianity can be seen as the one true religion when it is examined alongside all other religions.[17] The key idea here is that for Barth, as well as for all others who hold to the replacement model, Christianity has a place of privilege, not because of how it functions as a religion, but because it is the place where Christ is found.[18]

The replacement model is nuanced by the partial replacement model in Knitter's scheme. This model is held by those in what Knitter describes as "the Fundamentalist-Evangelical-Pentecostal precincts of Christianity"[19] who find the total replacement model to be too pessimistic regarding the value of other religions. These individuals make up the group that Knitter identifies as "the New Evangelicals," who are more open to ecumenism. The partial replacement model essentially argues that God is present in revelatory ways in other religious traditions. Knitter notes that this is typically accounted for by way of general revelation. This revelation communicates not only about the existence of God but about the

15. Barth writes, "Religion is unbelief. It is a concern, indeed, we must say that it is the one great concern of godless man. . . . From the standpoint of revelation, religion is clearly seen to be a human attempt to anticipate what God in his revelation wills to do and does do. It is the attempted replacement of the divine work by a human manufacture. The divine reality offered and manifested to us in revelation is replaced by a concept of God arbitrarily and willfully evolved by man" in *Church Dogmatics* I/2 (Edinburgh: T&T Clark, 1956), 299–300; quoted in Knitter, *Introducing Theologies of Religions*, 25.

16. Knitter, *Introducing Theologies of Religions*, 25. See also Martha Moore-Keish, "Karl Barth and John Thatamanil: Two Theologians against Religion," *Bangalore Theological Forum* 45, no. 2 (2013): 91–104.

17. Knitter's words are particularly helpful here: "Here we enter in to Barth's understanding of the paradoxical nature of experiencing God, 'by faith and grace and Christ alone.' Christianity is the true religion because it's the only religion that knows it is a false religion; and it knows, further, that despite it being a false and idolatrous religion, it is saved through Jesus Christ" *Introducing Theologies of Religions*, 26.

18. Ibid.

19. One problem with Knitter's delineation of the replacement model and the partial replacement model is that he sees these models as those held by "Fundamentalist/Evangelical" Christians. He doesn't seem to have a clear account of the significant distinctions between evangelicals and Protestant fundamentalists. At this point, he also includes Pentecostals in that group, though that seems to be for the purpose of identifying Pentecostal Christians as conservative Protestants (and this is sometimes true and sometimes not true).

existence of a personal God who is involved in the affairs of the world. At the same time, this view does not argue that other religions are salvific in themselves. In this model, only Christ brings about salvation, and only Christ makes salvation known.[20]

Knitter explores inclusivism in the form of the fulfillment model. He points to Rahner as a key proponent of this model.[21] For much of the history of the church, the attitude toward salvation was that it was not possible outside the church.[22] This was interpreted to mean that one had to be part of the visible church in order to be saved. Rahner, whose work, as noted above, was important at the Second Vatican Council, maintains the idea that salvation comes within the church, but he broadens the understanding of what counts as being within the church. Rahner's basic theological assumptions are discussed in chapter 3. Building on those assumptions, Rahner argues that God's grace is present in other religions precisely because it is operant throughout the world.[23] He argues that God wants all people to be saved.[24] Because God is God, if God really wants to save all people, God will make this possible. God, according to Rahner, communicates God's self to all people, and this is what Rahner means by arguing that God's grace is present throughout the world.[25] Knitter points out that Rahner held that grace must be embodied, and this is where other faiths come in. Rahner argues the religions of the world are some of the places where God's grace is embodied. Because of this, he argues that other religions can potentially provide ways to salvation.[26]

The third model offered by Knitter is the mutuality model. This model, which maps onto pluralism, sees the various religions as called into dialogue with one another. This model does not see Christianity as holding any kind of superior revelation to other faiths. Rather, these many faiths are called to dialogue and

---

20. Knitter, *Introducing Theologies of Religions*, 35–38.
21. Ibid., 70.
22. Ibid., 66.
23. Ibid., 70.
24. Rahner, *Foundations of Christian Faith*, 313.
25. Knitter, *Introducing Theologies of Religions*, 68.
26. Ibid., 70–71. Rahner's words are important here:

> When a non-Christian attains salvation through faith, hope and love, non-Christian religions cannot be understood in such a way that they do not play a role or play only a negative role in the attainment of justification and salvation. This proposition is not concerned about making a very definite Christian interpretation and judgment about a concrete non-Christian religion. Nor is there any question of making such a religion equal to Christian faith in its salvific significance, nor of denying its depravity or its provisional character in the history of salvation, nor of denying that such a concrete religion can also have negative effects on the event of salvation in a particular non-Christian. But presupposing all of this, we still have to say: if a non-Christian religion could not or may not have any positive influence at all on the supernatural event of salvation in an individual person who is a non-Christian, then we would be understanding this event of salvation in this person *in a completely ahistorical and asocial way*. (Rahner, *Foundation of Christian Faith*, 314, emphasis added)

work together. Most important, the mutuality model emphasizes the presence of God and God's love in other religions.[27]

For Christians who hold this model, traditional understandings of Christ create problems for entering into genuine dialogue with those of other religions. This leads to a reconsideration of some traditional Christian doctrines in light of an increasing awareness of other faiths. Knitter argues that this is the model that is receiving the most attention in theological circles today.[28]

Knitter discusses three fundamental assumptions for this view. The first assumption is a historical-philosophical one. It holds that all religions experience some degree of historical limitation, while also holding that it is at least possible that there is one reality behind the many religions. The second assumption is a religious-mystical one that holds that whatever God is (and here Knitter actually uses the term *the Divine*), God is certainly more than anything experienced by one religion, and yet God is also present in the experiences of all of them. The final assumption is one that Knitter calls the "ethical-practical." This assumption holds that problems that face the world today are a common concern for people of all faiths. Dialogue is necessary in order for those of other faiths to work together to address these problems.[29]

Knitter cites the work of Hick for the mutuality model and describes his ideas in much the same way that Markham does above. One point that Knitter stresses is that Hick's approach is based on the philosophical assumption above. This assumption is not the only way to get to the mutuality model, for the religious-mystical assumptions and the ethical-practical assumptions can also help one move to the mutuality model.[30]

Regardless of which assumption leads one toward the mutuality model, Knitter concedes that critics suggest that the mutuality model is not particularly mutual. The mutuality model can fall prey to the charge of imperialism, in which Christianity is still essentially privileged. Knitter notes that when this happens, Christians can be seen to use dialogue and relationships with those of other faiths to meet their own ends.[31]

27. Ibid., 109.

28. Ibid., 112. On this point Knitter cites Wolfgang Beinert and Francis Schüssler Fiorenza, *Handbook of Catholic Theology* (New York: Crossroad, 1995), 95, and Carl Braaten, "The Triune God: The Source and Model of Christian Unity and Mission," *Missiology* 18 (1990): 419.

29. Knitter, *Introducing Theologies of Religions*, 112–13. One model of this assumption is the work of Eboo Patel and the Interfaith Youth Core. For an account of this work, see Eboo Patel, *Acts of Faith: The Story of an American Muslim, the Struggle for the Soul of a Generation* (Boston: Beacon, 2007).

30. Knitter, *Introducing Theologies of Religions*, 114–23.

31. Knitter says,

Christians who follow this approach are so focused on dialogue and on getting along with others that they don't see how different each of the others really is. You might say that

Knitter's final model is one that does not map onto exclusivism, inclusivism, and pluralism in the way that the replacement, fulfillment, and mutuality models do. This is the acceptance model, and it came out of a realization that the other models are inadequate. Knitter argues that the problem with the earlier models is that they either stress the particularity of one faith to the detriment of all others or they stress the commonalities among all of them in a way that papers over any real differences.[32]

The acceptance model embraces diversity and all the ambiguities it may create. This model argues that diversity always dominates. When we look at the world around us, we always see that diversity prevails and that it cannot be undone, even though it exists in a world of relationships and interconnectedness. The key assumption for the acceptance model is that this diversity is also found in the realm of truth. Truth takes different shapes and is found in different places to the extent that it cannot be called one in any way. Truth also exists in diversity. Different people know different truths because they experience the world with different sets of experiences that shape the way in which they understand all that is around them.[33]

Because of this, there are many religions, and they have fundamental differences among them. Knitter outlines three different expressions of the acceptance model. First, he notes that the acceptance model has foundations in the work of George Lindbeck, as described in chapter 4. The second approach argues that the fact of many religions indicates many salvations. This is the approach of S. Mark Heim, as will be discussed below. The final approach is that of comparative theology, as also discussed below.[34]

Heim argues that the differences among the religions are simply matters of language or superficial practice. Rather, the differences are fundamental and ultimately get at their ends. While Lindbeck argues that religions are different because they have different languages, Heim turns this claim on its head by stating that the differences in languages come from the reality that the religions themselves are fundamentally different.[35] He argues that the existence of different religions means that there are different salvations. While this may initially sound somewhat like Hick's approach, Heim is careful to show how it is actually quite different.

---

mutualist Christians are so intent on nurturing one forest of religions that they miss, or even cut down, the forest for the trees. In other words, these Christians, in seeking to promote dialogue, end up as imperialists who, contrary to their own good intentions, take advantage of other religions for their own noble, but self-serving intents. (Ibid., 157)

32. Ibid., 173.

33. Ibid., 175.

34. Ibid., 177.

35. S. Mark Heim, *Salvations: Truth and Differences in Religion* (Maryknoll, NY: Orbis Books, 1995), 149.

In discussing questions about the afterlife, Heim emphasizes the differences between his model and that of Hick. He notes that the Christian understanding of communion with God after death and the Buddhist understanding of nirvana are fundamentally different.[36] While Hick's approach to differences among the religions is to do the work of reinterpretation until the seeming contradiction is no more, Heim forges a different path. He argues, "nirvana and communion with God are contradictory only if we assume that one or the other must be the sole fate for all human beings. True, they cannot both be true at the same time of the same person. But for different people, or the same person at different times, there is no necessary contradiction in both being true."[37] Under Hick's approach, if one version of the afterlife contradicts another, it must be that the truth is something beyond what the two versions describe. The distinctiveness of Heim's approach is that he shows an interest in letting both contradictory accounts stand as they are.[38]

To carry this further, Knitter points out that Heim moves in the direction of not just positing different ends but also positing different "ultimates." Heim offers three potential claims regarding the ultimate or ultimates. First, there is only one ultimate, and that ultimate is described in one of the many religions. This is the claim of the replacement and fulfillment models described above. Second, there is one ultimate, and that ultimate is described in the many religions. This is the claim of the mutuality model. Finally, there are many ultimates, rather than the one ultimate described by the other models. This is the direction that the acceptance model goes.[39]

Heim concedes that his claim does not fit well with traditional Christianity. At the same time, he argues that his view is fundamentally Christian because it is fundamentally trinitarian. Heim states that the doctrine of the Trinity gives us theological ground to acknowledge the potential for plurality in God. Christians have always claimed that God is not an undifferentiated reality, because they have held that God is in God's self social and plural. Heim argues that just as Christians have long held that there is a plurality to God, the plurality of the religions may fit into it.[40]

36. Ibid.

37. Ibid.

38. Heim writes, "Nirvana and communion with God are contradictory only if we assume that one or the other must be the sole fate for all human beings. True, they cannot both be true at the same time of the same person. But for different people, or the same person at different times, there is no necessary contradiction in both being true" (ibid.).

39. Knitter, *Introducing Theologies of Religions*, 194.

40. Knitter quotes Heim: "The perspective I am suggesting does not fit easily into traditional Christian theological frameworks. It requires fresh and imaginative thought" (ibid., 194–95). This is taken from S. Mark Heim, *The Depths of the Riches: A Trinitarian Theology of Religious Ends* (Grand

The Impasse

Where are we left now that we have considered the above approaches to religious pluralism? Whether we refer to them as exclusivism, inclusivism, and pluralism, or as the replacement, fulfillment, mutuality, and acceptance models, none of these approaches can satisfactorily answer the many questions raised about the religions and salvations. If exclusivism posits a God that would consign millions of people to eternal torment on the basis of religious belief, inclusivism suggests to members of other faiths that they are truly in agreement with Christians, even though they are not explicitly aware of that agreement. This sounds downright colonial. Pluralism is also unhelpful because of the many claims that it is actually a form of inclusivism and removes any differences among the various religions.

Because of this, scholars often argue that we are at an impasse on this topic. A number of solutions are proposed. Knitter presents the acceptance model as one way out of the impasse. His approach of "many true religions, so be it"[41] is attractive in a number of ways. At the same time, many people will find the claim that multiple ultimates result in multiple salvations to be problematic. Two other approaches require mention, and both take issue with the methodology of some of the models described above.

Hill Fletcher argues that feminist thought may have something to add to what has become a tired conversation.[42] Hill Fletcher's specific concern is that conversations about religious difference have been centered on concepts of sameness or difference. To the degree that the religious other is different and thus a threat, the current conversation within Christian theology encourages a retreat into sameness. Additionally, the religious other is always considered in terms of how he or she is like oneself.[43] Even though the standard three

---

Rapids: Eerdmans, 2001). Knitter goes on to say, "We can expect, in other words, that there will be multiple, really different (just as the divine persons of the Trinity are really different) ways in which creatures will relate to, and find their fulfillment in, God. God wants to relate to creation in really different ways, just as God relates to God's self in really different ways, and we can well expect that those different ways of relating are going to take concrete, living form in the religions of the world" (*Introducing Theologies of Religions*, 195).

41. Knitter, *Introducing Theologies of Religions*, 171.

42. Hill Fletcher writes, "The tired paradigms of exclusivism, inclusivism, and pluralism have been critiqued as often as they have been employed. Even the particularist approach of cultural linguists (e.g., George Lindbeck) is in need of an update. None of the positions seems accurate to the lived encounter with the religious 'other' that is often an encounter of sameness and difference. Perhaps more importantly, none can fully embrace the value of difference, while forging solidarity among religious communities" ("Shifting Identity," 7).

43. Hill Fletcher writes:

One way in which theologians have tried to explain the diversity of religious forms is to identify them in an underlying religious sameness. . . . One can see in this approach a self-referential construction of the other, where the person who is different is embraced according

positions of exclusivism, inclusivism, and pluralism can be shown to have key differences, the problem with all of them, according to Hill Fletcher, is that they are all fundamentally self-referential.[44] Even the particularist position (as articulated by Lindbeck) does not move the conversation forward, according to Hill Fletcher, because even with this approach the categories of religion are left intact. In other words, regardless of which of these approaches one takes, one is still Christian, or Buddhist, or atheist, or tribal, and so on. The problem here, according to Hill Fletcher, is that these religious categories organize and differentiate individuals on the basis of one facet of identity.[45]

This problem can be solved, according to Hill Fletcher, by considering the approach of feminist theory to the question of identity. For Hill Fletcher, the key idea that feminist theory can bring to this conversation is that actual identities of actual individuals are not constructed on a single descriptor. In other words, any one descriptor (e.g., gender, race, religion, economic status) is not sufficient to truly understand one's identity. Hill Fletcher traces this recognition in the United States to the advent of womanism, when African American feminists argued that their experiences were not the same as the experiences of white feminists owing to the added layer of race. She states that feminists took this idea even further and argued that multiple layers of identity inform every experience.[46]

Hill Fletcher concedes that many theologians would argue that to declare oneself a Christian means to indicate that one's religious identity and perhaps even one's whole identity has been shaped by Christianity. At the same time, though, she argues that if Christianity and one's understanding of what it means to be a Christian were truly found in one univocal identity, we would see far more agreement among individual Christians and groups of Christians. It is

---

to how he or she is similar to oneself. To interpret the diversity of religions through self-referential constructions of others eliminates both the distinctiveness of Christian witness, practice, and aim *and* the distinctiveness of the witness, practices, and aims of diverse religious communities. Here, difference is seen as a problem and we are encouraged to retreat to the security of sameness. (Ibid., 7–8)

44. Ibid., 9. Fletcher explains that pluralists either first see the shift from "self-centeredness" to "reality-centeredness" in Christ, thus using Christ as the foundation for turning to the diversity of the religions, or they first assume truth within Christianity before turning to other religions.

45. Ibid., 10. Hill Fletcher notes that this is following "a logic of identity" in which people are grouped together in their religious identity and seen as distinct from those who have different religious identities.

46. Hill Fletcher writes, "The identity of being a woman is intersected by race, class, education, ethnicity, age, sexual orientation, and other factors. This insight has implications for the construction of religious identity as well. Each element of identity and past experience combines with others in my own person and shapes my understanding and experience of Christian identity. Rethinking Christian identity using the resources of feminist thought, we find ways to embrace hybridity and forge new solidarities" (ibid., 14–15).

the reality of diversity within Christianity that indicates that Christians do not experience their faith as the totality of their identities.[47]

Hill Fletcher argues that it is the meeting of these identity categories that can account for the diversity within a particular religious tradition. Because these identity categories are never compartmentalized within individuals, one cannot ask about one of them without also accounting for the others.[48] These multiple identity categories result in hybrid identities, and these hybrid identities allow for solidarity in places where it would not be traditionally found. Hill Fletcher points out that solidarity across religious boundaries can be seen in parts of early feminist theology. There, we do not see an insistence on sameness or difference, but rather we see a commonality in feminism. Each writer in that stream displayed two aspects of her identity that came out: a feminist and an adherent of a particular religious tradition. Even though there were differences in religious traditions, the feminist part of the identity was something held in common, according to Hill Fletcher.[49] The reality of hybrid identities can thus help to move us beyond the sameness/difference dichotomy that seems to be the sticking point of the traditional approaches to religious pluralism.[50]

Comparative Theology

One final aspect of this conversation needs to be considered—the work of comparative theology. Knitter mentions comparative theology in his discussion of the acceptance model as another way to move beyond the impasse in the current discussion. The first thing that must be noted is that comparative theology is not the same thing as comparative religion, though many people conflate the two. Comparative theology seeks to look at religious texts or traditions side by side with the assumption that the "other" religious text will somehow inform one's reading of texts from one's own religious tradition. While comparative religious work is done by a detached scholar who has no stake in the outcome of his or her work, comparative theology is done by a theologian who is fully engaged in one or more religious traditions. Because of this, the theologian has a stake in the outcome and assumes that the work of bringing disparate texts together will result in some key insights into one's own tradition or traditions.

Francis Clooney offers a helpful explanation of comparative theology by noting that it is an act of "faith seeking understanding" that starts in a particular

47. Ibid., 15.
48. Ibid., 17.
49. Ibid., 20.
50. Ibid., 22.

faith tradition but ventures into other faith traditions. The desired result is learning that gives new insights into one's own tradition and also new insights to the "other" tradition.[51] Another key point made by Clooney is that there is nothing essentially Christian about comparative theology.[52] Unlike the approaches to theologies of religious pluralism described above, comparative theology can be done in conversation with the Christian tradition, but properly carried out, it will not privilege the Christian conversation. Clooney notes that if comparative theology were only done within Christianity without analogues in other traditions, an interreligious conversation would likely not result, because comparative theology would simply be a conversation among Christians. If theology is something that takes place in multiple traditions (and while that is debated, Clooney thinks that it does), then comparative theology can happen across traditions.[53]

John Thatamanil argues that the work of comparative theology is necessary because of the contemporary context. While in the past a wise person was typically someone who mastered one religious tradition, today, in order to have true wisdom, a person must engage with multiple traditions and see the world through multiple lenses.[54]

Clooney argues that a rich cross-fertilization can happen in the course of doing comparative theology. Because the work of comparative theology is not just a conversation held among Christians, there are ways in which it can enrich all traditions, rather than simply Christianity. Clooney argues that his own theology has been deeply informed by his study of Hinduism. He offers an example in his *Divine Mother, Blessed Mother*, in which he argues that Christian conversations about God and gender could be enriched by a consideration of how Hinduism treats divinity and gender.[55]

How does one do this work of comparative theology? Clooney argues that comparative theology "favors experiments, instances of learning."[56] The work of

51. Francis X. Clooney, *Comparative Theology: Deep Learning across Religious Borders* (Oxford: Wiley-Blackwell, 2010), 10.

52. Ibid., 11.

53. Ibid., 80.

54. John Thatamanil, "Binocular Wisdom: The Benefits of Participating in Multiple Religious Traditions," *Huffington Post Religion*, May 25, 2011, http://www.huffingtonpost.com/john-thatamanil /binocular-religious-wisdo_b_827793.html. Thatamanil writes, "In an older era, a person was accounted wise if he or she attained to a practical mastery of one tradition. Think St. Francis of Assisi. But our age requires also (not instead of) a new kind of wisdom: the capacity to see the world through more than one set of religious lenses and to integrate into one life, insofar as possible, what is disclosed through those lenses."

55. Clooney, *Comparative Theology*, 83. Here citing his earlier work, *Divine Mother, Blessed Mother* (New York: Oxford University Press, 2004).

56. Clooney, *Comparative Theology*, 57.

comparative theology involves reading religious texts that come out of various traditions. Perhaps what is most significant about Clooney's account of reading texts is that reading is an act in which the reader enters into one tradition and then reads from another tradition such that there is a movement back and forth between traditions.[57] Clooney argues that the work of reading must be focused on the text itself and the things to which the text points. He notes that the first obstacle to doing this kind of work is one of language. When one reads the text of a religious other, that is most often going to involve reading a text in a different language than one's own religious texts. If that is the case, one must either learn that language or be willing to work with translations (an option that Clooney says is quite legitimate). Once one is actually reading, Clooney says that the process should be "patient and persistent." He does say that the reader should be attentive to when the text points beyond itself to other contexts (whether these contexts are textual or historical). Ultimately, though, Clooney argues that the one who does this work of reading should emphasize insights that come from the work of reading itself, rather than by interpretations of things beyond the text.[58]

One difficulty that may come up when doing comparative theology has to do with reading unfamiliar texts from an initially unfamiliar tradition. Clooney wants to be clear that this reading is not to be done in isolation. Instead, reading should be done with the aid of commentary. Commentary recognizes that the text in question is one that has been passed down in a particular tradition and appreciated by earlier readers. Commentary also helps the reader to be aware of his or her own personal interests in approaching the text by showing differences between the way the text has been perceived by tradition and the way the reader may be inclined to read it.[59] Clooney concedes that the work of reading and understanding commentary is not easy and that results will not come quickly. In addition to learning the commentary and context around the text, it is also important to consider the standards for academic scholarship. While faith perspectives can have a role in commentary, it should not be hard

---

57. Clooney writes,

> Just as we learn religiously from going to a temple or hearing sacred recitation, comparative practice occurs when *acts* of reading have been undertaken, as we read back and forth across religious borders, examining multiple texts, individually, but then too in light of one another. To claim this is nothing extraordinary: texts have been central to most theologies as they have been to most disciplines in the humanities, and there is no reason to imagine that interreligious learning should be primarily non-textual learning. Reading can be primary even if religion is not lived only or mainly through books, and even if religious learning is not always a matter of book learning. (Ibid., 58)

58. Ibid., 60.
59. Ibid., 60–61.

to differentiate between a commentary on a text from a detached perspective and a commentary on a text from a particular religious perspective.[60]

Clooney ultimately argues that this work is a religious practice. Reading texts in other traditions and crossing from those traditions to one's own can have a deep impact on one's religious life. It is important to point out, though, that the question of religion itself is one that is not settled for many comparative theologians. For example, Thatamanil raises a key question about the continued resistance of many Christian theologians to the work of comparative theology. At the root of Thatamanil's question is the framework within which Christian theologians work. He notes that comparative theology has remained on the outskirts of contemporary theology as a whole and that most Christian theologians do not think that considering the commitments of other faiths is an important component of theological work. In response to this problem, Thatamanil asks, "Is not all theology *necessarily* comparative? What grounds the persistent dichotomy between systematic theology proper and comparative theology? Why is comparative work relegated to history of religions and not itself a constitutive feature of Christian theology?"[61]

Thatamanil argues that Christian thinkers do not often see other faiths as relevant to Christian theological reflection and that part of the problem may be in the use of religion as a category. He writes, "What might it mean for theology to think beyond and after 'religion'?"[62] To talk about interreligious work or interfaith dialogue is to assume that the world is naturally divided into various discrete religions. Thatamanil points out that postcolonial theorists raise some questions about this, noting that power is not divided equally among the various religious traditions.[63] This leads him to question the value of the category "religion" and consider whether it might be likened to race.

While a full discussion of his claims is not essential here, what is important to note is that Thatamanil questions religion as a category precisely because it seems to give Christian theologians a way to compartmentalize their work such that the claims and practices of other faiths do not need to be engaged. Thatamanil argues that this is a colonialist approach that has kept the work of comparative theology on the margins. He proposes thinking beyond religion as a category, which he argues will then make clear that the theological task is necessarily comparative.[64]

60. Ibid., 61–62.
61. John Thatamanil, "Comparative Theology after Religion," in *Planetary Loves: Postcoloniality, and Theology*, ed. Stephen D. Moore and Mayra Rivera (New York: Fordham University Press, 2011), 240.
62. Ibid., 246.
63. Ibid., 251.
64. Ibid., 238–57.

Conclusion

Some may ask why theologies of religious pluralism and comparative theology are covered in a book on theological method. To be sure, there are some clear differences between what has been covered in this chapter and in any other chapter in this book. At the same time, the concerns raised by a number of thinkers discussed in this chapter are fundamentally methodological concerns. This is nowhere more clear than with Thatamanil's question about whether all theology is inherently methodological. Certainly, comparative theology comes across as being quite different from what may be understood as traditional Christian theology. At its heart, though, is a fundamental methodological claim: that the experiences and beliefs of other faiths should serve as data for theological work. As a result, Christian theologians who ignore or marginalize comparative theology risk missing a theological movement that is seeking to understand how people of different faiths can enrich one another within their own traditions.

CONCLUSION

Where Do We Go from Here?

After examining many of the most important theologians of the twentieth and twenty-first centuries, it is clear that there is far from a consensus about theological method. Some may suggest that a lack of a consensus is a reason to set aside methodological concerns, and yet, as one can see after exploring the work of these various theologians, methodological differences yield significant theological differences. If Christians take seriously the idea that theological reflection matters deeply, theological methodology matters deeply as well.

Perhaps one of the clearest examples of differences in methodology leading to differences in theological reflection can be seen by placing Karl Barth and Karl Rahner side by side. Barth and Rahner are interesting figures to bring together. Barth is often considered the most important Protestant theologian of the twentieth century, while Rahner is often considered the most important Catholic theologian of the twentieth century. In comparing them, their methodological differences become apparent. Barth's insistence on God and the Word of God as the starting point for theology leads him to different conclusions than those of Rahner. Rahner insists that theology must start with the human being; before any theological work can be done, it is important to first establish that the human being can receive revelation from God should God choose self-disclosure to humanity. As a result, Rahner takes universal human religious experience as his starting point, whereas Barth holds that starting theological reflection with considerations of human beings is precisely what is wrong with the Protestant liberalism in which he was educated.

While there is great diversity within Protestantism and Catholicism, Barth and Rahner clearly reflect some key features of their respective traditions. Barth's early post–World War I work emphasizes the distinction between creator and creation. God's "no" emphasizes how God is totally other than the creation. Because of this, as noted earlier, Barth does not see general revelation as a source for fruitful theology. Rahner takes an analogical approach that emphasizes the many points of contact between creator and creation. This comes precisely from his assumption that the grace of God pervades all creation and that all human beings have contact with it in some way. For Rahner, general revelation can tell humanity many things about God, though this does not diminish the importance of special revelation.

What strengths and weaknesses do these positions have? Elizabeth Johnson points out that both approaches can be problematic if taken to the extreme. An overemphasis on points of contact between the creator and the creation can lead one into pantheism, a divinizing of all creation. Rahner is careful not to do to that, but an extreme version of his position could do that. An overemphasis on the distinctions between God and creation can lead to the opposite problem. Taken to the extreme, that position could suggest that it is impossible to know anything about God, which could lead to a functional atheism.[1] This is precisely why it is important to read Barth and Rahner in conversation with each other. They disagree, and their disagreements are important, but reading them side by side can serve as a powerful reminder of the potential pitfalls of one's own theological commitments, as well as those of others.

It wouldn't be fair to talk about weaknesses without also talking about strengths. Barth serves as a powerful reminder that God must be at the center of Christian theology. His critique of Protestant liberalism also makes clear the potential dangers in an anthropocentric approach to theology. Rahner makes clear the import of God's grace throughout creation. He serves as an important reminder that God is at work in the world and is constantly making grace available to human beings.

We can make similar observations about the other thinkers in this book. Certainly, George Lindbeck's work seeks to take seriously the importance of meeting other traditions on their own terms and not emphasizing consensus to the point of watering down one's own tradition or those of others. The insight that religious systems are learned in the same way as language and culture are learned has opened up new possibilities and new conversations with those in other theological circles. At the same time, Lindbeck's work does not seem to be entirely clear concerning the relationship between Christianity and other faiths, which has made it difficult to interpret his work.

The evangelical theologians remind all Christians about the importance of the biblical text and of living a Christlike life. Stanley Grenz's emphasis on

---

1. I am grateful to Elizabeth Johnson for this insight. Lecture at Fordham University, Spring 2006.

the believing community is important because it highlights another strength of evangelicalism: lived community. It is an interesting reality that, although Catholicism has a far more developed ecclesiology, Protestant evangelicalism can often have a more robust communal experience on the level of the local church. Grenz's work draws from that reality by offering a serious evangelical reflection on the nature of the community. At the same time, some theologians, including Kevin Vanhoozer, have raised questions about Grenz's interpretation of and commitment to the work of Lindbeck, arguing that Grenz has taken up some of the relativistic tendencies they see in Lindbeck's work.

The thinkers that fall under the umbrella of political theologies have emphasized the importance of doing theological work in context, on the ground. They have argued that talking about universal human religious experience can be problematic, because it insinuates that all human beings share common experiences and a common starting point. By trying to speak of human beings in a universal sense, the political theologians hold, the theologian has talked about no actual human beings. The political and feminist theologians have also pointed out the importance of connecting ethics to theological work. These theologians are not content to simply consider the being of God; rather, they seek to describe how God acts in the world and how Christians are called to act in response. At the same time, many people have argued that these theologians wed the political too closely to the theological and that they have sought to use theology to endorse their political or ethical commitments.

The theologians working on theologies of religious pluralism and comparative theology offer a reminder that Christianity does not exist in a vacuum. Rather, it exists in a world made up of a rich diversity of religious traditions. In the contemporary context, it is impossible for Christians to ignore questions about the status of other faiths and the relationship of those faiths to Christianity. If John Thatamanil is right, that all theology is fundamentally comparative, then Christian theologians must take seriously the work of comparative theology. Thatamanil rightly points out that comparative theology currently exists on the margins of Christian systemic theology; this is likely due to the many questions that remain concerning the relationship between the claims of other faiths and the claims of Christianity.

One final question might be posed to students of Christian theology: Who is Christ in each of these theological systems? While varying theological schools of thought understand Jesus in somewhat different ways, Christian theologians generally all agree that to be Christian implies placing the person of Christ in a position of prominence. Not all will argue for starting with Christ, but none will deny the importance of Christ. Exploring the question of who Christ is in each of these systems is an important step in understanding their methodologies and theological claims.

So where should a student of theology go from here? That is for the reader to decide. This book isn't interested in telling students which theological commitments to take up. Rather, it is interested in putting tools in the hands of students so that students can evaluate theological claims and the methodologies behind them. The truly interesting question is not about what the professor thinks but rather about what the student thinks.

Regardless of which position one takes up, one should take seriously Grenz's echo of Hans Frei's call for a generous orthodoxy. Frei and Grenz tend to talk about it in relation to evangelicalism and liberalism, but there is no reason a generous orthodoxy has to be limited to that. A generous orthodoxy for methodology might articulate a Christian center and allow room for elements of many or all of the perspectives outlined above. If every Christian is a theologian, the most important question to ask is whether one is a good theologian. By considering the varying assumptions, commitments, sources, and starting points of the theologians discussed throughout these pages, this study has aimed at moving the reader forward on the path to becoming a good theologian.

SUGGESTED READING LIST
FOR STUDENTS

Karl Barth, *Evangelical Theology*, chapter 2
James H. Cone, *A Black Theology of Liberation*, chapters 1–2
Avery Dulles, *The Craft of Theology*, chapters 5–6
Stanley J. Grenz, *Theology for the Community of God*, introduction
Gustavo Gutiérrez, *A Theology of Liberation*, chapters 1–2
Elizabeth A. Johnson, *She Who Is*, chapters 1–2
George Lindbeck, *The Nature of Doctrine*, chapter 4
Bernard Lonergan, *Method in Theology*, chapter 1
Wolfhart Pannenberg, *An Introduction to Systematic Theology*, chapter 1
Karl Rahner, *Foundations of Christian Faith*, introduction
Paul Tillich, *Systematic Theology*, vol. 1, chapter 1
Delores S. Williams, *Sisters in the Wilderness*, chapter 6

BIBLIOGRAPHY

Albrecht, Gloria. *Hitting Home: Feminist Ethics, Women's Work, and the Betrayal of Family Values*. New York: Continuum, 2004.

Barth, Karl. "Biblical Questions, Insights, and Vistas." In *The Word of God and Theology*, translated by Amy Marga, 71–100. New York: T&T Clark, 2011.

———. *Church Dogmatics*. 4 vols. Edited by G. W. Bromiley and T. F. Torrance. Edinburgh: T&T Clark, 1956.

———. *Evangelical Theology, an Introduction*. Translated by Grover Foley. New York: Holt, Rinehart & Winston, 1963.

———. "The Righteousness of God." In *The Word of God and Theology*, translated by Amy Marga, 1–14. New York: Harper Torchbooks, 1956.

The Catechism of the Catholic Church. 2nd ed. New York: Doubleday, 1995.

Clifford, Anne M. *Introducing Feminist Theology*. Maryknoll, NY: Orbis Books, 2001.

Clooney, Francis X. *Comparative Theology: Deep Learning across Religious Borders*. Oxford: Wiley-Blackwell, 2010.

Cone, James H. *Black Theology and Black Power*. 2nd ed. Maryknoll, NY: Orbis Books, 1989.

———. *A Black Theology of Liberation*. 20th anniversary ed. Maryknoll, NY: Orbis Books, 1990.

———. *God of the Oppressed*. Rev. ed. Maryknoll, NY: Orbis Books, 1997.

———. *Martin and Malcolm and America: A Dream or a Nightmare*. Maryknoll, NY: Orbis Books, 1992.

———. *My Soul Looks Back*. Maryknoll, NY: Orbis Books, 1986.

Conference of Latin American Bishops (CELAM). "Justice." September 6, 1968, Medellín, Colombia. http://theolibrary.shc.edu/resources/medjust.htm.

———. "Peace." September 6, 1968, Medellín, Colombia. http://theolibrary.shc.edu/resources/medpeace.htm.

———. "Poverty of the Church." September 6, 1968, Medellín, Colombia. http:// theolibrary.shc.edu/resources/medpov.htm.

Davies, Lizzy. "Pope Francis declares: 'I would like to see a church that is poor and is for the poor.'" *Guardian*, March 16, 2013. http://www.theguardian.com/world /2013/mar/16/pope-francis-church-poverty.

Dominus Iesus. http://www.vatican.va/roman_curia/congregations/cfaith/docu ments/rc_con_cfaith_doc_20000806_dominus-iesus_en.html.

Dulles, Avery. *The Craft of Theology: From Symbol to System.* Expanded ed. New York: Crossroad, 1995.

———. "A Life in Theology: 39th McGinley Lecture." *America*, April 21, 2008. http:// americamagazine.org/node/148690.

———. *Models of Revelation.* Maryknoll, NY: Orbis Books, 1992.

———. "Priesthood and Gender." In *Church and Society: The Lawrence J. McGinley Lectures, 1988–2007*, 205–20. New York: Fordham University Press, 2008.

———. *A Testimonial to Grace and Reflections on a Theological Journey.* New York: Sheed & Ward, 1996.

Erickson, Millard J. *The Evangelical Left: Encountering Postconservative Evangelical Theology.* Grand Rapids: Baker, 1997.

———. *Introducing Christian Doctrine.* Edited by L. Arnold Hustad. Grand Rapids: Baker, 1992.

Fodor, James. "Postliberal Theology." In *The Modern Theologians: An Introduction to Christian Theology since 1918*, edited by David F. Ford with Rachel Muirs, 229–48. Malden, MA: Blackwell, 2005.

Frei, Hans W. *The Eclipse of the Biblical Narrative: A Study in Eighteenth and Nineteenth Century Hermeneutics.* New Haven: Yale University Press, 1974.

———. "Remarks in Connection with a Theological Proposal." In *Theology and Narrative: Selected Essays*, edited by George Hunsinger and William C. Placher, 26–44. New York: Oxford University Press, 1993.

———. "Response to 'Narrative Theology: An Evangelical Appraisal.'" *Trinity Journal* 8 (1987): 21–24.

Gadamer, Hans Georg. *Truth and Method.* Translated by Garrett Barden and John Cumming. New York: Seabury Press, 1975.

Gaudium et Spes. In *The Documents of Vatican II*, edited by Walter M. Abbott, 199–308. New York: Guild Press, 1966. http://www.vatican.va/archive/hist_councils/ii_vati can_council/documents/vat-ii_const_19651207_gaudium-et-spes_en.html.

Goizueta, Roberto S. "Karl Rahner." In *Beyond the Pale: Reading Theology from the Margins*, edited by Miguel De La Torre and Stacey Thomas, 177–82. Louisville: Westminster John Knox, 2011.

González, Justo L. *A History of Christian Thought: From the Beginnings to the Council of Chalcedon.* Nashville: Abingdon, 1987.

Grenz, Stanley J. *The Named God and the Question of Being.* Louisville: Westminster John Knox, 2005.

———. *Reason for Hope: The Systematic Theology of Wolfhart Pannenberg.* 2nd ed. Grand Rapids: Eerdmans, 2005.

———. *Renewing the Center: Evangelical Theology in a Post-Theological Era.* 2nd ed. Grand Rapids: Baker Academic, 2006.

———. *Revisioning Evangelical Theology: A Fresh Agenda for the 21st Century.* Downers Grove, IL: InterVarsity, 1993.

———. *The Social God and the Relational Self: A Trinitarian Theology of the Imago Dei.* Louisville: Westminster John Knox, 2001.

———. *Theology for the Community of God.* 2nd ed. Grand Rapids: Eerdmans, 2000.

Grenz, Stanley J., David Guretzki, and Cherith Fee Nordling. *The Pocket Dictionary of Theological Terms.* Downers Grove, IL: InterVarsity, 1999.

Grenz, Stanley J., and Roger E. Olson. *20th-Century Theology: God and the World in a Transitional Age.* Downers Grove, IL: InterVarsity, 1992.

———. *Who Needs Theology? An Invitation to the Study of God.* Downers Grove, IL: InterVarsity, 1996.

Gutiérrez, Gustavo. *A Theology of Liberation.* Rev. ed. Maryknoll, NY: Orbis Books, 1988.

Hardy, Daniel W. "Karl Barth." In *The Modern Theologians: An Introduction to Christian Theology since 1918,* edited by David F. Ford with Rachel Muers, 21–42. Malden, MA: Blackwell, 2005.

Harnack, Adolf von. *What Is Christianity?* Translated by Thomas Bailey Saunders. New York: Harper, 1957.

Heim, S. Mark. *The Depths of the Riches: A Trinitarian Theology of Religious Ends.* Grand Rapids: Eerdmans, 2001.

———. *Salvations: Truth and Difference in Religion.* Maryknoll, NY: Orbis Books, 1995.

Hill Fletcher, Jeannine. "Shifting Identity: The Contribution of Feminist Thought to Theologies of Religious Pluralism." *Feminist Studies in Religion* 19, no. 2 (2003): 5–24.

Hunsinger, George. "What Can Evangelicals & Postliberals Learn from Each Other? The Carl Henry–Hans Frei Exchange Reconsidered." In *The Nature of Confession: Evangelicals and Postliberals in Conversation,* edited by Timothy R. Phillips and Dennis L. Okholm, 134–50. Downers Grove, IL: InterVarsity, 1996.

Johnson, Elizabeth A. "Forging Theology: A Conversation with Colleagues." In *Things New and Old: Essays on the Theology of Elizabeth A. Johnson,* edited by Phyllis Zagano and Terrence W. Tilley, 91–123. New York: Crossroad, 1999.

———. "Redeeming the Name of Christ." In *Freeing Theology: The Essentials of Theology in Feminist Perspective,* edited by Catherine Mowry LaCugna, 115–38. San Francisco: HarperSanFrancisco, 1993.

———. *She Who Is: The Mystery of God in Feminist Theological Discourse.* New York: Crossroad, 2002.

———. "Worth a Life." In *Vatican II: Fifty Personal Stories,* edited by William Madges and Michael J. Daley, 236–40. Maryknoll, NY: Orbis Books, 2012.

Johnson, Keith L. *Karl Barth and the* Analogia Entis. New York: Continuum, 2010.

Kegley, Charles W., and Robert W. Bretall, eds. *The Theology of Paul Tillich.* New York: Macmillan, 1964.

Kelsey, David H. "Paul Tillich." In *The Modern Theologians: An Introduction to Christian Theology Since 1918,* edited by David F. Ford with Rachel Muers, 62–75. Malden, MA: Blackwell, 2005.

Knitter, Paul F. *Introducing Theologies of Religions.* Maryknoll, NY: Orbis Books, 2002.

Koop, Doug. "Clark Pinnock Dies at 73." *Christianity Today,* August 17, 2010. http://www.christianitytoday.com/ct/2010/augustweb-only/43-22.0.html.

Krolokke, Charlotte, and Anne Scott Sorensen. *Gender Communication Theories: From Silence to Performance.* Thousand Oaks, CA: Sage, 2006.

Kwok Pui-lan. "Feminist Theology as Intercultural Discourse." In *The Cambridge Companion to Feminist Theology,* edited by Susan Frank Parsons, 23–39. Cambridge: Cambridge University Press, 2002.

Lindbeck, George A. *The Nature of Doctrine: Religion and Theology in a Postliberal Age.* Louisville: Westminster John Knox, 1984.

Lindbeck, George, George Hunsinger, Alister McGrath, and Gabriel Fackre. "A Panel Discussion." In *The Nature of Confession: Evangelicals and Postliberals in Conversation,* edited by Timothy R. Phillips and Dennis L. Okholm, 246–54. Downers Grove, IL: InterVarsity, 1996.

Lonergan, Bernard. *Insight: A Study of Human Understanding.* Toronto: University of Toronto Press, 1992.

———. "Insight Revisited." In *A Second Collection,* edited by William F. J. Ryan and Bernard J. Tyrrell, 263–78. Philadelphia: Westminster, 1974.

———. *Method in Theology.* 2nd ed. New York: Herder & Herder, 1972.

Lowen, James. *Lies My Teacher Told Me.* New York: Touchstone, 2007.

Lumen Gentium. http://www.vatican.va/archive/hist_councils/ii_vatican_council/documents/vat-ii_const_19641121_lumen-gentium_en.html.

Markham, Ian. "Christianity and Other Religions." In *The Blackwell Companion to Modern Theology,* edited by Gareth Jones, 405–17. Oxford: Blackwell, 2004.

Marmion, Declan. "Rahner and His Critics: Revisiting the Dialogue." *Irish Theological Quarterly* 68 (2003): 195–212.

Marx, Karl. "A Contribution to the Critique of Hegel's Philosophy of Right." *Deutsch-Französische Jahrbücher,* vols. 7 and 10, February 1844.

McFadden, Robert D. "Cardinal Avery Dulles, Theologian, Is Dead at 90." *New York Times,* December 12, 2008. http://www.nytimes.com/2008/12/13/us/13dulles.html.

McGrath, Alister E. *Christian Theology: An Introduction*. Oxford: Blackwell, 2006.

———. *Theology: The Basics*. 2nd ed. Malden, MA: Blackwell, 2008.

Metz, Johann Baptist. *Faith in History and Society: Toward a Practical Fundamental Theology*. Translated by J. Matthew Ashley. New York: Herder & Herder, 2007.

Migliore, Daniel L. *Faith Seeking Understanding: An Introduction to Christian Theology*. 2nd ed. Grand Rapids: Eerdmans, 2004.

Moore-Keish, Martha. "Karl Barth and John Thatamanil: Two Theologians against Religion." *Bangalore Theological Forum* 45, no. 2 (2013): 91–104.

Noll, Mark A. *Turning Points: Decisive Moments in the History of Christianity*. 3rd ed. Grand Rapids: Baker Academic, 2012.

Oden, Thomas C. *Classic Christianity: A Systematic Theology*. San Francisco: HarperOne, 2009.

Pannenberg, Wolfhart. *Basic Questions in Theology*. 2 vols. Philadelphia: Fortress, 1970.

———. "God's Presence in History." *Christian Century*, March 11, 1981, 260–63.

———. Introduction. In *Revelation as History*, 18–19. New York: Macmillan, 1968.

———. *An Introduction to Systematic Theology*, Grand Rapids: Eerdmans, 1991.

———. "Jesus' History and Our History." Translated by Ted Peters. *Perspectives in Religious Studies* 1, no. 2 (1974): 134–42.

———. *Systematic Theology*. 3 vols. Translated by Geoffrey W. Bromiley. Grand Rapids: Eerdmans, 1991.

———. "Theological Questions to Scientists." *Zygon* 16, no. 1 (March 1981): 65–77.

Patel, Eboo. *Acts of Faith: The Story of an American Muslim, the Struggle for the Soul of a Generation*. Boston: Beacon, 2007.

Phillips, Timothy R. and Dennis L. Okholm, eds. *The Nature of Confession: Evangelicals and Postliberals in Conversation*. Downers Grove, IL: InterVarsity, 1996.

Pinnock, Clark H. *Most Moved Mover: A Theology of God's Openness*. Grand Rapids: Baker Academic, 2001.

Placher, William C. *A History of Christian Theology: An Introduction*. Philadelphia: Westminster, 1983.

Rahner, Karl. Foreword to *Theology and Discovery: Essays in Honor of Karl Rahner, SJ*, edited by William J. Kelley, n.p. Milwaukee: Marquette University Press, 1980.

———. *Foundations of Christian Faith*. Translated by William V. Dych. New York: Crossroad, 1989.

———. *I Remember: An Autobiographical Interview*. Translated by Harvey D. Egan. New York: Crossroad, 1984.

———. *Karl Rahner in Dialogue: Conversations and Interviews, 1965–1982*. Edited by Paul Imhof and Hubert Biallowons. New York: Crossroad, 1986.

———. "Observations on the Problem of the Anonymous Christians." In *Theological Investigations*, vol. 14, translated by David Bourke, 280–94. London: Darton, Longman & Todd, 1976.

———. "Relationship between Nature and Grace: The Supernatural Existential." In *Theological Investigations*, vol. 1, translated by Cornelius Ernst, 297–319. Baltimore: Helcion, 1961.

———. *Theological Investigations*. Vol. 16. Translated by David Morland. London: Darton, Longman & Todd, 1979.

———. "Theology and Anthropology." In *Theological Investigations*, vol. 9, translated by Graham Harrison, 28–42. London: Darton, Longman & Todd, 1972.

Rahner, Karl, and Herbert Vorgrimler. "Nouvelle Theologie." In *Theological Dictionary*, 318–19. New York: Herder and Herder, 1965.

Schneewind, Jerome B. "Scottish Common Sense Philosophy." In *The Cambridge Dictionary of Philosophy*, ed. Robert Audi, 822–23. Cambridge: Cambridge University Press, 1999.

Stanton, Elizabeth Cady, and the Revising Committee. *The Woman's Bible*. New York: European Publishing, 1895–98.

Thatamanil, John. "Binocular Wisdom: The Benefits of Participating in Multiple Religious Traditions." *Huffington Post Religion*, May 25, 2011. http://www.huffingtonpost.com/john-thatamanil/binocular-religious-wisdo_b_827793.html.

———. "Comparative Theology after Religion." In *Planetary Loves: Spivak, Postcoloniality, and Theology*, edited by Stephen D. Moore and Mayra Rivera, 238–57. New York: Fordham University Press, 2011.

Thorsen, Don. *The Wesleyan Quadrilateral: Scripture, Tradition, Reason, and Experience as a Model of Evangelical Theology*. Lexington: Emeth, 2005.

Tillich, Paul. *Dynamics of Faith*. New York: Harper & Row, 1957.

———. *Systematic Theology*. 3 vols. Chicago: University of Chicago Press, 1951–63.

Vanhoozer, Kevin J. *The Drama of Doctrine: A Canonical-Linguistic Approach to Christian Theology*. Louisville: Westminster John Knox, 2005.

———. *First Theology: God, Scripture, and Hermeneutics*. Downers Grove, IL: InterVarsity, 2002.

Veeneman, Mary. "Relation and Person: Potential Contributions of Karl Rahner's Theology to Evangelical Trinitarian Debates." In *The New Evangelical Subordinationism? Perspectives on the Equality of God the Father and God the Son*, edited by Dennis W. Jowers and H. Wayne House, 311–24. Eugene, OR: Wipf & Stock, 2012.

Weinstein, Allen, and David Rubel. *The Story of America*. London: DK, 2002.

Williams, Delores S. "The Color of Feminism: Or Speaking the Black Woman's Tongue." *Journal of Religious Thought* 43, no. 1 (1986): 42–58.

———. *Sisters in the Wilderness: The Challenge of Womanist God-Talk*. Maryknoll, NY: Orbis Books, 1993.

———. "Womanist Theology: Black Women's Voices." In *Feminist Theology from the Third World: A Reader*, edited by Ursula King, 77–87. Maryknoll, NY: Orbis Books, 1994.

Yamauchi, Edwin M. "The Curse of Ham." *Criswell Theological Review* 6, no. 2 (Spring 2009): 45–60.

INDEX

abolitionist movement, 142
acceptance model, the, 177–79
accidentally necessary doctrines, 70
African-American theology, 126–40, 146–47, 158–67
Anabaptists, 134
analogy of being, 28–29
anonymous Christian, the, 52–55, 171
Anthony, Susan B., 142
anthropology, theological, 50–54, 57–58. *See also* humanity
anxiety, freedom and, 45–46
Apollinaris, 154–55
Arianism, 154
ascertainment, identification and, 163
atheism, 42–43, 188
atonement, 166–67. *See also* salvation
author, intention of, 19
authority, scriptural, 103–4

baptism, 96n71. *See also* sacraments, the
Barth, Karl
  exclusivism of, 173–74
  methodology of, 9, 14, 187–88
  situation of, 1–2
  theology of, 25–30, 38

being, analogy of, 28–29
Bergoglio, Jorge. *See* Francis (pope)
Bible, the
  the church and, 95, 99–100, 102–5
  doctrine and, 59
  evangelicalism and, 108–10
  feminism and, 141, 148–49, 152–53, 161–62
  interpretation of, 12, 75–77, 100–106
  in liberation theology, 133–34, 161–62
  neo-scholasticism and, 18–21
  as source of theology, 11–12, 18–21, 82–84, 89
  textuality of, 73–77
biblical theology, 19
black and white, liberation and, 139–40
Black Power, 131–32
black theology, 126–40, 146–47, 158–67
Black Theology and Black Power (Cone), 131–32
Black Theology of Liberation, A (Cone), 132–36

Calvin, John, 8–10
Canaan, curse of, 128–29
canonical-linguistic theology, 99–100, 102–6

capitalism, feminism and, 145–46
categories, magisterial, 23
catholicity, evangelicalism and, 102–3
CDF. *See* Congregation for the Doctrine of the Faith (CDF)
CELAM. *See* Conference of Latin American Bishops (CELAM)
cenobitic monasticism, 48–49
Christ
  anthropocentrism and, 51
  creation and, 29–30
  feminism and, 153–58
  incarnation of, 46–48, 170, 173
  liberation and, 137–39
  methodology and, 189
  pluralism and, 170, 173
  salvation and, 53–55, 153–56, 166–67
  as Word of God, 28
church, the
  ecclesiology and, 94–96
  evangelical theology and, 91–93
  feminism and, 154–56, 159, 160
  liberation and, 122–24, 131–32, 134–35
  scripture and, 99–100, 102–5

See also community; magisterium, Roman Catholic
church doctrines, 59
church hopping, 85n20
Cinderella, the Spirit as, 105n109
Clooney, Francis, 181–84
cognitive propositionalism, 63–64
Communion, Holy, 96n71. *See also* sacraments, the
community, 65–74, 84–96, 102–5, 162. *See also* church, the
comparative theology, 181–85, 189
concern, ultimate, 41–42
conditionally essential doctrines, 69–70
Cone, James, 130–40, 161–62
Conference of Latin American Bishops (CELAM), 115–17
conflict, doctrine and, 66–67, 87n24
Congregation for the Doctrine of the Faith (CDF), 22
conscientization, 122n52
consciousness, human, 57–58, 163
consciousness-raising groups, 144
construal, scriptural, 26, 100–102
context, 18, 90–91. *See also* situation, theological
continuity, scriptural, 104n104
contradiction, doctrinal, 87n24
conversion, doctrine and, 60
correlation, theological, 36–39
Council of Trent, 20
Craft of Theology, The (Dulles), 19–20
creation, 28–30, 31, 33, 34, 52
critical reflection, theology as, 118–19
cultural feminism, 144–45
culture, hermeneutics of, 19

death, humanity and, 44–46
Dei Verbum, 19, 21, 22
despair, estrangement and, 44–46
development, economic, 119, 145–46
dialogical intent, womanist, 159
didactic intent, womanist, 159–60
difference, pluralism and, 173, 177–81. *See also* diversity
disputes, doctrinal, 66–67, 87n24
dissent, theological, 22–25
diversity, 160, 173, 177–81
divine revelation. *See* revelation, divine
doctrine
  the Bible as, 19
  community and, 65–74, 91–93
  methodology and, 59–60, 166–67
  in postliberal theology, 62–74
  in Protestant liberalism, 25–26
  rule theory of, 64–67, 86–87
  theology and, 67–68, 72–74
Dominus Iesus, 171–72
dramatic, theology as, 103–5
dreaming innocence, 44–46
dream states, 57n89
Dulles, Avery, 15–25, 155–56

ecclesiology, community and, 94–96. *See also* church, the
ecofeminism, 147
economic development, 119, 145–46
Emancipation Proclamation, 126
empirical consciousness, 57–58
encounter, vertical, 163
epistemology, 57–58, 91n48, 164
Erickson, Millard, 81–84
eschatology, realist, 32–33

essential doctrines, conditional, 69–70
estrangement, humanity and, 44–48
ethical-practical assumption, pluralist, 176
ethics, methodology and, 189. *See also* praxis
Eucharist, the, 96n71. *See also* sacraments, the
evangelicalism
  community and, 84–96, 102–5
  generous orthodoxy and, 96–97
  postliberalism and, 77–78
  scripture and, 81–84, 98–106
  sources of, 89–91, 108–10
exclusivism, religious, 170–71, 173–75
exegesis, spiritual, 19
existence, God's, 43
existential hermeneutics, 19
experience
  community, 85n19, 135
  in epistemology, 57
  hermeneutics of, 19
  theology and, 13, 34, 133, 135, 189
  womanist, 163–66
experiential expressivism, 19, 63–64
extratextuality, 72

fall, the, 44–46
Feminine Mystique, The (Friedan), 143
feminist theologies, 141–67, 179–81
finitude, human, 44–46
first-wave feminism, 142–43
flat hermeneutic, 3
flesh, incarnation and, 47
foundationalism, 84, 91–92, 98–100
Francis (pope), 111
freedom, human, 44–46
Frei, Hans, 74–78
Friedan, Betty, 143
fulfillment model, the, 175
functional atheism, 188

fundamentalism, religious, 37
future, the, 107–8

Gaudium et Spes, 115, 150–51
general revelation, 11, 28–30, 174–75
generous orthodoxy, 96–97, 190
genocide, oppression and, 159n57
God
  as black, 136
  history and, 32–33, 107–9
  language for, 151–53, 160
  revelation and, 11, 32–33
  scripture and, 100–105
  as triune, 93
  as ultimate concern, 41–43
grace, humanity and, 51–52, 175
Grenz, Stanley, 84–97, 188–89
Gutiérrez, Gustavo, 118–26

Hagar, 161–62, 164–65
Ham, sin of, 127–30
Harnack, Adolf von, 1, 26
Heim, S. Mark, 177–78
hermeneutics
  biblical, 12, 75–77, 99–106, 108–10
  flat, 3
  neo-scholastic, 19–20
  trilateral, 108
Hick, John, 170, 172, 173, 176, 177–78
Hill Fletcher, Jeannine, 173, 179–81
historical location. *See* location, historical
historical reconstruction, 19
history
  Christ and, 137–38
  God and, 32–33, 107–9
  location in, 10, 112–14
  pluralism and, 176
  revelation through, 31–33
history of dogma movement, 25–26
Holy Spirit, the, 105, 160
horizontal experience, the, 163
Humani Generis, 20

humanity, 44–46, 50–54, 57–58, 120–24, 153–56
Hunsinger, George, 77–78

identification-ascertainment, 163
identity, pluralism and, 180
immortality, doctrine and, 70–71
impasse, pluralist, 173, 179–81
incarnation, the, 46–48, 170, 173
inclusive language, 151–53, 160
inclusivism, religious, 171–73, 175. *See also* pluralism, religious
infallibility, biblical, 133–34
innocence, estrangement and, 44–46
Insight (Lonergan), 55
integral, the, 120–24
intellectual consciousness, 57–58
intention, authorial, 19
intents, womanist, 159–61
intermediator, theology as, 88
interpretation. *See* hermeneutics
intratextuality, 72–74
Introducing Theologies of Religions (Knitter), 173–78
irreversible doctrines, 70
Isasi-Díaz, Ada Maria, 147

Jesuits, the, 48–49
Jesus. *See* Christ
Jim Crow period, 126–27, 130
Johnson, Elizabeth, 149–58, 188

Kelsey, David, 100–102
kerygmatic theology, 37–38
Knitter, Paul, 78, 173–78
knowledge, human. *See* epistemology
kyriarchy, 148

language, 19, 28–29, 151–53, 160
law of love, 69
liberal feminism, 144

liberalism, Protestant, 1–2, 25–26
liberation, definition of, 119–20
liberation theology, 19, 111–26, 132–36, 161–66
light experience, Pannenberg's, 30–31
Lindbeck, George, 61–74, 86–87, 88n29, 177, 188
linguistic hermeneutics, 19
liturgical intent, womanist, 159
location, historical, 10, 112–14. *See also* history; situation, theological
Logos, the, 47
Lonergan, Bernard, 55–60
Lord's Supper, the, 96n71. *See also* sacraments, the
love, 51–52, 69, 136
Luke, Gospel of, 138–39
Luther, Martin, 11–12, 38, 134
lynching, 127

magisterium, Roman Catholic, 20n16, 22–25. *See also* church, the
Malcolm X, 131–32
male, Christ as, 153–56
manuals, theology of the, 17
Marcion, 136n104
Markham, Ian, 170–72
marks of the church, 94–95
Marx, Karl, 124–25
Medellín, conference at, 115–17
membership, church, 85n20
mendicant orders, 48–49
message, theological, 36–39, 59. *See also* truth, theological
Method in Theology (Lonergan), 55–60
methodological doctrine, 60
Metz, Johann Baptist, 112–40
monasticism, 48–49
monuments of tradition, 21
moral superiority, female, 143, 145
Mott, Lucrecia, 142

mujerista, 147
multidialogical intent, womanist, 159
mutuality model, the, 175–76

NAACP, lynching and, 127
narrative theology, 75–77
Nature of Doctrine, The (Lindbeck), 62
Nazareth, rejection at, 138–39
necessary doctrines, 69–70
neo-orthodox theology, 25–34
neo-scholasticism, 17–18
New Evangelicals, the, 174–75
new perspective on Paul, 3
nonfoundationalism, 98, 99
"normative" interpretations, 76
norms, theological, 135–36. *See also* situation, theological
Nouvelle Théologie. See ressourcement theology

official doctrines, 65–66
open theism, 107–8
operational doctrines, 65–66
oppressed, the, 122–24, 134, 136–40, 147–48. *See also* poor, the
ordination, maleness and, 154–56
orienting questions, 4, 13–14
origins, doctrinal, 25–26, 59
orthodoxy, generous, 96–97, 190
orthodoxy, Protestant, 38n14
other, difference and the, 173, 179–81

pacifism, 69
Pannenberg, Wolfhart, 30–34, 88n29
pantheism, 188
parachurch organizations, 94n63
partial replacement model, 174–75
patriarchy, 147–48
Paul, the apostle, 3

perfection, the fall and, 44–45
permanent conditional doctrines, 69
person, God as, 153n37
philosophical assumption, pluralist, 176
Pietism, 38n14
pillars, theological, 89n37
Pinnock, Clark, 106–10
pluralism, religious, 170–81, 189
political theologies, 111–40, 189
poor, the, 111–12, 122–24, 137–39. *See also* liberation theology; oppressed, the
postfoundationalism, 98–100
postliberal theology, 61–79
praxis, 113n5, 118–19, 189
prayer, monasticism and, 49
primary sources, theological, 3–4, 10–14
progress, human, 1–2, 26–27
prolegomena, definition of, 2n6
proof-texting, biblical, 109
propositionalism, 63–64, 84n16
Protestantism, 1–2, 25–26, 38n14
Proving Doctrine: The Use of Scripture in Modern Theology (Kelsey), 100–102

Quadrilateral, Wesleyan, 13
questions, theological, 4, 13–14

race, liberation and, 139–40
radical feminism, 145
Rahner, Karl
    methodology of, 9–10, 13–14, 187–88
    pluralism and, 171–72, 175
    political theologies and, 112–14, 121
    theology of, 48–55
ransom theory, salvific, 167
rational consciousness, 57–58
real, the, 170, 172
realism, 32–33, 99

reason, 13
reconstruction, historical, 19
reconstructionist Christian feminist theologians, 149
Reconstruction period, 126
reflection, critical, 118–19
reform feminism, 144–45
reformist Christian feminist theologians, 148
religion, unbelief and, 173–74
religious experience. *See* experience
religious-mystical assumption, pluralist, 176
Renewing the Center (Grenz), 93, 96–97
replacement model, the, 173–75
responsibility, consciousness and, 57–58
ressourcement theology, 15–25
resurrection, the, 32–33
revelation, divine
    general, 11, 28–30, 174–75
    humanity and, 50–54, 135
    incarnation and, 47
    pluralism and, 174–75
    special, 11
    through history, 31–33, 133
    two-source, 20
reversible doctrines, 70
Revisioning Evangelical Theology (Grenz), 84–93
revolution, liberation and, 121–24
revolutionary feminist theologians, 148
righteousness, God's, 136
Ritschl, Albrecht, 1
romantic feminism, 144–45
rule theory, Lindbeck's, 64–67, 86–87

sacraments, the, 95, 96n71, 155–56
salvation, 52–55, 121, 153–56, 166–67, 170–81
sameness, pluralism and, 173, 179–81
Sarah (wife of Abraham), 161–62

scholasticism, 17–18
science, natural, 33–34,
  56–57
scripture. *See* Bible, the
second-wave feminism,
  143–46
Seneca Falls Convention, 142
signs, symbolism and, 39–40
sin, 46, 120, 124, 127–30,
  139–40
situation, theological
  history and, 10, 112–14
  humanity and, 50–51,
    107–9, 135–36
  as source of theology,
    90–91
  truth and, 18, 36–39,
    87–88, 108
slavery, 70, 126–30, 133n89,
  161–62
socialist feminism, 145–46
Society of Jesus, 48–49
sola scriptura, 11–12, 102–5
Sophia, Christ as, 156–58
soul, the, 70–71
sources, theological
  evangelical, 89–91, 108–10
  liberation, 124–26, 133–35
  primary, 3–4
  types of, 10–14
special revelation, 11
Spirit, the, 105, 160
spiritual exegesis, 19
Stanton, Elizabeth Cady,
  141–42
starting point, theological,
  4, 14
substitutionary atonement,
  166–67. *See also* salvation
subversive, priests as, 123
suffragist movement, 142–43
superiority, female, 143, 145

supernatural, the, 120–24
supernatural existential, the,
  51–54
surrogacy, salvific, 167
symbolism, theological,
  39–40, 42–43
systematic theology, 59–60

teaching, magisterial, 20n16,
  22–25
temporary conditional doctrines, 69–70
temptation of Jesus, 137
textuality, theological, 72–74,
  75–77. *See also* Bible, the
Thatamanil, John, 182,
  184–85, 189
theism, open, 107–8
theocentrism, 50–51
theological doctrines, 59–60
theology, definition of, 7–8.
  See also doctrine
third-wave feminism,
  146–47
Thirteenth Amendment, the,
  126
Thomas Aquinas, 8–10,
  28–29, 153n37
Tillich, Paul, 35–48
tradition
  community and, 93
  in liberation theology, 126,
    134–35
  scripture and, 20–21
  as source of theology,
    12–13, 89–90
transcendental method, epistemological, 57–58
transformations of con-
  sciousness, 163
Trent, Council of, 20
trilateral hermeneutic, 108

Trinity, the, 93, 178. *See also*
  God
Troeltsch, Ernst, 1–2
Truth, Sojourner, 164–65
truth, theological, 36–39,
  87–88, 177–78
Tubman, Harriet, 165
two-source revelation, 20

ultimate concern, 41–42
ultimates, pluralism and, 178
unbelief, religion as, 173–74
unconditionally necessary
  doctrines, 69

Vanhoozer, Kevin, 97–106
Vatican II, 20–21, 54–55,
  114–17, 171–72
verbal infallibility, 133–34
vertical encounter, the, 163
violence, 124, 127, 130. *See
  also* revolution, liberation and
vocation, prayer and, 49
voting, feminism and, 142–43

Walker, Alice, 146, 158, 160
war, participation in, 69
Wesleyan Quadrilateral, 13
white, black and, 139–40
wilderness experience, the,
  164–66
Williams, Delores, 158–67
Wisdom, Christ as, 156–58
womanism, 146–47, 158–67
Woman's Bible, The (Stanton),
  141, 142
Word, the, 47
Word theology, 19, 27–28
work, theological, 8–10
World War I, 1–2, 26, 35
wrath, God's, 136